ALSO BY THOMAS CHRISTOPHER

In Search of Lost Roses

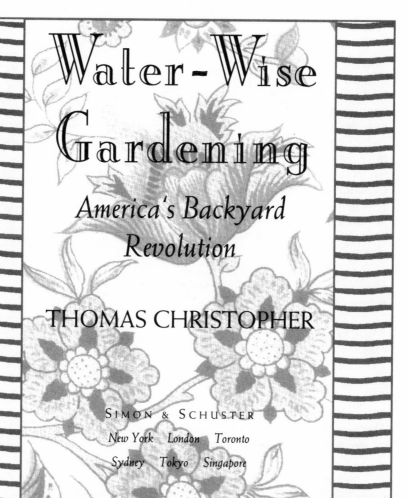

Water-Wise Gardening

America's Backyard Revolution

THOMAS CHRISTOPHER

SIMON & SCHUSTER

New York   London   Toronto

Sydney   Tokyo   Singapore

SIMON & SCHUSTER
Rockefeller Center
1230 Avenue of the Americas
New York, New York 10020

Designed by Marysarah Quinn
Manufactured in the United States of America

10   9   8   7   6   5   4   3   2   1

Library of Congress Cataloging in Publication Data
Christopher, Thomas.
    Water-wise gardening / America's backyard revolution / Thomas Christopher.
        p.   cm.
    Includes bibliographical references and index.
    1. Landscape gardening—United States—Water conservation.   2. Xeriscaping—
United States.   I. Title.
SB475.83.C48   1994
635.9'17—dc20   93-39688
                                                                   CIP

ISBN: 0-671-73856-9

Photo Credits
1, 2, 3, 4: Robert Kourik. 5, 6, 8, 9–14, 17–34, 38–48: Suzanne O'Connell. 7: Owen Dell. 15, 16:
William Welch. 35: Neil Diboll. 36: John Biever. 37: Saxon Holt.

Acknowledgments

Among the many people who helped with the research and writing of this book, I would like to extend special thanks to all those water-wise souls who so generously shared their gardens and experiences. I'd also like to thank Dr. William Welch of Texas A&M University for his hospitality, sage advice, and introductions. Thanks to Ruth Lively for her invaluable help with the manuscript. And of course, deepest gratitude to my wife, Suzanne, for three years of photography, shrewd literary criticism, and unfailing support and encouragement.

For my father, Robert Collins Christopher
(1924–1992)
Editor and Gardener
Who wasted neither water nor words

Contents

Introduction:

The Challenge

merican gardeners are confronting a crisis. It's the greatest challenge they have faced since their ancestors began nibbling away at virgin forest with fire and ax. We are running out of the one thing our plants cannot do without: water. Or at least, our demand is outstripping the available supply.

Even a few decades ago, no reasonable person could have believed this would ever occur. According to the most recent government study, the runoff from precipitation—the water that swells our river streams and lakes—totals approximately 1.23 trillion gallons each day. Of this we use only 265 billion gallons, though we pump a further 73.3 billion from our underground reservoirs, the aquifers. Taken together, that's an impressive withdrawal—a year's worth would be enough to flood the whole of the forty-eight conterminous states to a depth of 2.4 inches. Yet during that same period, natural precipitation bathes our country in roughly thirty inches of water. So how could there be a shortage?

The water's very abundance has been, indirectly, one cause of the problem. It has encouraged us to think that we could never exhaust this resource, and so we have squandered and polluted it.

This is a problem nearly everywhere, but it tends to be most severe where we can least afford it, in the population areas where the need for fresh water is the greatest. For example, in my home state of Connecticut, one of the most heavily industrialized and densely populated states, 116 of the 169 townships report wells contaminated by pesticides, nitrates from turf fertilizers, landfill leachate, or other by-products of ignorance and carelessness. In most instances the damage is for all practical purposes irreversible. As a result, since 1980, 150,000 of my neighbors (in a state of just 3 million) have joined those who depend on the public water supply system, increasing pressure on the reservoirs at the same time as our alternatives disappear.

Even as we were reducing the supply, we've allowed our thirst to increase unchecked. We've kept adding to our population—there are 174 million more people in the United States now than there were ninety years ago—and we've increased our personal water use by almost 80 percent, from 95 gallons per capita per day in 1900 to an average of 165 today. What's worse, we've concentrated so much of our expansion in a few metropolitan areas that communities once famous for their water supplies, for example, Los Angeles and New York, now draw more than their systems' so-called safe yields. The safe yield is the amount that a system's wells and reservoirs can deliver even in dry years; when average daily consumption exceeds this amount the city in question begins to feel the effect of a drought almost at once. New York City's reservoirs (which store a nearly unimaginable 550 *billion* gallons) were sufficient to see that community through four years of severe drought in the 1960s. By 1991, though, just a dry summer, one with rainfall ten inches (23 percent) below average, forced the metropolitan area into a water alert.

Nor is this danger limited to a few metropolitan giants. A poll of mayors found that at least half of the major U.S. cities suffered from a water shortage of some severity during the summer of 1990. In many cases the shortfall could be dismissed as a temporary inconvenience, the result of unusually low levels of precipitation. But 26 percent of the mayors reported that the expansion of their water supply was not keeping pace with the growth of demand and that in the foreseeable future the shortage would become chronic.

Compounding these man-made problems are some natural trends. When the Colorado River's water was divided up in 1922, the annual flow measured at 17 million acre-feet (an acre-foot is the quantity of water that would cover one acre of ground to a depth of one foot—325,850 gallons). In their "Colorado River Compact," the seven states in that watershed (Arizona, California, Colorado, Nevada, New Mexico, Utah, and Wyoming) claimed between them 15 million acre-feet of water, and guaranteed a further 1.5 million to Mexico. Since 1930, however, the flow has averaged only 14 million acre-feet annually. This deficit didn't matter as long as the Colorado basin remained largely undeveloped, and the signators to the compact didn't need their full allotments. Today, with 21 million people and 2 million acres of farmland competing for the river's water, there is never enough to go around.

In the past, easterners have complacently regarded that kind of bad news as a problem peculiar to the West. But spurred by recent droughts, scientists have been reconstructing histories of climate east of the Mississippi. The source of their data has been a Boy Scout's bit of wood lore. Like a nine-year-old looking for the year of Columbus's landing as he runs his finger over the rings on a fresh-cut stump, the researchers have counted backward through cores taken from tree trunks, identifying the years of good and poor growth in the fat and thin bands of wood. By examining trees on water-poor sites—rocky hillsides, for example—where a drop in rainfall plunged trees into an immediate state of stress, researchers have been able to chart the relative abundance of precipitation. What they are learning is that we may have taken far too much for granted.

At Columbia University, the dendrochronologists (tree-ring interpreters) have discovered that the post–World War II building boom in the Hudson River Valley coincided with a period of unusually benign weather. Having charted precipitation back to 1694 through a study of five different species (eastern hemlock, pitch pine, eastern white pine, chestnut oak, and white oak), they ascertained that the fluctuations between years of high and low precipitation were depressed by some 48 percent from 1931 until 1960. In other words, suburbanization came during a period of unusually reliable rainfall. What this suggests is that the recurrent "drought emergencies" of the last twenty years are, unfortunately, a return to normalcy.

Meanwhile, in North Carolina stands of first-growth bald cypress revealed that over the past fifteen centuries the weather has run in cycles of about thirty years, with three decades of abundant rainfall followed by equal periods of drought. If this is indeed the pattern, then the droughts that gripped North Carolina in 1985 and 1988 may be not aberrations but announcements of a climatic change that will last well into the twenty-first century.

If what we have been labeling "droughts" are in many instances closer to a region's standard climate, then almost certainly, a water supply system that sufficed for the last generation will not prove adequate for the next one—unless we change our ways. Dr. Michael D. Hudlow, director of the National Oceanic and Atmospheric Administration's Office of Hydrology, put it this way in a press conference of November 23, 1990: "As we move toward the 21st century, short supplies of clean water could rival expensive oil as one of the nation's most serious concerns unless we start now to implement strategies to better manage our water supplies."

Traditionally, our solution to a water shortage has been to build another dam, tap another river, and impound another reservoir. This has been especially true west of the Mississippi, where dam building has been regarded as a holy mission, an answer to the Bible's injunction to make the desert bloom, so that 37,000 such structures now flood vast tracts of once arid rangeland. But even there it is generally admitted (strictly off the record) that the best sites, the ones that offer a high rate of return in gallons for dollars spent, are all used up. Yet economics alone won't stop the engineers. For decades they have been pouring concrete in spite of figures that clearly showed that the water would cost far more to deliver than the crops or industry it supported could earn. What has been proving far more troublesome is the public's increasing unwillingness to pay the environmental price.

The most dramatic confrontation of this sort came at a spot west of Denver called Two Forks. The City of Denver had been planning to dam the South Platte River there for sixty years when it finally got ready to start building in 1982. When completed, this project would have boosted the city's water supply by some 98,000 acre-feet. It would also have flooded thirty-one miles of scenic Cheesman Canyon.

Hikers, kayakers, bird watchers, and fishermen all united against the project. Yet in the end it was probably the Army Corps of Engineers, one of the Two Forks project's most enthusiastic supporters, that killed it. In its $37 million environmental impact study, it let slip the fact that "single-family homes consume 65 percent of the water [from all sources in Denver's water system] and represent the greatest user of all the water in the metropolitan area. *One-half of the water consumed by single-family homes is for lawn irrigation.*" (Emphasis added.) This bit of information persuaded the Environmental Protection Agency to join in the opposition to the project. If Denver really needed more water, chief administrator Wiliam K. Reilly decided, it could secure it at a far more reasonable cost through smaller, less destructive projects—and through conservation. On November 24, 1990, Reilly formally vetoed construction of the Two Forks Dam.

In the conservation program that the Denver Water Department is now promoting, it is gardeners who are expected to make the greatest sacrifice. They are an easy target, because society as a whole views gardening as a luxury.

That's a mistake. Quite apart from the issue of quality of life, gardening can provide benefits of the most measurable, practical sort. A study in Florida found that a judicious arrangement of trees, shrubs, and vines around the home cut the use of air conditioning by 58 percent. Another study, by scientists of Lawrence Livermore Laboratory near San Francisco, linked commercial development and the felling of orchards and native oaks to a 9°F rise in the average local temperature. And in the North, an evergreen hedge, if properly sited to block prevailing winds, can reduce the gas or oil consumption of a furnace by 10 to 30 percent.

But the fact remains that most Americans view gardening as a frill, and as such, expendable. During the several serious droughts that have occurred since I first turned my hand to horticulture— the ones that parched the Northeast in 1977 and 1980–1981, again in 1985, and 1987–1988—the first conservation measure adopted has always been a ban on landscape irrigation.

I hate to envision a future in which watching my garden wither becomes a regular experience. But no matter how much I believe in the importance of gardens, I must admit that we gardeners are gluttons when it comes to water. *Grounds Maintenance,* a journal that circulates to professionals in the horticultural industry, has calculated that the owner of a typical single-family dwelling in the United States lavishes 90,000 gallons of water annually on his or her landscape.

Although this quantity may sound immense, really, it's not hard to calculate where it goes. Gardening guides recommend that you give your lawn a minimum of an inch of water (that is, enough water so that, if none ran off or soaked in, the turf would be covered uniformly to a depth of one inch) every time a week of hot weather passes without a rainstorm. So figure that your lawn spreads over half an acre; to give this area the inch of water consumes 1,815 cubic feet of water. That's 13,577 gallons *per watering*. At that rate, it doesn't take very many dry weeks to use up the average annual allotment.

Of course, gardeners in arid regions use far more water than that 90,000 gallon average. In Phoenix, Arizona, I found the residential lots surrounded by continuous, low berms. When I asked the purpose of this, owners explained that they water their turf by flooding. At least once a week throughout the hot season—that is, from spring through fall—these gardeners turn their entire lots into shallow lakes. That's outrageous behavior for the residents of a desert city; yet there are even worse examples of waste. On the dry, eastern face of the Cascade Mountains there's a famous nine-acre alpine garden that the gardeners keep green by sprinkling every summer night. That garden consumes 130,000 gallons— every day.

The fact is that Denver is not an exception, for in the summertime irrigating the home landscape consumes 50 percent of all available water in many American municipalities. That's something which, increasingly, nongardeners don't feel they can afford. They are right, too. The capacity of a municipal water system is based on peak demand. It's the water you give your lawn, your tomatoes, and your petunias in August that raises the peak and forces the town to drill another well or negotiate a bigger (and more expensive) contract with the state aqueduct system.

From Tampa to Los Angeles, communities are voting to make restrictions on landscape watering—measures once invoked only in emergencies—permanent. If this sounds threatening to you, as a gardener, it really isn't. There is no reason why these watering restrictions should hamper your gardening at all. The chances are very good that you can reduce the water you use for irrigation by 80 percent, and in the process develop a far more interesting, original, and beautiful landscape.

You can still have as many flowers, fruits, and vegetables as you want, too. Less water does not translate into reductions in yield if you achieve your water savings through more precise irrigation. In addition, reduced irrigation produces another, incidental benefit, one that will please any but the hopeless spendthrift and workaholic: it will curb your landscape's hunger for fertilizers and pesticides, and cut the work of maintenance to a minimum. As any experienced gardener knows, excessive watering encourages excessive growth; not only does this increase the plants' need for nutrients, but it encourages them to produce soft, flabby tissue that is irresistible to predatory insects and diseases. Keeping your landscape on a high-nutrient, high-water diet increases the work of clipping and pruning, and it also encourages the growth of weeds. If you give your plantings exactly the water they need and no more, there won't be any left over for those invaders.

Given all these benefits, it's not surprising that water-thrifty gardening is taking hold in virtually every region of the country. *Xeriscaping* is the term most widely used for this kind of landscape design, *xeros* being the Greek word (and so the botanical term) for drought. As of 1991, the promoter of this particular school, the National Xeriscape Council, claimed 800 members in forty American states, two Canadian provinces, Israel, Tasmania, and Aruba.

But there are many other types of water-thrifty design, each adapted to its own region. In the Los Angeles region it's called "Landscaping Southern California Style"; the foremost practitioner in New England calls his creations "Mesiscapes" (since, as he points out, there are no truly xeric landscapes there, only moderately dry, or mesic, ones). Actually, I've met any number of gardeners who practice the principles of water conservation without giving their gardens any special label. What unites all these gardeners is their willingness to embrace change rather than resist it.

Indeed, in travels around the United States over the last few years, I've learned that the need for water conservation has become the driving force of a gardening renaissance. The challenge is extraordinary, for water is *the* fundamental resource for plants. Yet this extraordinary challenge, the demand that gardeners turn off the taps, is stimulating an equally extraordinary imaginativeness. Through the adoption of new technologies and the revival of old, forgotten ones, through bold, revolutionary strategies of design and cultivation, American gardeners are creating landscapes that flourish with little more water than nature provides. And these new landscapes are wedded to the land as our gardens never have been before.

To achieve the goal of water conservation, gardeners have to study closely the earth they cultivate. They have to determine not just what can be made to survive there, but what will thrive without coddling—they have to identify the plants that really *like* their climate. At the same time, they have to learn how to collaborate with nature in the arrangement of these plants, to learn which ones harmonize physically as well as visually with each other. They must learn how best to manage their particular soil, whether it's a red Georgia clay, an organic-rich prairie loam, or a southwestern adobe, and not just force it into production with imported resources. In short, they must rediscover the principles of good gardening. That is what is happening, and the gardens that are appearing as a result are among the most exciting I've ever seen.

As an apprentice horticulturist, I was indoctrinated in what I call the "tour de force" school of gardening. The gardener whom my teachers held up for emulation was, typically, the man who kept a collection of high-mountain plants alive on the hot, humid coast, or the woman who somehow wintered over tender southern specimens in the frigid north. Since then, though, through my work in the profession, I have come to know how thankless such a task is. At best it is a skillfully managed lost cause; you may win any number of battles, but nature dictates that you will lose the campaign. Sooner or later a particularly hot, wet summer will turn the alpines to pools of stinking mush, and an early, unexpected frost will blacken the out-of-place subtropical shrubbery. But even during the temporary periods of success, to contradict the rules of nature seems to me not a triumph but an obscenity.

Obscene or not, tour-de-force horticulture is something water-conserving gardeners cannot afford. Their creations—at least the successful ones—must be in harmony with the world around them. Keyed to the local climate and environment, they seem most often like subtly refined versions of their natural setting. Even those planted entirely with exotic species appear securely and unselfconsciously rooted into that locale.

This brings me to another aspect of gardening in America that I find troubling: our emulation of all things English. I am a sincere admirer of English gardeners; they do what they do superbly well, and there's nothing I like better than an English garden—when I am in England. But it makes no sense to impose that foreign tradition on our soil.

In all the other arts—architecture, painting, music, etc.—we long ago matured enough to stop copying the Old World masters, to accept the value of their traditions but to begin pursuing our own journeys. But in gardening we still buy English spades to plant English hybrids according to plans we take from English books. The result is boring gardens, and gardens at odds with their environment.

Water-conserving gardeners can't afford to be so derivative in their thinking. Nowhere in the United States, except maybe in the Pacific Northwest, is it possible to garden as if one were in rainy old England and still create self-sufficient landscapes. Instead, water-wise gardeners must consult nature itself wherever they happen to be, and plant according to its plan. This, I have found, makes their gardens as varied as the face of the land itself.

In southern Arizona, for example, I learned that the water-conserving landscapes mirror the desert, drawing not only on cacti, succulents, desert shrubs, and trees but also the indigenous Indian and Hispanic traditions. In the Midwest such landscapes are more likely to employ prairie flowers and grasses, while on the southern California coast they draw their inspiration from the chaparral. Certain themes unite them all—a new interest in the native flora and a spirit of cooperation with nature are always prominent—and certain technologies are common throughout. Yet of all the water-wise landscapes I have visited, no two have ever been exactly alike.

When I began researching this subject, I set out to describe "the new American garden"—a catch phrase these days in the gardening press (and, trust the federal bureaucracy, the name of a display garden recently added to the National Arboretum). In the course of my travels, however, I found not one new style but dozens of them. In this book I've included visits to more than thirty gardens; this selection can only suggest the richness of what's appearing now.

In describing the gardens, I've grouped them together as I found them, in tours of each geographical region. Thus the gardens are seen in the context of their community—and this is crucial to understanding such intensely regional landscapes. Besides, this type of organization highlights the gardens' astonishing originality. For even when the gardeners were neighbors, responding to identical challenges, the differences in their planting were what was most striking.

In between the tours, you'll find chapters focusing on the how-to's of water-wise gardening. By helping you understand how these gardens were created, this information should increase your appreciation and enjoyment. More importantly, it will help you plan a water-wise garden of your own.

This book is not only about a challenge; I intend it to be one itself. Someday in the not too distant future, you will have to learn how to garden better. You will have to learn how to cultivate your landscape with a more precise budget of water. That will be a necessity, but a most exciting opportunity, too. Who knows what kind of new American garden you will create?

One

Watering Arts and Science

t seems so simple. Just tip the can or open the tap and let the water flow. Give the plants a good soak. Give them a drink. What could be easier than watering the garden?

In fact, that sort of watering is liable to do the plants as much harm as good. Really, there is no such thing as a "good" soak; giving a plant too much water is as bad as not giving it enough. Watering accurately is *the* skill that divides a master gardener from a black-thumbed novice. Part art, part science, watering is indeed a fairly simple process. But you have to understand what you are doing.

That is impossible for most gardeners, because they know virtually nothing about water, especially as it works in relationship to plants. The fault really is not theirs—the reason for our ignorance is too successful engineering.

Why should we value something that is cheaper than dirt? When I set up as a landscape contractor in 1977, a cubic yard of topsoil cost me $14.00, delivered; 100 cubic feet of water—just under four cubic yards of water, water that had been filtered, chlorinated, and that tested pure enough to drink—cost $1.10. I was busy, and if I left the sprinkler running for a few hours too long while I slipped off to talk to another customer or pick up some plants at the nursery, well, that was good business—even if it was bad gardening.

A widely circulated bit of trivia observes that a human being is 66 percent water. That may seem impressive, but it would be a fatal level of dehydration for most plants. Water accounts for 95 percent of the mass of most annual and perennial flowers, and even a seemingly solid Douglas fir is 85 percent water. I've heard Iceberg lettuce disparaged as "textured water"; actually, that's an apt description of all plant life.

So it's not surprising that the availability of water is the primary factor in determining the lushness of plant growth in any region. There are other factors involved, of course—the richness and depth of soil, heat and cold, intensity and duration of sunlight— but water is the determinant. Given two trees of the same species and age and growing in the same region, 80 to 90 percent of any difference in their trunks' diameters can be traced directly to differences in the trees' water supply.

Nor is man, with all his hoses and sprinklers, capable of erasing the inequities between different plants. Water available to one plant may be unavailable to another, because plants differ in the ways that they gather moisture. The most primitive plants, the algae, absorb moisture into their cells directly from the water around them, and many land plants preserve the ability to take up water into the tissues of their leaves and stems directly from the surrounding atmosphere. Epiphytes—"air plants"—such as Spanish moss, derive all their moisture in this fashion, and the coast redwoods of California are believed to absorb significant amounts of water into their foliage from the fogs that bathe the north Pacific coast. But for the overwhelming number of trees, shrubs, and flowers, the plants of which our gardens are made, the essential supply comes through the roots.

Perhaps the best measure of this organ's importance to the average plant is its relative size. According to one botanist's measurements, a single rye plant, a grass that stands five feet tall, sent out roots that if laid end to end would stretch for 380 miles. The drier the environment, the more of the plant hides underground. In an oak forest—an ecological community of well-watered regions —10 percent of the biomass (the total mass of the living material) typically lies underground. On a tall-grass prairie (a community that developed in response to regular droughts), the percentage is closer to 50 percent. In the desert, 90 percent of a plant may lie beneath the surface of the soil.

Water has a tendency to flow from areas of higher concentration to areas of lower concentration. So if the soil is moist, the water will tend to move in through the membranes that surround root cells, because the cellular sap is higher in dissolved substances (and therefore relatively poorer in water) than the liquid resting in the spaces between the soil particles. But there is a tug-of-war at work here; there is also a physical attraction of water to soil particle, a force that tends to counteract the pull of the roots, so that when the soil moisture drops to a certain point (and I'll discuss this in more detail in Chapter Four) water may still surround the roots and yet be unavailable to the plant.

Curiously, despite the tremendous extent of their root systems, few plants seek deep enough to tap the underground reservoirs we call groundwater. There are exceptions to this rule, in North America most notably those thorny southwestern trees, the mesquites. In 1960, an open-pit mining operation near Tucson found roots of mesquites growing to a depth of 175 feet. This deep-rootedness, with the ability it gives the plant to find water no matter what the weather, accounts for the mesquite's rapid spread through lands we have desertified through overgrazing or soil erosion.

In general, though, roots do not hunt so deep. Corn (*Zea mays*) typically explores only five feet downward, while broad-leaved shade trees—our oaks, maples, etc.—confine the bulk of their feeder roots to the top six inches of the soil, the area richest in organic materials. Knowing the approximate penetration of *your* plants' roots is a key to effective irrigation.

"Water deeply" was the rule I was given when I was a student, the supposition being that this would encourage plants to make deeper root systems, and so enhance their ability to withstand drought. In fact, that isn't necessarily so. Deep watering is good for deep-rooted species, and will encourage them to develop their roots to the full potential. But it's sheer waste when the species you are irrigating are naturally shallow-rooted.

To some degree, the gardener can control the depth of moisture penetration by thorough preparation of the soil before planting. In all but the sandiest areas, water will soak down quickly only as far as the soil has been loosened through digging and amendment with grit such as coarse sand or organic matter such as compost. Still, the careful gardener will want to supplement this with the use of a soil sampler, an inexpensive hand tool which may be ordered from horticultural supply houses.* Briefly, by extracting a core as much as twenty inches deep from the soil, the sampler allows the gardener both to check the depth of the plants' roots and to see if the moisture is reaching down that far. Ideally, the water should penetrate just a bit deeper than the roots, for my teachers' goal was correct. Plants should be encouraged to root as deeply as possible —but not by wasting water.

Pinpointing the differences in root depth is important, but the fundamental fact is that few plants reach down to the water table, and that means your landscape must rely on irrigation—either natural irrigation by rain and snow, or artificial irrigation by man. The overwhelming majority of landscape plants are utterly dependent in this matter. Yet they are nevertheless astonishingly extravagant in their water consumption.

An acre of corn, for example, will extract from the soil more than 3,500 gallons on a sunny day; over the course of a single growing season, this crop uses a quantity of water that if applied all at once would flood the field to a depth of fifteen inches. Advocates of reforestation may be surprised to learn that a forest can be even greedier. The hardwood trees in a southern Appalachian cove, for example, require a bath of more than twenty-one inches per year.

This difference in demand is what gives the lie to another of the traditional rules of thumb—that you must make sure your plants get an inch of water (whether from rain or irrigation) every week. That may indeed suit a bluegrass lawn in the northeastern states, but it would harm rather than help a southwestern desert-scape. A plant's need for watering should be minimal if you plant your landscape correctly; in any case, irrigation must be regulated by the plants' needs (and I will tell you how to recognize that a little farther on).

What the plants get from their extravagant consumption seems to be slight. One botanist found that a birch drew 317 ounces of

* My favorite source of tools, A. M. Leonard, Inc. (P.O. Box 816, Piqua, OH 45356), offers one for $39.66 that samples to a depth of twenty-one inches.

water from the soil for each ounce of solids ("dry matter," a scientist calls this) that it added to its bulk. An English oak drew even more —344 ounces—to achieve a similar result.

The reason for this seeming inefficiency is that 90 percent of the water which enters a plant through its roots is drawn right out through the leaves and into the atmosphere by a process called transpiration. To carry on the chemical processes by which it captures solar energy, then manufactures food and metabolizes it, a plant's green tissues must breathe; they must be able to absorb and expel both oxygen and carbon dioxide from the atmosphere. This makes the plant vulnerable to dehydration as moisture commonly escapes with the gases, evaporating into the drier surrounding air.

But though lost, this water isn't wasted, since transpiration serves a couple of useful purposes. To begin with, it cools the plant, since the water absorbs heat energy as it evaporates and carries it off when it escapes as water vapor. This cooling effect is significant, especially on a clear day when sunlight is heating the leaves. A large shade tree—a sugar maple, say—may release into the atmosphere 100 gallons of water on a hot day, and its cooling effect is equal to that of five average-sized air conditioners (machines with a capacity of 2,500 kcal/hr) running twenty hours continuously.

This cooling is pleasant for anyone sitting underneath a tree in summertime, of course, but to the plant it is essential. Enzymes that facilitate a plant's basic chemical processes operate effectively within a fairly narrow range of temperatures. In corn, to return again to that basic American crop, the interior temperature must stay between 77° and 88°F; in cucumbers, it's 93° to 100°. If any plant's internal temperature should climb above the ideal, essential processes such as food production and waste elimination slow and eventually stop. Ultimately, unless the plant can reduce its temperature, it dies.

Besides regulating internal temperatures, transpiration also serves plants as an inexpensive way of moving water and nutrients upward. As water evaporates off leaf surfaces, more water moves in to replace it, and the net effect is that moisture is sucked up through the plant's stem like soda up a straw. In sunny weather transpiration works like a pump, continuously pulling water (and with it, nutrients) from the soil, through the roots and stems, and up into the leaves.

The best part of this process, from the plant's perspective, is that it's free; the solar power it consumes costs the plant nothing. The savings can be tremendous, too. A first-growth sequoia will, on average, transpire 2,500 pounds of water in the course of a day, and to lift this weight to the top of its 300-foot-tall crown involves an expenditure of energy that would be sufficient to launch a can of soda into a low earth orbit.

There can be many reasons why a plant runs short of water. Drought is the most obvious cause, but plants may suffer from dehydration because of damage done to their roots, because conditions in the soil prevent the roots from working properly (for more information about this, again see Chapter Four), or simply because on a hot sunny day transpiration sucks water from the leaves faster than the roots can replace it.

In any case, the effect is more or less the same. Some plants, the so-called xerophytes ("dry plants"—species that evolved in arid or semi-arid regions), are better equipped to withstand dehydration. They suffer less permanent damage from thirst and are more likely to recover. But they experience the same distress. Learning to recognize the early symptoms of water stress, so that you can correct it before it injures the plant, is an essential skill for successful gardening. It is also the key to putting your garden on a tight water budget.

Before exploring the symptoms of dehydration, I should explain why *too much* water is just as harmful to most plants as too little. Flooding the soil, saturating it with water, drives all the oxygen from the spaces between its particles, and without a supply of oxygen the roots cannot digest the food sent to them by the leaves. They then cease to function, so that although there may be water, water everywhere, none of it reaches the leaves.

To return to dehydration: the first and most visible response of a plant to this kind of trouble is to reduce its evaporative surfaces. The plant is losing most water through its leaves, and so it has to somehow reduce them. Rhododendrons roll their large, broad leaves into cylinders in times of drought; once this has been completed, only the outermost layer of each leaf-roll is exposed to the dehydrating air. Other plants, such as broad-leaved, deciduous trees, simply jettison much of their foliage; the autumn of 1980 was one of the least colorful in memory in the northeastern states since the forests had already shed most of their leaves during the preceding, extremely dry summer.

Even a brief period of water stress will cause flowers to abort and fruits to shrink. If prolonged, it can stunt a plant's growth by interfering with the plant's metabolism, and by starving it of the nutrients and minerals water brings with it from the soil. This may suit the bonsai fancier, who mimics a drought's effect by cutting back the roots of the trees he wishes to dwarf, and so limits their ability to absorb water. To the average gardener, though, this is not so welcome.

It's bad enough that water stress should destroy your plants' vitality. Even worse is the fact that it calls in all of their microscopic and insect enemies at the same time.

Why pests and diseases should be attracted to dehydrated plants is not entirely clear. In part it is opportunism, a response to a weakening of defenses. Many plants infiltrate their tissues with resins that make them distasteful to plant-eating insects (and most larger animals, too, for that matter). Along with all the other internal processes it inhibits, water stress slows or stops the protection of these natural pest repellents.

Drought also favors certain kinds of microscopic parasites. I know from personal experience that powdery mildew, a fungal disease that blights the leaves of lilacs, roses, phloxes, and many other garden plants, spreads more swiftly in dry weather, and I've read that the cankers that infect many trees find dry barks easier to invade. But recent studies indicate that water stress doesn't just open the gates, it actually broadcasts signals of distress to the predators.

Water stress makes plants more visible to insects. It's long been common knowledge among greenhouse operators that the color yellow attracts certain types of insects; I remember twenty years ago being taught to hang adhesive-coated yellow squares above the hothouse benches to serve as insect traps. At the time I wondered why this worked, but I never got an answer until I began researching water stress. One of the effects of dehydration is to make a plant's leaves turn yellow; a water deficiency inhibits the production of the green pigment chlorophyll.

Apparently, this unnatural and bright color catches the insects' eyes, alerting them to the presence of a defenseless plant. At the same time as water stress turns plant foliage yellow, of course, it also heats it up by putting an end to transpiration. To insects, whose vision (unlike man's) may extend to the infrared wavelengths of light, these overheated plants will seem to glow like neon signs.

Even more fatal than these visual SOS's may be the audible ones. A recent study of drought-stressed plants suggested that in times of severe water deficit they may actually call pests in to the feast. As moisture in the soil decreases and roots can no longer supply the upward flow, the pull of the transpiring leaves on the water already inside the conductive tissue, the xylem, increases until finally the tubes shatter with a high-pitched squeak. Researchers speculate that this sound, though inaudible to the human ear, may alert insect predators who *can* hear sounds in the ultrasonic range.

It's unfortunate that we gardeners do not have eyes and ears like a grasshopper. Watering accurately is largely a matter of responding promptly to a threat of drought; the ideal is to give the plant the water it needs just when it needs it—that is, just as it is beginning to experience stress—and it would be a great help if we could hear and see the distress signals. Since we can't, we have learned to rely on rules of thumb.

There are any number of these, as I learned during my apprenticeship at the New York Botanical Garden. Each of the gardeners there knew a different set, and each insisted in Bronx/Sicilian dialect that I learn his.

Mike, the native plants curator, told me how he'd been taught to tap a pot (the botanical garden still grew all its greenhouse plants in clay pots then—this trick works only with a clay pot) with a hose's nozzle, and listen to the tone. A dull thud meant the soil was evenly moist, while a hollow, ringing tone meant it was dry.

Frankie raised the crops for the seasonal shows; he was the one who was entrusted with bringing the endless files of potted poinsettias and tulips into peak bloom together on the appointed day. He had been given this job largely because he was an artist with the hose. There were two clues that Frankie used to watch for, signals that the plant was calling for water. First he watched for "flagging"—the first wilting of the foliage. But it was a sign of Frankie's expertise that he didn't need to wait until a leaf actually drooped before he recognized flagging's onset. A subtle change in the leaf color, a slight dulling of the green, alerted him.

Frankie wouldn't have explained it this way, but he knew from experience that flagging can result from excessive transpiration as well as dry soil. In the middle of a sunny afternoon a plant may be wilting simply because the leaves are calling for water faster than the roots can supply it, and in that case irrigation will do no good. So he generally applied a second test. Squeezing a bit of earth in his hand, he would check whether it was still moist enough to stick into a ball. If not, he knew that it was time to get out the hose.

By eye and by instinct—that was how the old-time gardeners watered. Incredibly science, until recently, had nothing much else to offer. An irrigation textbook of as recent a vintage as 1980 still listed plant color, leaf movement, and the "feel" of the soil as criteria to consider when judging a crop's need for water. In other words, it recommended Frankie's approach. From working with him I know that this method of assessing water needs can work beautifully. But I also know that to develop the necessary discrimination requires years of constant practice.

Fortunately, I have found hints of something new, of a method more objective and exact. That textbook also included a discussion of "ET," and I've since learned that in many regions of the country —the Southwest especially, but also some areas of Virginia, Massachusetts, and New York—agricultural extension agencies have begun making ET data available to local residents, whether farmers or gardeners. Often you'll find the daily ET number with the weather report in the newspaper.

What is ET? It's an abbreviation of "evapotranspiration," which is an estimation of the amount of water drawn from the soil in a specified period through evaporation and plant transpiration. Typically, ET is expressed in inches of water per day.

How does it work? If, say, you live in Plainview, Long Island, and the Nassau County Cooperative Extension agent tells you that the ET for Kentucky bluegrass in your town has been .25 inch per day since you last watered two days ago (and such was the case as of this writing), you can easily determine that you must give the lawn .50 inch of irrigation this evening (Nassau County only allows watering on alternate days, so you have to double the daily ET figure) to make up the deficit. That's what you apply—no more, no less.

Equipped with this number, even the most casual weekend groundsman can quickly learn to give various plantings something very close to the exact amount of water they require. Better yet, he or she can give the plants that water before a deficit develops—with a reading of the daily ET rate, a gardener doesn't have to wait for distress signals to know that it's time to uncoil the hose.

So far, ET sounds blessedly simple, but there are, alas, some complicating factors. To begin with, in calculating the water you must apply, you have to factor in rainfall, offsetting the amount gained in this fashion against the amount lost through ET. If your ET in Plainview has been .25 inch for the last two days, but a shower dumped a quarter inch of rainfall (.25 inch) on the lawn, then the forty-eight-hour deficit is only .25 inch of water total, rather than .5. So you give the lawn .25 inch of water.

To keep track, you can look at the weather report in the local newspaper, which generally includes rainfall, but you'd do better to install a rain gauge in your yard. This need be nothing fancier than an empty can set upright out in the open, away from sheltering trees or overhanging roofs, but you must remember to measure the water accumulated there after every rainstorm. Consistency in this matter is important, and the gardeners I know who use ET most successfully keep a chart on which they record both the daily ET and rainfall together.

A far more serious difficulty confronting the would-be scientific irrigator is the fact that an extension agent generally gives the ET rate only for a single crop, typically the locally most popular turf. This makes sense, since turf irrigation accounts for the vast majority of water applied to the landscape. But since other species of plants transpire at different rates, that turf ET won't correspond exactly to the water lost from your bed of lettuces or your home apple orchard.

Still, the turf ET does furnish an objective reading of one plant's water needs, and that's a benchmark from which you can, with a little experience, calculate the needs of all your plantings. Keep track of the amount of water you apply to various areas of your garden—that's easy if you use one of the new drip irrigation systems which deliver water at a prescribed rate, so you can just keep track of how long and how often you run it. If you won't give up your sprinklers, use the simple output measurement system I've included in Chapter Five (page 168).

In either case, cut back on your watering until you've reached the minimum amount the plants must have—water, then wait until the plants flag before watering again. Compare the amount measured out in this fashion with what the published ET called for in the same period, and you've got a proportion you can use to convert future ET figures.

Quite likely this talk of numbers, inches of rainfall, and calculations sounds too complicated (though it can save you a great deal of money if you live in an area where water costs are high, especially if you insist on watering your lawn). Maybe you like the immediacy of the traditional pinch-the-soil-and-eye-the-plant system for regulating irrigation. That can be made to work fairly efficiently, too, especially if you use some of the simple aids outlined on the following page. Whatever system you use, however, you will find that watering precisely not only saves money, it produces better plants.

So whether you treat watering as an art or science, learn some respect for an endlessly renewable but always irreplaceable resource, and do put your garden on a budget.

Rules of Thumb

Install a rain gauge in an open area of your yard (the top of a fence post makes a convenient pedestal) and use this to keep track of the water deposited through natural precipitation. Newspapers often include a total of precipitation for the year to date, and for the current month, in their weather reports, together with the average precipitation for the same periods. Though these may differ from the exact figures for your location, they will help you establish whether your landscape is enjoying more or less natural irrigation than usual.

Let the plant set the watering schedule. If readings of the local ET are available, use them to identify when your landscape is developing a water deficit. Otherwise, watch for a dulling of the foliage color or "flagging"—drooping of leaves—and let these be the signal to irrigate.

Don't overreact to distress signals. Flagging in the middle of a hot, sunny afternoon may just be evidence that roots can't supply water fast enough to replace moisture lost through transpiration. If you think that may be the case, wait until morning to see if nighttime's cooler temperatures and relief from solar radiation perk up plants. Wilting can also be a sign that a plant's roots are drowning; it's always a good idea to check soil moisture with a soil sampler before irrigating.

Identify the area of your yard that dries out first: an exposed patch of turf that dries out most quickly, a patch of impatiens that is the first to droop. By watching this spot you can forecast a water deficit in other areas of your landscape before it actually occurs.

Avoid frequent light waterings that moisten only the soil's surface. This treatment encourages plants to make shallow root systems that are especially vulnerable to drought. Water to a depth just slightly below the root zone of your plants. A soil sampler can help you establish the depth to which both plant roots and moisture are penetrating.

To check the moisture of soil from the sampler, squeeze a handful to see if it adheres easily together in a ball that holds together when you open your hand again. If not, your soil needs water.

Water when the air is still and the sun is low—this will help reduce the water wasted through evaporation.

When watering, keep in mind the normal life cycle of the plant. Many plants (most turf grasses, for example, and species from areas with regular summer dry seasons) respond to high temperatures by going dormant. Irrigating heavily during dormancy won't help the plant and may actually harm it, so save the water for the flush of new growth that comes with cooler weather.

Santa Barbara, California

"Reclaimed water" was what Art Gonzalez was delivering; he was quick to correct me when I called it treated sewage. By early 1991, many other members of Santa Barbara's Hispanic Gardeners Association had been driven out of business by the four-year-long drought—who's going to pay you to cut a lawn that's dead? But Art had not only survived, he'd prospered. He'd bought a tank truck and taken out a license to pick up the outflow from the water treatment plant. It wasn't fit to drink, but the plants liked it fine. Art's customers liked it too. With the regulations the city had put in place against other kinds of landscape irrigation—tap water you could only apply manually, with a bucket, and not to lawns—Art had found lots of buyers. After all, his reclaimed water was practically the only alternative to brownscape.

The only *legal* alternative, anyway. The city was full of rumors of a black market. Certainly, water in Santa Barbara had become a rare and precious commodity. To encourage conservation, the water department had boosted the billing rate five times in four years, and I had spoken to one serious gardener who paid $800 per month the previous summer just to keep her half-acre of trees and shrubs alive.

Figures like that could catch the attention of thieves, and I had heard reports of tank trucks backing up into the driveways of vacationing homeowners to fill up with thousands of stolen gallons. Does that sound like paranoia? Maybe, but water commissioner Charles Meyer was taking the reports seriously. "I think there has been quite a bit more water theft than people realize," he had told a reporter from the local newspaper.

Water was on everyone's mind when I arrived in Santa Barbara in late May of 1991. There had been four years of drought; 1990 had been drier there than in Saudi Arabia. Heavy storms, dubbed "the March miracle" by the grateful Santa Barbarans, had rescued the city from immediate disaster that spring by dumping twelve to thirteen inches of water in a couple of weeks (the city only gets eighteen inches in a typical year). Still, May is the beginning of the region's dry season, and at the time of my visit Lake Cachuma, Santa Barbara's principal reservoir, stood at only 35 percent of its capacity.

Santa Barbarans were wondering if they were facing a fifth year of drought, and if so, how they would cope. Proof of just how seriously the public was taking this was the referendum that was coming to a vote in a few days: the electorate would have a choice of committing $440 million toward linking up with the state aqueduct system, or building a desalinization plant at a cost of $37.4 million.

No matter which option the city chose, however, the cost of water was going to rise even more. Cost estimates for state-delivered and desalinated water varied wildly, but the bill seemed liable to be at least twenty times as much per acre-foot as that drawn from Lake Cachuma. Yet the gardeners I was meeting were excited, and I could understand why. They were engaged in making something wonderfully new; a landscape that was as complex, rich, and satisfyingly dry (in California parlance) as a fine chardonnay.

"It's utterly bullet-proof," Owen Dell remarked. What he was showing me was not a kevlar vest or armor-plated BMW but a luxuriant clump of Mexican bush sage (*Salvia leucantha*). "One of my favorite plants," he added. Who, I wondered, would take a shot at those graceful spikes of velvety purple, with their bristling armature of small, white trumpets? Nor did the soft, cool billows of flowers and foliage spreading out around us seem a likely hideout for gunslingers.

Yet this landscape *had* been under fire when Owen first saw it two years before. The energy giant ARCO had built a conference center down by the Santa Barbara beach, a place where executives could come to relax and exchange ideas. Back in the spring of 1989, the conference center had enclosed within its red brick walls five acres of manicured lawns. To keep these green, the gardeners were using three times as much water as the water district was willing to allot them.

ARCO had immediately moved to correct this situation—but not by abandoning its landscape. Instead, management sought a creative solution by contacting the local landscape architect who had most closely identified himself with the cause of water conservation—Owen. What he accomplished here was helping to solidify his reputation as a designer who really understands the southern California landscape, one who can be depended on for imaginative yet practical responses to its challenges. It was here he chose to introduce me to his work.

I'd arrived right at 9:00 A.M., to find Owen—panama hat, checked shirt, and neatly trimmed beard—already waiting in the parking lot. As he took me in through the gate, Owen told me how, when he presented his proposals for landscape conversion to the ARCO management, he had met with an unexpected ally in the company's no-nonsense chairman. "He loves flowers," Owen explained. "He thinks they're the next best thing to oil." So Owen and his crew descended on the conference center "like locusts"; the very first day on the job, they stripped away 70 percent of the lawns. People were shocked . . . and pleased. "Why didn't we do that years ago?" they demanded.

The fact is that turf has become the default landscape solution all across the United States. If an area suggests no other kind of treatment, then we automatically plant it to lawn. That's forgivable in areas where turf grasses flourish naturally, but in southern California they demand a commitment to heavy, regular watering. In Santa Barbara, according to Owen Dell, sowing grass seed or rolling out the sod shouldn't be a reflex, it's got to be a decision.

Lawns weren't the only thing to disappear from the conference center grounds with Owen's arrival. Azaleas, begonias, hibiscus, and all the other colorful but poorly adapted plantings were torn out, too. In their place, and over the former lawn too, came the plants that would flourish with only minimal irrigation.

They bloomed all around us as we toured the grounds, the drifts and sweeps of pink daisy-like flowers of fleabanes (*Erigerons*), and pale yellow to cream-colored, delicate falls of the iris-like fortnightly lilies (*Dietes vegeta*); the great bunches of statice (*Limonium perezii*) with their enormous, rich, blue-purple heads; the silver mounds of Artemisia 'Powys Castle', larger here than I have ever seen them before, and the clouds of blue-flowered Russian sage (*Perovskia*).

Some were natives, like the California bush anemone (*Carpenteria californica*) Owen had tucked in at the foot of a building. That's so rare in the wild, Owen said, that for thirty years after it was first collected it was thought to be extinct. It seemed happy here, the five-foot-tall twigs of glossy, narrow leaves and peeling, silvery bark holding out for our inspection clusters of sweet-scented pure white flowers, each one of them fully three inches across. Many more of the plants were exotic, like the blue hibiscus (*Alyogyne huegelii*), which is really not a hibiscus but a purple-flowered relative from arid lands of southern and western Australia.

As a horticulturist, I am continually disappointed by the poverty of the average landscape architect's vocabulary. Most know only a handful of reliable and undemanding plants, which they use constantly and without reflection, like a tough teenager with his Anglo-Saxonisms. The result is that all their plantings look alike.

Owen, by contrast, was speaking in tongues—there was something unfamiliar and striking everywhere I looked. Owen credits this diversity to the local nurseries, whose stock, he says, is amazing, the richest and most diverse in the country. I don't doubt that, but I believe the richness of Owen's gardens have more to do with his background. It was a fascination with ecology that brought him to landscaping, and the wild landscape has been Owen's mentor.

He was an undergraduate studying botany—his major kept changing, Owen recalls, but an interest in plant sciences was a constant—and field trips took him out into the California countryside. The immediate effect of that was entirely predictable. Like every visitor since John Muir, Owen was fascinated by what he saw there, for wild California, even after a century and a half of man's abuse, still casts a spell. Less predictable was the aftermath of that experience. Upon his return to town, Owen looked around with an increasingly critical eye.

It was the early 1970s, and southern California suburbs were an endless vista of junipers, podocarpus, and hibiscus. "The palette," he recalls, "was about fifty plants, if that. Environmentalism hadn't been invented yet, really, and we were going around on field trips looking at the most beautiful places, and I thought what a discrepancy there was between them and what people did on their property. It just kept eating away at me. Something snapped in me, and I said, this is not right, I've got to change this. That's why I do what I do."

What Owen does is largely art and partly a pragmatic response to ways in which people use a property. In the course of his twenty years in landscape design, he has lost his initial insistence on native plants. Still, at the heart of his work seemed to me to be a set of sensitive, highly imaginative variations on the themes of the natural landscape.

Within the conference center grounds, for example, I found reminders of the grasslands that once covered this coast: a bank planted to blue hair grass, the Miscanthus by the entrance to a driveway, eruptions of red fountain grass that framed the tennis court. There were scenes drawn from the wildflower meadows of inland valleys, luxurious (if compact) tapestries where spires of deep purple penstemon flowers (*Penstemon* 'Midnight') soared from a ground of the blush pink saucers of Mexican evening primrose (*Oenothera berlandieri*), and yellow, hovering disks of Achillea 'Moonshine' blossoms.

On the drier slopes, especially to the seaward edge of the property, there were dense aromatic tangles I had to believe were inspired by chaparral, the evergreen scrub that used to come down almost to the beach and that still clothes the upper reaches of the foothills where building has not yet penetrated. Owen had interwoven gray santolinas (called lavender cottons for their soft foliage and clean, sweet smell) with Spanish and French lavenders, and fine-leaved *Geranium incanum* (true geraniums, not the gaudy, red-flowered annuals we call by that name) with his favorite Mexican bush sage. Dwarf chaparral broom flanked the drives, as much at home in that dry, sunny spot as in the California foothills and seaside strands where it grows wild.

What I didn't find anywhere in this garden were the clichés of suburban gardening with which I had been raised. I wasn't surprised to find the Bermuda grass lawn reduced from the usual flood to narrow rivulets of walkways; my readings about water conservation had prepared me for that. But where were the carpets of low-maintenance ground covers? Owen disdains those "creepy-crawlies," because, like turf, they must be irrigated by old-fashioned and inefficient sprinkler systems. To save ARCO water, he'd converted the whole landscape (except the remnants of turf) to drip irrigation. With its 15,000 "emitters" (individual tiny nozzles), he believes that this is the most extensive drip irrigation system in any ornamental landscape in southern California.

Between the new planting and the improved irrigation system, Owen's design cut ARCO's water usage by almost half from the day it was installed. As the landscape has matured and the plants have sent roots deeper into the soil, the need for watering has continued to decline, so that by the time of my tour usage was down to less than 30 percent of what it had been before the redesign. That meant ARCO had been consistently using less water than was allowed to it, even as the drought worsened and the allotment dropped.*

* As of spring 1993 the drought had ended, but ARCO continues to conserve—the return to normal rainfall has not diminished its enthusiasm for the new landscape.

The crucial part of this success has been Owen's personal involvement. He continues to visit the site at least weekly to extract a core from the ground and check soil moisture, and to reset the electronic controls for the watering system. Given his choice, he'd eliminate those altogether; watering by the clock is an absurdity, he points out, yet that is what automatic irrigation systems do. On Tuesday it's overcast and cool, yet the electronic control gives the flowers two hours of irrigation; on Wednesday, when it's hot and dry, it gives the plants nothing at all.

The decision to water *must* be kept in the hands of human beings, not left to digital technology, where, Owen says firmly, it does not belong. Whenever he can, Owen persuades his clients to substitute Bermadon valves for conventional "clock"-type controllers; the Bermadon, an Israeli device, must be turned on manually, but it turns itself off after a set amount of water passes through it. This guarantees that the gardener chooses the time to irrigate, yet makes the process as easy and simple as possible.

We returned at last to the gate, where Owen pointed to a windbreak of towering eucalyptus trees across the street, and talked of biomass. The area on which we stood was originally grassland. Introducing trees and shrubs is not only fighting nature; it, along with population growth, has created Santa Barbara's water shortage. The city has become famous for the diversity of its flora, and Owen treasures that. Yet he is persuading at least some of his clients to move toward finer, sparer plantings. But a return to anything like the original vegetation isn't practical, and he knows that in Santa Barbara, conflict between horticulture and ecology is inevitable. It is his job to be the mediator.

I left Owen Dell with his clocks and valves—what he termed, mockingly, "the life-support system." In fact, though, that's just what an irrigation system is in Santa Barbara. "You've got to have it," Owen admitted. "You put plants in the ground without irrigation, and they're going to die. You have to deal with that constraint every single time."

Unfortunately, that life-support system was daily growing more difficult to maintain. The drought had drawn an impressive response from Santa Barbarans. Many are wealthy people—Santa Barbara ranks among the twenty-five most affluent metropolitan areas in the country—who had come here because of the city's reputation for fashionable ease. Besides, retirees make up a disproportionate share of the population, and I wouldn't have guessed that they'd be eager for new challenges. I was wrong; for they'd joined everyone else (or virtually everyone) in accepting considerable discomfort to cut their water use by 41 percent in 1990, and by 48 percent (48 percent of the pre-drought average, that is) in the first months of 1991.

I found an outstanding example of this civic-mindedness in another of Owen's clients, Dr. Jerry Griffith. He's a retired physician living in Goleta (the community to the west of downtown Santa Barbara). He had replaced all the toilets in his home on Ronda Drive with "ultra low flush" models that used one-fourth as much water per flush, and installed "low-flow" shower heads that reduced the expenditure there by one-half to four-fifths. His wife prefers baths, which involve a bigger investment of water than a shower (eight to twelve gallons per day), but with the help of an electric pump, they use the water from the tub to flush the toilet and so use it twice.

Dr. Griffith knows how much water is coming into Santa Barbara County's water supply system—he's got a rain gauge in the backyard, and he's kept records of rainfall since the early 1970s. He has a chart on the kitchen wall where he records the weekly precipitation and the status of Lake Cachuma, how much water flows into the reservoir, and how much is lost through evaporation. He keeps track of his end of the equation, too, for he knows where all the gallons go once they pass through his meter.

Fourteen hundred gallons a week is how much he allows his plants. He arrived at that quota through simple arithmetic. By looking at his bills for the months of February and March (the Goleta Water District bills on a bimonthly basis) a rainy period normally when he doesn't have to irrigate at all, Dr. Griffith established what his household usage is: it runs from fifty-five to sixty gallons a day (in a state where daily usage for a household of two averages more than four hundred gallons). That number he subtracted from the basic allotment Goleta suggests for a family of four or less—2,200 cubic feet per billing period. This calculation gave him the quantity he could allow for use outside the house: 1,400 gallons a week, enough to operate his drip irrigation system for two hours.

He figured this out in 1987, even before Goleta began rationing water (because it depends mainly on reservoirs and has fewer wells on which to draw, Goleta was hit even harder by the drought than the city of Santa Barbara). Dr. Griffith's childhood vacations on a family homestead in the San Bernardino Mountains made him thrifty. When you have to haul all your water in buckets from a pump a mile and a half away, you learn not to waste. In addition to conservation, however, he had another motive. He was tired of "fighting the lawn." Turf had never flourished in his sloping front yard. Dr. Griffith speculated that the soil was badly compacted when the builder carved the homesite out of an old walnut grove. Anyway, he was fed up with mowing, trimming, and fertilizing something that never did look particularly attractive.

He found Owen's name in the Yellow Pages in an advertisement for xeriscaping, and called him up. Dr. Griffith had two requirements: he wanted something informal—the landscape should "look as if it just happened that way"; and it should harmonize with the blue, white, and yellow color scheme his wife had chosen for the house.

What he got was a boulder-strewn hillside buried under a mulch of shredded bark and a cosmopolitan avalanche of dryland flowers. One Australian, the blue hibiscus (*Alyogyne* 'Santa Cruz'), I recognized from my visit to ARCO's conference center; the other, a dense mat of dark green leaves sprinkled with mauve, tubular flowers, Dr. Griffith identified for me as fanflower (*Scaevola* 'Mauve Clusters'). The statice came from the Canary Islands (at least originally), while the lily of the Nile (*Agapanthus africanus*), a blue-flowered bulb like a bolder amaryllis, the fortnight lily (*Dietes* 'Lemon Drop'), and the *Euryops pectinatus* (a gray-leaved, yellow daisy-flowered shrub rare enough that it has no common name) all hailed from southern Africa.

The basket of gold (*Aurinia saxatilis*), the gray-leaved tuft with small but vivid yellow flowers, was seeding itself around the slope —Dr. Griffith noted that it rarely persisted where planted, preferring to find its own niche. That came from Turkey, while the mountain lilac (*Ceanothus* 'Ray Hartman') was a domesticated offspring of the California chaparral native, and the island bush poppy (*Dendromecon harfordii*), a rounded, yellow-flowered shrub that would grow to a tree eighteen feet tall, came from Santa Cruz Island, the mist-shrouded giant that dominated the view from every Santa Barbara beach.

All that remained from the previous landscape was the wave of jasmine that rolls down the property line—Dr. Griffith insisted on keeping that. He doesn't miss the rest. "The front lawn was total dissatisfaction," he told me. "This is really easy to live with." It should be, because all he must do to maintain it is spot spray with weed killer and occasionally unclog one of the 500 drip emitters. Like the conference center, this landscape's efficiency is increasing as it matures, so that now even during dry months Dr. Griffith uses only 75 to 80 percent of the water allotted him by the Goleta Water District.

Dr. Griffith is by no means the only retiree who has made his mark in water conservation. The press was treating as heroes the Santa Barbara couple who had built a 2,000-gallon concrete cistern to collect rainwater from their downspouts. Certainly, they were determined; although at the time of the interviews they had used the rainwater only to irrigate their trees and yard, they insisted that "we'd boil it and drink it if we had to."

Still, I suspect I gained a truer picture of the senior community at my next stop, on Fortunato Drive back in the city of Santa Barbara. There, facing each other across a quiet residential street, were the Polans and the Clarkes, two retired couples that were both clients of Owen Dell.

The Clarkes had found Owen first, again through an advertisement. Howard Clarke, a professor of Classics recently retired from the University of California at Santa Barbara, had also been tired of mowing and spraying. Yet he wanted to keep the front yard open. He'd read an article tracing our liking for clipped turf to an instinctive preference for open fields where predators could not approach unobserved, and he told Owen that he, Howard Clarke, was particularly worried about vandals—and Huns and Visigoths, too. Owen responded with a list of perennials guaranteed to repel Vandals and Visigoths; for problems with Huns, he directed Dr. Clarke to the agricultural commissioner.

What Owen planted for the Clarkes was a wildflower meadow, some of which I recognized from the conference center. There was Achillea 'Moonshine' again, *Geranium incanum* with its mounds of delicately cut leaves and magenta flowers, and *Penstemon* 'Midnight'; but the backbone of olive trees, the Texas privet (*Ligustrum japonicum var. texanum*), and Heavenly Bamboo (*Nandina Domestica*), gave this smaller site a feeling of intimacy.

Dr. Clarke appreciated the reduced maintenance—I found him

strolling about with a pair of shears, snipping fading flower heads from the Achilleas, and he says that's about all he does now. He admired the hardiness of the plants; he showed me how the geraniums had hopped the fence to colonize an uncultivated bit of the neighbors' property. He appreciates the difference in water needs when the bills arrive. In the past he used to haul out the sprinklers twice a week; over the whole past summer he had turned on the new drip system only twice. But what really delights him are the olive trees.

Olives are a species so persistent, even on the parched, rocky slopes of southern Europe, that the ancients regarded this tree as virtually immortal. Besides, in Santa Barbara they practically qualify as natives, since they arrived there with the first Spanish padres. The Spanish planted olives for their fruit; Owen, in the interest of neatness, selected trees that the nursery had guaranteed to be fruitless cultivars (*Olea 'Wilson'*). Still Dr. Clarke wasn't surprised when his trees fruited. After all, the olive's irrepressible fecundity had been the mainstay of the ancient Greek economy.

"As any classicist knows, an olive tree's sole purpose for existence is to bear fruit." So he'd had the opportunity to taste a fresh olive for the first time, and the experience had filled him with wonder at the ingenuity of the human race. How could man ever guess that anything which tasted so horrible was actually edible?

Watching from across the street, Russell and June Polan had decided that they wanted the very same thing that the Clarkes had. Owen refused. Then he told them that he'd give them something that would be theirs alone. In this case he'd played off the burgundy-colored trim of the house, planting Indian Hawthorn (*Raphiolepis* 'Springtime'), a glossy-leaved evergreen whose new growth is purplish red. For contrast, he had framed these with the blue blossoms of Verbena 'Designer Lavender' and French lavender, and the bluish foliage of matilija poppies (Romneya coulteri). This last, an eight-foot-tall Californian perennial, helped cool the composition with spectacular flowers four to eight inches in diameter, blossoms of white, crepe-like petals and golden centers; and he'd further tempered the whole with the green foliage of McMinn Manzanita, an expansive western relative of the eastern, mat-forming bearberry.

New Zealand tea trees (*Leptospermum scoparium* 'Burgundy Queen')

—fine-leaved shrubs, really—reiterated (in season) the keynote with their burgundy-colored, quince-like blossoms. It was the Red Fountain Grass, though, that stole the show. Like the Clarkes' olives, it was mislabeled; although sold to Owen as dwarfs, the plants proved full-sized, cresting at a height of six feet. These spectacular jets of crimson remind the Polans of the ocean when the wind sets them rippling, and the maintenance is far easier than that of turf grasses. They cut the clumps of red fountain grass back to the ground once a year. "When should we do this?" they had asked Owen. "When you can't stand them anymore," he'd replied, and that point seems to come in December.

The Polans appreciate the thriftiness of their landscape. They water more than the Clarkes, but only once a month or so, and they are pleased that they no longer have to pay a gardener to mow and edge weekly. But what they like best is the freedom it gives them. They travel often; last year they drove to Maine, and they were preparing for a trip to Greece when I talked to them. They wanted a landscape that could take care of itself while they were away, and still look neat when they returned. They got it—their yard made a pleasant contrast to the dead lawns all around them.

For a while, turf almost qualified as an endangered species in Santa Barbara. It earned this status when the city outlawed lawn watering in February of 1990, threatening anyone who ignored this ordinance with first a warning and then a summons and a fine. To enforce this rule, and to help seek out car washers, those with leaking toilets, and all other kinds of water wasters, Santa Barbara hired a squad of "water cops." The officers' zeal and their reliance on anonymous tips had made them distinctly unpopular; land-scapers Chris Cullen and Gillian Christie, hosts of "Garden Gossip," the gardening program on the local radio station, had nicknamed them "H_2O Gestapo," and the name stuck.

Some of the offenses, however, were spectacular. A corporate raider from Texas, Harold Simmons, had refused to stop watering the twenty-three-acre lawn he'd carved out of an avocado grove in the neighboring town of Montecito, and since Montecito and Santa Barbara draw from the same sources, city residents were infuriated. Simmons was using 10 million gallons of water annually for this luxury—enough to support a typical family of four for thirty years. He'd ignored summons after summons, and a bill of $25,504 for excess usage didn't even make the rich man blink. When, finally, Montecito turned down Simmons's water pressure so that his irrigation system wouldn't work, he drilled his own well.

I was told by a local nurseryman that Simmons had actually expanded his lawn during the drought, and that his conspicuous consumption had inspired imitation among some of his wealthy and competitive neighbors. A neighbor from the other camp, a woman who favored preserving the native flora, complained that her oak trees were dying as a result of the changes in the local ecology caused by the ever-widening circle of sprinklers. She was right, too; continually wetting the base of the oaks increases their susceptibility to a fatal fungus, *Armillaria*, that is endemic now all through southern California.

Despite such unrepentant guzzlers, though, conservation had regularly exceeded every target set by the city water department. But it wasn't enough. Even with the reduced consumption, the supply was shrinking as stored water in the reservoirs was depleted, and the water in the ground, the aquifer, continued to drop. In May of 1991, Santa Barbarans faced a shortfall between supply and demand of 20 to 50 percent if the drought continued another three years—and seven-year droughts are a regular pattern in southern California.

Indeed, weather records stretching back over 120 years included four droughts more severe than the present one. Besides, the water department couldn't afford the conservation. After the March rains it had asked for and gotten repeal of the anti-lawn-watering ordinance. The reason for this move was simple dollars and cents. Water use citywide had dropped to 9,200 acre-feet per year, little more than half the pre-drought level, and the water department had to sell 13,000 acre-feet to break even.

I took a crash course in Santa Barbara history *and* climatology the next day with Sydney Baumgartner. She, too, is a landscape architect, and she's the professional heir to a team that was central to making Santa Barbara gardens famous in the early part of this century. Sydney apprenticed with Elizabeth de Forest, the widow and former partner of Lockwood de Forest.

Lockwood de Forest had cut quite a figure in the Santa Barbara of the 1920s, '30s, and '40s. An heir to the Tiffany fortune, he met on equal terms with the wealthy easterners who were coming then to build lavish winter refuges. But de Forest was more than just *the* fashionable designer; he was also an inspired plantsman who drew on floras from similar climatic regions all over the world—Australia, South Africa, and the Mediterranean—to enrich the local landscape without violating it. He was the man who, as much as any other, transformed the old Spanish mission town into the "Riviera of southern California."

As my first lesson, Sydney took me to the de Forests' own home, and along the way she told me about the Santa Barbara climate. The peaks I could see standing at attention behind the town are part of the only mountain range on the Pacific Coast that runs from east to west; they act as solar collectors, absorbing the heat of the sun on their southern slopes, and as a giant windbreak, fending off the cold north winds. This has given the region an unusually mild climate, one that gardening books commonly describe as Mediterranean.

In fact, it is far milder, for it escapes the extremes of the Mediterranean basin. Summers along the southern California coast are not typically searing hot; in Santa Barbara, 70° to 80°F and clear is the norm, and sea fogs often roll in to refresh the town in the morning. Nor do the Santa Barbara winters have any chilling winds like the Mediterranean's frozen mistral—the mountains see to that.

To say that this region has no weather, however, as many people do, annoys Sydney Baumgartner. That's judging southern California against a northern European tradition, one that expects dramatic shifts from day to day. Weather is more predictable in Santa Barbara, since the changes are gradual. But as if in compensation, the region gets five seasons rather than four.

There are two springs, two summers, and a rainy season. The first spring comes after the early rains in late fall (typically, in November) and lasts only a few weeks, but it's long enough to coax a bloom from the jasmine, bougainvillaea, hibiscus, oleander, and other subtropical imports. This makes a brief summer that is soon swallowed up by three months of rain (except in drought years): January, February, and March. The second spring begins in April and is ended by the "Santa Ana" winds that blow in hot and dry from the desert in May. This marks the beginning of the *real* summer, the six months during which it quite likely will not rain at all.

Many gardeners regard this last as a period of hardship, but to Sydney this time of golds and russets, the season when the native plants fall dormant, is one of southern California's chief attractions.

Yet although she herself is a native, she admits that she didn't appreciate the southern California summers fully until she'd spent several years working abroad, in Germany and England.

"I came home, and it was August, and I thought, God, for the first time in a couple of years I feel really clean. It felt so good to dry out again." Understanding the beauty of the dry season, she believes, is a crucial part of coming to terms with the natural landscape in Santa Barbara. Coming to terms with Santa Barbara also involves admitting that conventional American landscape plants are as out of place here as a conventional calendar.

Elizabeth and Lockwood de Forest understood this well. I recognized the trees that lined their drive, but only because I share with Howard Clarke a classical education. The gnarled trunks and gray-green leaves could only belong to olives. But the trees of the *allée* were a traditional choice (at least in Santa Barbara); the turf that embraced them was not.

It was Kikuyu grass from East Africa. This was the first lawn of its type in southern California, and it proved ideally suited to the climate, since it flourishes with no irrigation at all. Kikuyu survives the dry season by going dormant, and in summertime it dries to a golden brown. This was all to the good, as far as the de Forests were concerned. The color of the dormant Kikuyu nicely matches the midsummer hue of La Cumbre peak, the focus of their garden's main vista, and the lawn seems to invite the wild majesty around the house. With the return of the rains, both mountainside and lawn quickly green again.

Though they had promoted Kikuyu grass very actively among their clients and neighbors, the de Forests made only a limited number of converts. Kikuyu makes a rougher lawn than our traditional turf grasses, and until recently most Santa Barbarans didn't care about saving water. What impressed me was the obvious durability of this grass. Later I learned that Kikuyu is a common choice for sports fields in South Africa because of its toughness and wear resistance, but at the time I only knew that this lawn was healthy. It has seen sixty summers now in a climate where turf is generally considered a short-lived planting, and it doesn't have the benefit of an owner's care, since the de Forests' son has moved to Australia. Even so, this lawn was thriving, and that made it a striking contrast to those all around it.

In April, Sydney told me, this imported meadow bursts into

bloom with South African bulbs—homerias, ixias, sparaxis—the particolored "harlequin flowers," babianas, lapeirousias, and little blue "peacock" moraeas—trumpets, cups, and strings of stars more delicate than the familiar Dutch bulbs, but vivid, as colorful as their names. All of these, like the Kikuyu grass, are accustomed to a cycle of wet and dry, and won't thrive without a summer drought. I saw kniphofias ("red-hot pokers"), another native to South Africa, blooming in the cutting garden, and sword-like leaves of irises and alstroemerias, dryland perennials whose fleshy roots and rhizomes had made them as drought resistant and persistent as the lawn.

This is a landscape that has aged well. Indeed, it had improved over the years, at least from the water department's point of view. After an initial flirtation with roses, Elizabeth and Lockwood had replaced the thirsty rose bed they had planted in the side garden with a far less routine collection of drought-proof lavenders. I paused to admire the South African proteas—shrubs with flowers like spray-painted artichokes—and the espaliered figs (another Mediterranean plant). Then it was on to the next demonstration. Once again, this was preceded by a lecture.

As we drove to the next garden along, Sydney advised me to look up the old volumes of *The Santa Barbara Gardener*, the monthly magazine that the de Forests had published from 1925 up until Lockwood enlisted in an Army camouflage unit in 1942. Sydney told me that in its pages I'd find previews of many techniques now being presented as "cutting edge" (the highest term of praise in southern California).

"This hasn't been the first big drought [a severe one gripped the area from 1928 to 1934]. They were writing articles back then on the use of gray [waste] water in the landscape, drought tolerant plants . . ."

Months afterward, sifting through crumble-cornered pages, I found, along with the month-by-month accounting of the rainfall, not only plugs for the virtues of Kikuyu grass and notes about which plants had best withstood the roasting of the latest Santa Ana, but even directions for designing a summer garden in shades of brown.

We stopped at an estate formerly owned by the British wife of a well-known actor (Sydney forbore to tell me which one). The previous owner had filled the site with English-style lawns and flower borders; the current ones, a Calfornia rancher and his wife, had called in Sydney to create something more at home in Santa Barbara.

She had accomplished this largely through the use of native plants—by using them, as she noted, "in a way nobody had ever seen before." Instead of trying to reproduce the look of untouched nature, she had disciplined the natives in formal plantings. For example, she had espaliered trees and shrubs, training them with trellises and shears into living fences and trellises to outline courts and soften walls.

Espaliering is a centuries-old European technique, one that's typically applied to apple or pear trees, or other Old World plants. Yet it worked equally well here with western redbuds (*Cercis occidentalis*), small, multi-trunked deciduous trees of handsome blue-green foliage that bear bunches of brilliant magenta flowers in springtime.

It worked with the lemonade berries (*Rhus integrifolia*), too. These evergreen shrubs bear foliage as handsome and glossy as that of their relative the poison ivy, though the lemonade berry's leaves aren't toxic, and in late winter bear dense clusters of white or pinkish flowers, too, a bloom that gives way to sour and edible berries. Espaliering also helped tame a prostrate form of ceanothus, a creeping variety of the common chaparral shrub known as "wild lilac." And despite the unaccustomed discipline, these shrubs hadn't lost their native thrift—even in the garden, they still prefer the natural budget of water to the sprinkler's spray.

I appreciated the elegance of the formal plantings. What went straight to the heart, though, was the meadow of western wildflowers Sydney had planted not far away. I spotted nemophilas and lupines with blossoms as blue as a desert sky, raspberry-colored clarkias, and golden California poppies. Gazing at this display, I was struck by a sad reversal. Horticulturists have introduced so much foreign vegetation into Santa Barbara (over 500 species, according to a botanist at the Santa Barbara Museum of Natural History), that now it is natives which impress the eye as exotic.

With a half-dozen fat lemons picked from a tree in the estate's orchard, we drove back into town and past the Red Lion Inn, whose grounds Sydney had designed eight years before. The inn's owners had insisted on broad sweeps of lawn. Their customers expected it, they insisted. The town, short of water even before the drought, had demurred. To break the impasse, Sydney arranged to run a pipe to the sewage treatment plant.

Now the Red Lion can water its lawns without further draining Lake Cachuma. The city has taken note: it applies more of the "reclaimed water" (whatever it doesn't sell to door-to-door vendors) to its parks. Who would have predicted a decade ago that the city's sewage treatment plant would be touted as a natural resource in 1991? But it is capable of reclaiming 5,000 acre-feet of water a year, about a third as much as the city's total pre-drought usage.

If the afternoon with Sydney had been a return to Santa Barbara's past, the next morning was a glimpse of what the future will be— if Art Ludwig has anything to say about the matter. "The free market jungle" is what Art Ludwig calls the existing city, and he believes that its water problems are inherent in its economic system. Given an opportunity, he'd reorganize the town entirely. Property lines, he believes, should be drawn to coincide with watersheds.

Nor is it enough for Santa Barbarans to change their style of gardening. As far as he's concerned, the architecture of their houses is also wrong for the climate. He spent nine months traveling through the Pacific rim countries, researching alternative living systems for the program in ecological design he completed at the University of California at Berkeley. But now he was back in the town he grew up in, building his own living space and marketing "Oasis," the laundry detergent he developed as the subject of his thesis.

That may sound suspiciously like plain old capitalism, but it really isn't. Oasis is more than a commodity and a means of cleansing dirty clothes, it's a step toward what Art calls natural design— "integrating human culture, technology, and economics with nature." He believes that water, as the most crucial resource, must be a focal point of home design.

"Every house," he has written, "especially in dry climates, should be surrounded with an oasis of biological productivity nourished by the flow of water and nutrients through the home."* It *is* a waste to buy water at a high price, as Santa Barbaran homeowners do, and then pour it down the drain. Art wants to save and recycle this gray water (as it is commonly called) through "biological land

---

* Art Ludwig, *Living with Nature* (Santa Barbara, Calif.: Natural Designs, 1989), p. 32.

treatment"—that is, he wants to apply it to the landscape right around the home, and let the plants purify it. This isn't practical if the water has been poisoned with conventional detergents, since these fill it with sodium, chlorine and boron, chemicals that are toxic to plants. So Art invented a cleaner that is actually a mild fertilizer.

Oasis is the only detergent I know of that is sold in nurseries, and that lists its ingredients in a numerical ratio. I'm used to picking up a bag of 5-10-5 (5 percent nitrogen, 10 percent phosphorus, and 5 percent potassium) when I want to feed the vegetables or flowers, but I admit I was dubious about applying Art's 4-3-6 to my shirts. It worked. And Art has proved that it's good for plants.

In the trials he conducted at Berkeley, Art raised a flourishing crop of tomato and bean plants in the university greenhouse, feeding them nothing but various solutions of water and Oasis. Pure water left plants hungry and stunted, while a solution of *Tide* (the commercial laundry detergent) and water destroyed them in as few as twelve days. That result does not make *Tide* a special villain (Art chose it as a standard of comparison on the basis of its popularity). Something that emerged from Art's study was the fact that virtually *all* brands of detergents, even the biodegradable ones, are death to plants.

After patenting his invention and finding a family-owned detergent manufacturer which agreed to manufacture Oasis, Art introduced it onto the market on Earth Day, 1990. He was shipping only eighty cases a month when I interviewed him—that's enough for a little over eight thousand loads of laundry. But as he pointed out, his sales are limited to individuals who have already installed gray-water irrigation systems in their landscapes, and it was only in August of 1989 that Santa Barbara County became the first county in the nation to make that legal. Elsewhere, outdated health codes still prohibit any such do-it-yourself water recycling, and that has stifled the demand for Oasis.

According to Art, gray water use still has a long way to go. He believes that the current systems are based on a fundamental mistake. To date, the emphasis has been on taking gray water out from the house and to the plants through a skein of plastic tubes. They are all unnecessarily complicated and technology dependent, since according to Art, the water never should have been inside the house—at least in California.

"In this climate," he explained, "it's so rare that you need the full degree of shelter." So why not just live in your garden? he asks. He himself has slept outside nearly every night since 1982. He's also integrated most other aspects of daily life into his landscape. A spigot poised over a rock-lined basin is where he washes his dishes, and he bathes himself in an open-air shower in warm weather, and in the cooler months in an old claw-footed bathtub set up on a stone firebox. Bending over to scoop a nervous lizard out of the empty bath, Art explained how a small fire of clippings and brush can keep the water comfortably warm even on the chilliest evenings.

To some degree, Art's comfort has dictated the disposition of these facilities. His sleeping mat under the California pepper tree faces toward the winter solstice, so that the tarp roof catches the first light and maximum radiation on the coldest days. Likewise, his shower faces southward, and it's backed by a shrub that blocks the north wind. Equally decisive, though, have been the needs of the plants. Art believes in bringing the water to them.

So the outflows from tub, shower, and faucet serve as springs within the landscape, each one nourishing a different cluster of plants. Water from the tub, for example, runs into pits, where it soaks down to the roots of persimmon and loquat, while runoff from the roof of his office (Art keeps his computer and photocopier indoors) irrigates the vegetable garden. A luxuriant squash plant catches the water from the shower. Water from the gravel driveway at the top of Art's hillside lot drains into a shallow swale that empties onto a grassy terrace; this serves as a reservoir of moisture for the plantings below.

This system not only irrigates plants inexpensively, it also very effectively purifies the wastewater. With plant roots grabbing all the nutrients they can, the water emerges from Art's "pet ecosystem" far cleaner than the stuff that pours out of Santa Barbara's wastewater treatment plant. Art is sure of that, because he collects water the way his neighbors collect wines.

He keeps the different vintages in a row of jugs on the shelf that runs shoulder high around the walls of his office. There's the brown, tannic rainwater that dripped down from the leaves of his oak tree—the rain washes nutrients out of the leaves and down into the ground, where the roots take them up again. There's the sediment and debris-filled stuff Art drew from Mission Creek up in the mountains; the sample he collected further down is more particle free, but murky with algae from fertilizers and natural nutrients washed out of the soil.

The jug of rainwater is clear. In contrast to Santa Barbara's well water, which contains as much as 1,000 parts per million of dissolved solids, the rain yields just 4. Yet in some ecosystems, such as alpine meadows and hillsides, the traces of nitric acid rainwater contains are nevertheless a crucial source of nutrition for plants. As clear as the rainwater is the jug of water Art collected from his own subsoil. The plants have removed virtually all pollutants, even pathogenic viruses, which, Art notes, are something that conventional processing, even tertiary treatment, won't touch.

Art admits that his landscape is still in its infancy. He has built low mounds along the property lines to keep the rainwater in, and broken its downhill run with swales and basins so that even during the heavy rains of the previous March virtually 100 percent of the water that landed on his soil was absorbed. But he plans to install a water garden, and he notes that the hot water from his bathtub could be used to warm as well as irrigate tropicals such as bananas. He plans a greenhouse, and he's rooting grape vines.

Ideally, he says, water would be "cascaded" down through a series of household uses—cooking water serving to wash dishes after the meal, water from the hot tub feeding the washing machine, and then purified through a hierarchy of plants. What he dreams of, though, is something much more ambitious than this "pet ecosystem." He would like to build an ecological research village, where he can bring all the different aspects of a sustainable lifestyle—"water, transport, architecture, land use, work, etc." together for the first time. He's setting aside his profits from Oasis to buy the land.

I won't be moving outdoors, certainly not in my native New England. I probably wouldn't do so even if I moved to Santa Barbara. Still, I believe there's a value in questioning basic assumptions. Art Ludwig is purposely out of step in a way that would have delighted Henry David Thoreau. Anyway, I found Art's eccentric landscape far more appealing than the half-dead, suburban plant-by-the-numbers all around it. It, at least, is based on a genuine intimacy with his surroundings. Art experiences nature, he says, "in a lot of different moods, and after a while you get it, how these different systems work." The garden he calls home is his response, and it made me understand this region just a little bit better.

A few nights later on State Street, over beers at Joe's, Owen Dell told me that what fascinates him about gardening in Santa Barbara is the variety. Step across a hill in Santa Barbara County, and you find the climate and vegetation transformed. He told me that if I went thirty miles up the coast and drove through the Gaviota tunnel, in the quarter mile underground I would pass from southern to northern California, from sun to fog, and one flora to another. Or if I liked, he told me, I could tune the climate by climbing— every thousand feet of additional altitude would lower the average temperature by six degrees. In Santa Barbara you can grow not only banana trees but also redwoods. You can grow nearly anything, in fact, as long as you can get water.

Yet he half seriously supports a movement proposed by water-issues specialist Marc Reisner: "Californians for Drought."

"I could be dead wrong, but I see that the drought has been a tremendous force in what I hope will be permanent change. We had our drought in the seventies; it wasn't as bad as this, it produced some dilettante thinking but then customers went back to installing sod lawns. But this time there have been substantive changes. Everybody's got a low-flow toilet, everybody's been carrying water from showers to the lawn. There has been no dearth of two- or three-thousand-dollar water bills, and that gets your attention real fast. But it's not just that. People wanted to do the right thing."

The next morning, June 5, my last in Santa Barbara, I read in the newspaper that residents had voted to grab all the water they could. Instead of choosing between options, they had demanded both: they were going to build the desalinization plant *and* bring in state water. But I remembered Owen's insistence that for gardeners the election was irrelevant.

"It [water] is never going to be cheap again. It's never going to be abundant again. I think we have a life's work digging up front lawns. This is the best thing that ever happened to the landscape industry. Californians for drought? You bet."

Two

Xeriscaping, Not Zero-scaping

here is a place I always go when I need information about subjects horticultural: the vertical file of the New York Botanical Garden Library. Running all around the walls of one basement storage room snakes a row of twenty-three battered, five-drawer metal file cabinets. Into these the librarians have fed forty-five years' worth of newspaper and magazine clippings on every imaginable horticultural and botanical topic, from A—"Acid Rain, Politics" to Z—"Zen Gardens" and "Zombies." It has become a matter of course that whenever I have a question on gardening matters, I head down those stairs. So I was taken aback when I looked for a file on "xeriscaping" one day, and found nothing among the X's.

Then in a flash of inspiration, I turned to the Z's. Sure enough, there was the folder I wanted, correctly titled but filed under "zero."

Xeriscaping, through a well-managed publicity campaign, has become the best-known school of water-conserving landscaping. Indeed, it is the only one that has penetrated every major region of the country. And yet, ironically, xeriscaping suffers from an image problem. For the library clerk's mistake typifies the attitude of too many gardeners who have never actually seen a xeriscape.

We Americans equate conservation with deprivation, and when told that a landscape is designed to reduce water consumption, we imagine the result as a sterile waste of gravel and boulders, with maybe the stark silhouette of a cactus lurking in the background. In truth, that is precisely what xeriscaping is intended to prevent.

"Green but not greedy" could be the motto of this movement. Xeriscaping *did* originate in the semi-arid West, and its guidelines were put together by water-conservation officers. But the designers were people committed to the quality of life in their communities, and they were smart enough to know that belt-tightening doesn't sell well to Americans. So they planned their alternative in such a way that it would actually increase the luxuriance of the local yards.

In town after town, wherever xeriscaping has taken hold, it has helped break the grip of a sterile suburban tradition. Skilled gardeners have criticized the movement, arguing that xeriscape is nothing more than a fancy name for principles that good gardeners have always practiced. They miss the point. The majority of homeowners in this country have never been gardeners, and they practiced landscaping as an unpleasant necessity, as a reflex rather than an art. As soon as the house is finished, you roll out the sod, pop in the foundation planting, then mow and clip, mow and clip, mow and spray, and mow and clip some more. Xeriscape has encouraged these people to aim higher.

What exactly is xeriscaping? To answer that requires a little bit of history.

Colorado—a state that has in a real sense become a meeting place for east and west and a magnet for well-educated (human) transplants—was the movement's birthplace. In 1977, six years before the opening shots in the battle over the Two Forks dam, the Denver Water Board signed something called the Foothills Settlement Decree. It hadn't done this altogether willingly; in point of fact, the Environmental Protection Agency had forced the board to sign in return for granting the city a permit to build yet another water project.

Fundamentally, this "decree" was a commitment by the water board to a program of water conservation (failure to achieve its goals would later be the basis for the E.P.A.'s rejection of Two Forks). A cornerstone of this program would be cutting water use by residential customers, and to help them do that the water authority developed a seven-step program in 1981; it was a secretary there who came up with the name. As noted in the introduction, *xeros* is the Greek word meaning dry and the botanical term for drought, and since the water board's new principles of landscaping were designed to foster drier landscapes—and a controlled drought by comparison with the water-wasting styles then current in Denver —"xeriscaping" they became.

As word spread through magazines and newspapers, other cities with water shortages began setting up their own xeriscape programs. For several years Denver continued as the new movement's center, with the unofficial headquarters being the back room of Highland's Tru-Value Nursery and Hardware. In 1986, however, the Denver group called for a general meeting at the annual xeriscape conference hosted by the City of Los Angeles.

The goal was to form a national organization, not only to coordinate promotion of the xeriscape concept but also to protect it. Local governments and water authorities had been changing key parts of the program to suit their own agendas, and responsible members of the xeriscape movement feared that this "bastardization" of the message would confuse the public. Far more troubling, though, was the way in which commercial landscapers in arid regions were trying to capitalize on xeriscaping's prestige. They were incorporating the words "xeriscape" and "xeriscaping" into their advertising and even their company names, often without observing its principles in their work. This unscrupulous activity threatened to discredit xeriscaping, and was making promotion of xeriscaping by governmental groups or public utilities look like a conflict of interest.

So the name "xeriscape" and the process were registered as a trademark, and Austin, Texas, was chosen as the headquarters for the new National Xeriscape Council. The decision to locate in Austin was due in some degree to the presence in that city of a "multimanagement company," a firm that specialized in the management of trade associations and societies, which could provide the machinery for the new council's day-to-day operations. More important, though, was the extraordinary commitment of the City of Austin to xeriscaping and the extremely active educational campaign being waged by Martha Latta, a landscape architect on the city payroll. Headquarters have since moved to Roswell, Georgia.* However, by virtue of enthusiasm, if nothing else, Austin remains the de facto center of the movement, and it was through the brochures issuing from Austin that I learned xeriscaping.

Briefly (and in my own words, though I'm following closely the materials I've received from the National Council) the seven steps to xeriscaping are as follows.

1. Planning and Design

A water-conserving landscape doesn't happen by accident. An informed choice of plants, a sensitive treatment of the site, and the grouping of plants together by their water needs—this is called "zoning"—are all fundamental to success and must be worked out on paper ahead of time. As in any garden or landscape, the design should organize itself around your needs and ideas of what's attractive. The gardener's urge to fill the plot with foliage, fruit, and flowers must accommodate the need for a play area, areas for outdoor entertainment, for pets, and maybe even a pool. But in a xeriscape another imperative, the need to use water efficiently, shapes the design as well.

Matching the plant to the site, setting shade-loving plants in the shadow of a tree, and locating sun lovers out in the open is a fundamental (and obvious) rule of successful gardening. The xeriscaper, though, takes this a step farther. He or she matches plant to plant, too, grouping species according to their relative thirst for water. In this way it is possible to avoid the situation that wastes so much water in the typical garden: by planting one thirsty rose bush amid a dozen drought-resistant junipers, the gardener who plans purely by aesthetics ensures that the whole area will have to be irrigated enough to satisfy the rose, and so guarantees that the junipers will be always overwatered.

* For further information about xeriscaping and help in contacting local chapters, write to:
National Xeriscape Council
P.O. Box 767936
Roswell, GA 30076-7936

Organizing plants into zones of uniform water needs makes precise watering possible, but even greater savings can be realized through a rational arrangement of the different zones. For the sake of simplicity, the National Xeriscape Council suggests dividing the landscape into high-, medium-, and low-water-use zones. Most commonly, xeriscape design calls for keeping the high-water, lusher zones small. At the same time, it maximizes their impact by setting them right next to the house, distributing them around decks, terraces, and other outdoor seating areas to create what xeriscapers call a "mini-oasis." As you move away from the house, the xeriscape typically becomes less intensively cultivated (and watered), progressing through medium-water-use zones to a periphery of low-water-use plantings, a zone that may receive no artificial irrigation at all once the plantings have rooted into the soil.

Every guide to xeriscape design I have seen makes clear that this pattern for arranging the zones *must* be adapted to suit the site and individual. If the only spot with sun enough for roses (your passion) lies at the far end of the backyard, then you create a high-water-use zone there. It is important to avoid jumping directly from zones of low to high water usage, since that practically guarantees waste through overwatering along the edge of the low-water-use zone—irrigation devices, whether automatic sprinkler systems or hand-held watering cans, do not irrigate precisely to a line.

2. *Soil Analysis*

One of the chief goals of the xeriscaper is to increase the water-holding capacity of his or her soil so that the maximum amount of rainwater and snowmelt is retained and the need for artificial irrigation is reduced as much as possible. But, as Chapter Three explains in detail, soil is a highly variable commodity. It can vary in texture and chemistry from site to site, and even from one area of yard to another. As a result, the treatment that will benefit your yard may be very different from the one your friend right across the fence used successfully.

Simply adding peat moss (as your nurseryman probably advises) will not necessarily improve your soil. Because it boosts the soil's organic content, a dose of peat will often increase your soil's ability to absorb water, but in many cases it is not the best material for this purpose. Peat has a distinctly acidifying effect on the soil, and in areas such as the Northeast, where the soil naturally tends to be acidic, you may not want to encourage that tendency, especially in this era of acid rain. Besides, for many soils, organic matter alone is not remedy enough.

My introduction to xeriscaping came during the four years that I lived in central Texas, in the town of College Station, and the soil I was tilling then was a leaden gray clay. It actually would hold a fair amount of water, but it resisted wetting—irrigation water, whether natural or artificial, commonly drained off across my yard's surface without penetrating. Digging in humus—I used the spent compost that I picked up cheaply at a local mushroom farm—helped, but I also blended an inch-deep layer of coarse sand into each bed, to permanently change the soil's texture.

In Chapter Three I'll focus in more detail on prescriptions for various problem soils, but the essential first step every time is to take a sample to your Cooperative Extension agent (see Chapter Four, pages 123–25 for complete instructions) and have a complete analysis carried out. This will involve two tests. One, the so-called nutrient analysis, tests for your soil's nutrient content and pH (its relative acidity or alkalinity); the other, the mechanical analysis, will inform you about the soil's texture (whether it is a clay or loam, etc.) and about its organic content. The costs of these tests vary somewhat from state to state, but in general they are extraordinarily reasonable. In fact, they may be the greatest bargain in gardening today, for in Connecticut at least (my present home—I moved here in 1989), you can still have them both done for a total of twelve dollars. The soil analysis enables you to attack any problem rationally and efficiently rather than by clumsy, often misguided guesswork. It may also convince you to live with the problem. If, for example, the soil tests reveal that improving your sandy, nutrient-poor seaside yard will require dump truck loads of humus and hundreds of pounds of fertilizers, you may decide instead to explore the beauties of the natural dune flora.

3. *Efficient Irrigation*

I had always considered myself a fair hand with the hose—as a former student of Frankie, Mike, and all the gardeners at the New York Botanical Garden, I knew how to water properly. Then, in Texas, the xeriscapers showed me how much water I was wasting.

I had thought I was being efficient by irrigating only when my plants clearly needed water. But as I learned, that was not the only factor to consider in scheduling my sessions with the hose. I had been watering when it was convenient for me; in fact, I most often set the schedule to suit my writing rather than my plants. Watering became an activity I used to stretch and relax during my breaks from the word processor in midmorning and midafternon.

As the xeriscapers pointed out, those hours of full sunshine were the worst possible choice, since that was when the sunlight was most intense and air temperatures were highest. On a clear, breezy day, as much as half the water droplets that left my sprinkler nozzle evaporated in midspray, before they ever reached the earth. And of the water that did reach the ground, much never soaked in to the plants' root zone; instead, it too evaporated back into the air. Ultimately, I calculate that for each drop of water that my sprinkler actually delivered to the roots of my plants, it wasted three or four.

I could have reduced the wastage substantially simply by re-scheduling. Xeriscapers habitually water in the early morning, late in the evening, or even at night, at times when the air is still and relatively cool, and when the solar radiation is minimal. That would cut the water stolen by evaporation. But, as the xeriscapers pointed out, adjusting the schedule was only a first step for a convert like me. What I had to do next was to retire my sprinkler altogether— or at least confine it to lawn watering.

As yet, there is no effective replacement for the sprinkler when it comes to irrigating turf grasses—the heavy, evenly dispersed shower of water it provides is just what a lawn needs. But using a sprinkler to water flowers, shrubs, trees, or vegetables, plants with distinct root systems rather than the turf grasses' even network, is like taking a sawed-off shotgun to the target range. You'll hit the bull's-eye, all right, but in the process you'll spread an awful lot of shot around where it does no good. Luckily, Texas xeriscapers introduced me to several other irrigation devices that could hit the target, and nothing else.

The one I came to rely on most in Texas (where irrigation was a constant duty) was drip irrigation. There are several different types of drip systems (I'll discuss them all, as well as a number of other methods of precision irrigation, in Chapter Five), but all rely on the same principle. Any drip system uses plastic tubes to deliver water at very low pressure exactly to the root zone of the plant. Because it's easy to control the delivery rate of this tubing, a drip system allows the xeriscaper to give each plant almost exactly the amount of water it needs, without waste.

I eventually installed no less than five different types of drip systems in different areas of our small Texan garden, and found that they provided a number of unanticipated benefits. By connecting the supply pipe to an electronic timer, I was able to water at midnight without going out in my pajamas to turn valves on and off. In addition, drip irrigation proved better at keeping the garden free of weeds than the most toxic herbicide. This is a virtue drip irrigation shares with any precisely targeted watering system.

Dandelions, chickweed, plantains, and all those other weedy invaders rely on a strategy of fecundity—some of these pests will bear a quarter of a million seeds *per plant*. They broadcast this impressive crop as far as they can, counting on at least a fraction of it to land in a hospitable spot. Millions of seeds are sown in this fashion every year in your home landscape, and if you insist on watering with sprinklers and wetting the whole surface of your yard, you are encouraging every single one of the invaders to germinate. In contrast, the xeriscaper who keeps most of the soil's surface dry, and wets the remainder only where desirable plants can seize upon the moisture immediately, leaves weed seeds high and dry and gives garden plants a long head start.

For gardeners with an aversion to complex technology, xeriscaping offers a number of other alternatives, most of them centuries-old devices thoroughly tried and tested by peoples of arid lands. I'll discuss these in detail, too, in Chapter Five; all share drip irrigation's ability to deliver water slowly, at a rate the soil can absorb it, and directly to the root area of the plants.

4. *Practical Turf Areas*

Until 1990, the National Xeriscape Council called for "limited turf," recommending that this type of planting be eliminated wherever possible. Since then, it has modified this stance somewhat, recognizing that with the new turf grasses that are appearing on the market, and with improved methods of management, a lawn need not be an eco-villain, as politically correct gardeners still insist it is. In fact, throughout large areas of the United States, notably the Northeast and upper Midwest, an intelligently designed lawn can be maintained with *no* supplemental irrigation.

Nevertheless, it is true that the traditional emerald-green turf is one of the thirstiest kinds of landscape treatment. When managed in the conventional way, especially by commercial chemical lawn methods (which grows grass hydroponically), Kentucky bluegrass uses two to four times as much water as more drought-resistant ground covers. Jim Knopf, a landscape architect from Boulder, Colorado, and author of an excellent guide to xeriscaping in the Rocky Mountain region, calculates that in Denver, Kentucky bluegrass needs as much as ten times more water over the twenty-week growing season than a low-water ground cover such as fernleaf yarrow (*Achillea filipendulina*).

For that reason, xeriscape manuals recommend restricting grass to areas of the landscape where its special qualities are really needed: play areas for the children, high-traffic areas adjacent to the house, etc. Turf, as Owen Dell pointed out to me in Santa Barbara, has become the default solution for American gardeners— when they can't think of any other treatment for a patch of earth, they bury it under a sheet of grass. The result is that our landscapes include far more turf than they should, not only from the standpoint of water conservation but from an aesthetic point of view as well. In College Station, I found that I was watering far less than the man across the street once I converted my front yard to a cottage-garden-type tapestry of flowers and shrubs, and it was my yard that passers-by stopped to admire, not his St. Augustine grass.

When drought-proofing an existing landscape, xeriscapers recommend replacing turf wherever practical with hardscape: a deck, a terrace, or an expanse of gravel. Its tolerance for foot traffic is a primary rationale for using turf, for no other ground cover is as resistant to that kind of abuse. But hardscape is even more durable, and it not only reduces the need for irrigation but can even increase the amount of rainwater other plants receive, if you make sure to give the hardscape a permeable surface. Setting flagstones in sand, for example, rather than on a concrete slab, allows passage of precipitation down into the soil and so to roots.

If your design really needs the cool sweep that only a lawn can provide, xeriscapers suggest making the turf a focal point of the design and locating it most prominently so that you can achieve the desired effect with the minimum square footage of turf. A xeriscape trick for controlling the water needs of turf is to keep any lawn as level as possible, so that rain or irrigation water soaks in rather than running off. Above all, never plant a steep slope to turf, since it will be nearly impossible to supply the soil with enough moisture to keep the grass green in that situation.

Finally, keep in mind that a geometrically compact lawn—a circle or square, say—consumes less water per unit of area than an amoebic lawn of many peninsulas and a long, complicated perimeter. Partly, this is because complicated shapes are impossible to water without waste; some of the sprinkler's pattern of spray is going to fall on non-turf areas. In addition, the turf at the edge of a lawn, grass that abuts a curb or driveway, or even the trimmed edge of a flower bed will dry out faster than does the grass at the lawn's interior. The heat radiating off pavement increases the local ET, and cutting or confining the turf's roots (as you do at the lawn's edge) reduces its ability to absorb water.

You'll find that to keep the grass at the lawn's edges green, you'll have to water it more. So the more edge, the more water you use. For this reason, the long narrow strips of turf, like those we set between the sidewalk and road, are the worst water wasters and are anathema to xeriscapers.

5. Appropriate Plant Selection

The conventional gardener chooses plants mainly on the basis of aesthetics and utility. That is, if it looks good to him, if it will do the job he has in mind (cover the ground and keep it free of weeds, rise up to block an unsightly view, furnish flowers in springtime, or colored foliage in the fall, etc.) and will survive in that climate, then the plant is acceptable. He's striving for a composition that's pleasing to the eye, and usually he's not interested in the preferences of the plants, as long as they will grow where he sets them. That's why the cliché plants of the classic suburban foundation planting—the rhododendrons, junipers, and yews—are so common. They flourish in a wide range of conditions; apply enough water and fertilizer, and they'll grow adequately on a rocky hillside or a humid coastal plain.

The xeriscaper approaches the matter of plant selection from a very different perspective. He wants plants that will contribute to the beauty and usefulness of his design, of course, but he insists that they be adapted to his soil and climate as well.

That's why an interest in native floras is common among xeriscapers. By choosing from among the trees, shrubs, and wildflowers that grew on a site before it was disturbed, they hope to secure plants that will flourish there now without much human assistance. Sometimes that works, though other xeriscapers maintain that they get better results by importing plants from distant areas of similar climate (for an exploration of this controversy, see Chapter Four). In any case, few of us really want a garden that is indistinguishable from the natural landscape. We may admire a stand of untouched woodland or tallgrass prairie, and enjoy exploring it, but we wouldn't find it a comfortable setting for daily life.

Nor will you find that the plants with the lowest need for water are necessarily the appropriate choice for your garden. As I discovered in College Station, those ultimate desert survivors, the cacti, do not adapt well to the humidity of central Texas. In south Florida, an area experiencing severe problems with the water supply because of excessive, unplanned development, any xeriscape plants must enjoy six months of drenching showers. The best plants for a xeriscape vary depending on where you live, and how exactly you intend to dispose them. That's why the National Xeriscape Council maintains that virtually any plant is potential material for the xeriscape.

Anyway, plant selection is always a matter of compromise for xeriscapers, since every gardener, even the most ardent water saver, admires some water-thirsty plants so much that he or she can't imagine a garden without them. Roses are my weakness—I like the types, such as rugosas, that can stand drought without help, but I must have besides some of the splendid old garden favorites that need regular watering through every dry spell. Vegetable crops, too, from lettuce to bell peppers, won't produce well if forced to contend with a water shortage. There are ways to reduce water usage by food crops (see Chapter Five). But unless you are willing to depend entirely on the supermarket or accept the simplicity of a Digger Indian's diet (I'm not, though it would doubtless benefit both my waistline and my health), you can't stop watering altogether.

In the western states, many water departments and public utilities have compiled lists of garden plants that will flourish locally with no or only modest irrigation. In the East, it is more often the agricultural schools, such as Cornell and Rutgers, that can supply this information. No matter where you live, however, the National Xeriscape Council can tell you where to go for this information. Such a list will serve you as the palette with which to paint your water-conserving landscape.

6. Use Mulches

Any properly educated gardener knows that a blanket of mulch, by protecting the soil from the sun and wind, can keep it cooler and moister. So there's nothing unusual in xeriscapers' endorsement of mulches. What's uncommon is their adroitness in manipulating this horticultural commonplace.

It was from xeriscapers that I learned to appreciate (and take advantage of) the differences of various mulches. Organic mulches such as shredded leaves provide the greatest rewards, because they not only do the best job of protecting soil from dehydration, they also increase its water-holding capacity by adding to its humus content as they decompose (see Chapter Four, pages 129 ff., for a fuller explanation of this). Black plastic, while effective in suppressing weeds, does *not* significantly increase soil moisture; and a gravel mulch, while it cools the soil below, may actually heat the air and plants above. On a sunny summer day, a sheet of gravel or crushed rock will typically increase the ambient temperature in a garden by 10° to 15°F.

Although the practical benefits they provide may be the reason landscapers bring mulches onto the site, xeriscaping has turned this expedient into a source of aesthetic rewards, too. Matching the mulch to the planting is the secret of this. A layer of pine needles enhances the woodland look of a clump of evergreens; and a meander of rounded pebbles can create an impression of a waterway where there usually is none—except in a season of heavy rain, when the pebble mulch will channel runoff to areas of the landscape where it will be absorbed and used.

Through their skill in the use of mulches, xeriscapers are helping to give them the place of importance they deserve in garden design. Xeriscapers are also, I find, the best source of information about locally abundant and inexpensive materials. Chipped tree trimmings are a standby everywhere, of course, but on Long Island, I've been told, you can supplement them with eelgrass gathered from the beach. Austin, Texas, has no seaweed, but old newspapers are there in stacks for the taking, and a local xeriscaper shared information about the types that are free from toxins. Even more important is the part that xeriscapers' advice has played in steering gardeners away from mulches that come with too high an environmental price tag. So, xeriscapers in south Florida are discouraging the use of shredded cypress wood, for though it mats well, weathers to an attractive shade of silver, and resists decay, its use contributes to the destruction of cypress swamps, a biologically rich and increasingly rare habitat.

7. Appropriate Maintenance

Planning and planting skillfully aren't enough; the way you manage your xeriscape also determines the amount of water you save.

Setting the blade of your lawn mower at the machine's highest setting, for example, reduces the amount of water required by a lawn. It might seem that longer leaf blades would increase transpiration, but in practice the extra cover seems to act as a living mulch. (For more information about water-wise lawns, see Chapter Six).

Yet if the cause of water conservation is served by less severe mowing, it benefits from more rigorous pruning. Judicious thinning of trees and shrubs reduces their leaf area, which lowers their rate of transpiration. When they lose less water in that way, those plants need less irrigation.

Reducing the amount of fertilizer you give your plants is another important element of xeriscape maintenance. The exact amount of actual nutrients you should apply varies from plant to plant and soil to soil, but at the least try cutting back to one-half the standard recommendation. It's easy enough to feed again if plants yellow or show other symptoms of distress. Be especially sparing with native plants. In talks with xeriscapers, I was warned again and again not to "push" native plants with extra nutrients and water. That, according to their observations, forces gangling, unsound growth, and hurries the plant to an early death.

Of all the tasks of xeriscape maintenance, none is more important than weeding. As I've noted, the xeriscaper's more precise watering should decimate the invading host, and the mulches should discourage them further, but even a single weed in the xeriscape is too much. A principal weapon weeds use for overwhelming more desirable plants is their superiority in extracting water from the soil. Let them be and the weeds' water thievery will soon put a hole in your irrigation budget.

Even if xeriscapes need a special kind of care, on the whole they demand far less work than conventional landscapes. Once the plants are well rooted in and have knit a canopy of foliage over the garden, the xeriscaper generally finds that this type of planting approaches very closely to the ideal of self-sufficiency. In the end that, not water conservation, was the feature of xeriscaping I heard praised most enthusiastically by those who followed its principles. Not one of them took for granted the emancipation from the hard, unpleasant chores of conventional garden maintenance.

That suits me, too. In College Station I found that I liked spending my gardening time musing and savoring rather than stooping and spraying. Reducing the amount of water I drew from the main markedly improved the health of my plants, too (I explain why on pages 133–34. As important to me as the practical benefits of xeriscaping, though, was the interest it added to my gardening.

Gardening with less water involved me in a very active dialogue with the Texan climate and soil. I had moved to Texas a horticultural carpetbagger. Like many other recent arrivals, all I knew to do was to try, through lavish use of resources, to force a Yankee character onto the landscape. With each step in the process of building a xeriscape, I had to consult what the land suggested. I had to know my soil, know the weather in all its seasonal variations, and I had to know every corner of my lot.

For I learned in Texas that successful xeriscapers are above all opportunists. If my College Station mentors found a low spot in the yard, a hollow that collects rainwater, or the water from lawn irrigation, that is where they planted the crepe myrtle (*Lagerstroemia indica*), whose elegantly mottled, muscular trunk and delicately shaded, long-lasting flowers of white, pink, red, or purple have made it Texas's most universally admired shrub. It is a relatively thirsty plant, demanding thirty inches of water a year and regular irrigation through protracted droughts if it is to look its best, but a hollow sees to that. The sheltered spot in the northwest corner of the fence by the kitchen door—that's where I planted the subtropical Chinese climbing rose ('Fortune's Double Yellow') that craved full sun but needed protection from the dehydrating winds.

Exploiting microclimates, those nooks and corners within every site where the regional climate is modified by a trick of exposure or topography, is another standby of all skillful gardeners. But the xeriscapers' ability to *create* microclimates was something new to me. A hedge planted where it blocked the prevailing wind gave them a band of calm air downwind for a distance equivalent to three times the height of the windbreak—a good haven for annual flowers, salad greens, or any crop not naturally drought resistant, ones whose ET would skyrocket when the wind played across their broad leaves. Shade trees were planted as a summertime haven for people, of course, but also for St. Augustine grass, which can tolerate the shade but won't stand exposure to the full sun of summer without frequent sprinkling.

The xeriscapers taught me to garden like an ecologist. Whereas before, like the other gardeners I knew, I assembled what were really collections of individual plants, forcing species with different needs to coexist, the xeriscapers encouraged me to copy nature's way by planting in communities. In a xeriscape, plants are chosen to complement each other not only visually but culturally. Within each zone, and even from zone to zone, all the plants, trees, shrubs, and herbaceous material should interrelate.

The plants in a single zone all share similar needs for water, and collaborate to create the environment each one needs—while the tree with its canopy filters the sunlight for the ground cover, the ground cover acts as a living mulch to protect the roots of the taller neighbors. The moisture that nourishes the mini-oasis seeps down to feed the roots of surrounding shrubbery, or it may work its way farther downhill to help support the deep-rooted meadow flowers of the low-water-use zone.

An ecologist defines a community as populations of organisms (plants or animals) that not only share an environment, but also interact. Through this interaction—competition and cooperation—they create something greater than the sum of the individual members; they begin to function as a whole, with stable, self-sustaining patterns of organization and structure. That's a very fair description of a xeriscape too.

Austin, Texas

"I am *not* a gardener," Wilbur Davis insisted, speaking emphatically, yet so softly that I had to strain to hear. White-haired, neatly dressed in slacks and sport shirt, Mr. Davis had perfected an ability I have observed only in older Texans: he somehow combined an old-fashioned, stately diction with a thoroughly informal warmth of manner. He was telling me why he was flabbergasted when an agricultural extension agent from San Antonio called him one Sunday morning in 1985.

The agent said he wanted to photograph Wilbur Davis's xeriscape; it was one of the best examples of this kind of landscaping, the agent said, that he had ever seen. "I don't know what you are talking about," Wilbur had replied.

He really didn't. Because Wilbur had developed his horticultural style entirely independently. What he had done was to respond logically to a particular situation, proceeding step by step and without any preconceived idea of where he would end up. All he knew was that what he and his neighbors had been doing was wrong.

I had seen a good deal of that kind of wrong during my years in central Texas. When I first arrived in the the mid-1980s, central Texas didn't have a native style of gardening, or at least not one that you'd find in the yards of well-to-do suburbanites. In College Station we used a mixture of Asian plants—Burford hollies (*Ilex cornuta rotunda burfordii* from eastern China), holly ferns (*Cyrtomium falcatum* from Japan), and Asiatic jasmine vines (*Trachelospermum asiaticum*) to give the yellow brick shotgun shacks a lush, "English" look. Even in sophisticated Houston, if you drove through the neighborhoods of the oil-rich all you saw were grander versions of our College Station landscapes. Everything was calculated to make you think you were somewhere else.

That's why, soon after Christmas, the conscientious central Texas gardener planted the bulbs that had been chilling in the refrigerator, so that by late February the front yard would be a postcard from Holland. Then, in another month his azaleas (and they were a bear to grow—they hated the alkaline soil) would explode in lurid bloom, stirring memories of Tara and the antebellum South. A few weeks after that, the hot-colored hybrid annual flowers and English perennials (which central Texas gardeners had to replant every year) would go in by the flatful. They ushered in a tea-and-crumpets interlude that lasted until the heat and humidity of our semitropical summers killed them both. Then in fall, gardeners would emerge from the air conditioning to clear away summer's casualties and set the stage for another round-the-world tour.

Though a transplant myself, I couldn't understand why the Texans—a people who take extreme pride in their heritage—had ever practiced this rootless kind of gardening. By 1986, though, this question was becoming moot, since the more knowledgeable gardeners were beginning to make a change. They were taking an obvious yet radical step: they were figuring out a landscaping style that suited Texas. What intrigued me about Wilbur Davis was that he had arrived at the same point without reference to gardening columns or books, without consultation with extension agents until after the fact. He was no gardener, he was just doing what worked.

. . .

It had been a big change for Wilbur when he moved to Austin's west side in 1983. He had lived in the city all his life, but always on the east side, an area that had originally been blackland prairie. Now he had moved up into the Hill Country, the rugged limestone escarpment that with its cedars and small, arthritic oaks looks oddly Mediterranean—a pasture in Sicily, say, or maybe a derelict olive grove in Tuscany. The vistas were as romantic as even the Texans claimed.

But Wilbur's own half-acre had not been romantic at all when he and his wife had arrived there. The photograph he shared with me showed a house perched on a desert. The builder, a man Wilbur had known since high school, had bulldozed away the native cedars and hollies to lay down St. Augustine grass sod. He'd regraded the site, too, as Wilbur discovered when the handful of relict trees died a year later. The arborist Wilbur called in found that five feet of soil had been pushed over the trees' roots.

So Wilbur had set to work putting in the standard foundation planting of pittosporums and other exotics. The first winter wiped him out again.

"Probably the best thing that happened to us," Wilbur mused. "We had this bad, bad freeze in 1983. Everything froze. Even the grass." Everything died, too, except for a few dwarf yaupons—native hollies—that the builder had planted.

That set Wilbur thinking. He might not be a gardener, but he had done his own yard work and he knew that the Austin climate was difficult for the standard (mostly exotic) landscape plants. The weather alternated between hot and humid, and hot and very dry—yet winters usually brought a couple of dozen days when the temperature dipped below the freezing point. Besides, plants from out of state mostly didn't like the limy, very alkaline soil of the Hill Country. So why did the homeowners of Austin plant these things? One night at a bridge game he voiced this question, and a lady across the table told him that she had just been to a lecture on that very subject at her garden club. The speaker had suggested that Austinites would experience fewer problems in their gardening if they relied on the native flora. They'd have far less need to irrigate, too.

That suited Wilbur. Austin was experiencing a water shortage.

The city government issued the usual warning—that the cost of expanding the existing system of supply would be ruinous—and it was raising the cost of water all the time. So Wilbur decided that while he relandscaped with natives he would also redesign his yard to conserve water. He soon learned that he had to plan for floods, too.

While Austin may get only a moderate thirty-two inches of rain a year, it comes in bursts, in storms that the Texans have aptly named "gullywashers." Wilbur had paid a contractor two thousand dollars to relandscape the slope overlooking his house. The man had set it with boulders and spread topsoil over the concrete-like native caliche* soil, and Wilbur was so proud, taking photographs and showing the new landscape off to neighbors. Then, six weeks later, nature descended with a seven-inch rainfall.

"And the whole thing, rocks, the whole nine yards, ended up at the bottom of the hill. I couldn't pay to have it done again, so I rebuilt the hill myself." He excavated a cascading spillway that splashed out over a huge rock and down into an artificial creek bed that he and his son ran across the backyard. Then he anchored the hillside with native buttonbush (*Cephalanthus occidentalis*—an eight-foot bush with sputnik-like clusters of whitish flowers) and kidney-wood (*Eysenhardtia texana*—a six-foot shrub with the feathery foliage of the pea family, and in springtime falls of white flowers reminiscent of sweet peas).

Finding Texan trees and shrubs wasn't easy, even though Wilbur lived in the state capital. Back in the mid-1980s only one nursery dealt in native plants (several do now), and Wilbur found that as rarities, the natives were expensive. In the end, the landscaping cost him about twenty thousand dollars. He expects the price would be far less today, since increased production has brought down the cost of the plants. Anyway, Wilbur made a lot of mistakes, since he was learning as he went along, so that much of his landscape had to be planted twice.

---

* I got my introduction to caliche at a xeriscape planting party in the town of San Marcos, Texas. A group of volunteers assembled one Saturday morning to install a model xeriscape in a public park, and I joined them for the affair. As we dug holes for plants donated by a local nursery, I encountered, about ten inches down, a gray granular material that did indeed look and feel like decayed concrete. I carried a handful over to Cliff Caskey, the Cooperative Extension agent who had organized the party. After a careful inspection he remarked dispassionately that if the quality was a little better, it would be what they use for roadbeds; "and in a couple of hundred years, it'll be what we call soil." That was caliche.

Even at the price he paid, Wilbur believes that his landscape was a bargain. It has cut the need for irrigation almost to nothing—when I visited him in mid-April, he told me he had watered the whole yard only once since the previous October, and even his bed of hybrid tea roses had only been watered twice. So he saves money that way. But the big savings is in maintenance. Much of this he achieved by simply reducing the size of his lawn.

"I really don't spend much time out there. What turf grass we have left I can edge, and weed, and cut, and totally groom in an hour and fifteen minutes. And that ain't too shabby. I was spending probably three hours when I had the traditional landscape."

There's another benefit, too, one that's hard to express in dollars and cents. It pleases Wilbur every time strangers, people just walking by, stop to tell him how pretty his yard is. He's developed a personal relationship with his plants, too. That became abundantly clear in the course of the tour he gave me.

There was the cedar elm (*Ulmus crassifolia*) coming up by the mailbox, for instance. That was a volunteer that came up from a windblown seed. "I just got tired of cutting it back," Wilbur told me. So now it has a place in the plan. By contrast, the native Texas persimmon (*Diospyros texana*) toward the house had arrived as a hitchhiker—Wilbur noticed it popping up from the root ball of a Texas mountain laurel (*Sophora secundiflora*) he had brought home from the nursery.

Even if the persimmon arrived uninvited, however, Wilbur approves of it now, for the contrast it poses to the laurel is striking. The glossy, broad-leaved mounded mountain laurel is an evergreen shrub that will, if left unpruned, reach a height of six feet; its mass emphasizes all the more the delicacy of the gray-barked, fine-branched persimmon. The persimmon bears modest black fruits in fall; the laurel splurges in springtime, bearing bunches of bright purple blossoms whose smell recalls the childhood pleasures of grape Kool-Aid.

What accident had sprinkled the beds with the simple purple blossoms of wild petunia (*Ruellia brittoniana*)? Wilbur didn't know. But this native perennial blooms every year now—without replanting. Wilbur didn't want to dwell on that, though. Instead, he hurried over to the agarita (*Mahonia trifoliata*) by his house's foundation, to show me how the mockingbirds eat the fruit. The spiny, holly-like shrub bore only small yellow flowers at the time of my visit in April. But once the tassels of red berries appear, a mocker will descend to start feeding at one side of the bush, pecking red berries as he moves across just like you'd eat an ear of corn.

"This is Mexican marigold-mint (*Tagetes lucida*)," Wilbur noted as he stooped to pick a leaf, crushed it between his fingers, and then held the aromatic thing up to my nose. Then he handed me a tiny, lance-shaped leaf of Mexican oregano (*Poliomentha longiflora*) to smell. Wilbur grows the compact, mounded plant for the lavender-pink, trumpet-like blooms it bears from late spring through summer. "Course, they use that as a spice in Mexico."

Wild bermuda grass crept in to replace the St. Augustine grass that died in the freeze, and the result, though not as neat as the neighbors' turf, demands much less water. Wilbur waters his lawn no more than once a week now, even in the hottest, driest weather. Most of the turf has disappeared altogether, replaced by curved and sweeping beds of flowers, shrubs, and trees.

"I don't plead guilty to having much talent at abstract design," Wilbur said as we surveyed this effort. Though he ended up making a career in his family's dry-cleaning business, Wilbur's training was in mechanical engineering, and even when landscaping he thinks like an engineer: "I think of things in symmetrical patterns and evenly spaced. I really had to struggle with myself a great deal to do random planting and free-form beds, and things like that. It really was against my nature to do that."

He didn't have much choice. The untamed profiles and vigorous growth of the central Texas natives don't lend themselves to formal design. Even when it is possible to keep a tree or shrub cut to shape, the labor involved in repressing such vigorous plants would be considerable. One Texas redbud (*Cercis canadensis* var. *texensis*) in Wilbur Davis's backyard has grown to a height of fifteen feet in just five years, and to trim it back would be to cripple branches that bear springtime flowers of salmon pink.

Wilbur also finds an informal design more forgiving. That's important when as much of your planting is experimental as his has been. "One of the neat things about asymmetrical planting is that if something dies, you just pull it up or cut it down and nobody knows it was there. But if you have a row of ten junipers and one dies, you just got a gap."

Whatever the reason, the results of Wilbur's planting were

colorful and lush, in striking contrast to the green sterility of the other yards up and down the block. There was cypress vine (*Ipomea quamoclit*) a red-flowered tropical relative of the morning glory (Wilbur the engineer, I gathered, is a pragmatist, not a native plants purist) that returns from seed every year to wreath the mailbox. To the right of the driveway rise the brilliant red spires of the misnamed autumn sage (*Salvia greggii*—despite the common name, it was blooming well during my springtime visit) and the indigo blue spikes of mealy-cup sage (*S. farinacea*). Blackfoot daisy (*Melampodium leucanthum*), lantana (*Lantana camara*), gay feather (*Liatris*), turk's cap (*Malvaviscus arboreus*) with its curious scarlet spirals of petals, and of course Texas sage (*Salvia coccinea*) seemed to me much preferable to the turf they had replaced.

Wilbur spreads thirty bags of pine-bark mulch over the beds every spring to help them keep their moisture through the dry spells. To help them shed the periodic downpours, he has raised their level above the surrounding soil, edging them with low walls of the local limestone. This, too, he hired done, only to find it not up to his standards, so he has reset all the stonework—"it's kinda like doing a jigsaw puzzle."

A row of evergreen sumacs (*Rhus virens*—twelve-foot trees that bear clusters of five-petaled white flowers in summertime) and another redbud line the grassy path to the backyard, and also screen the view of the neighbors' yard. Wilbur plucked a leaf from an Encino (*Quercus pungens* var. *pungens*), a "sandpaper oak," to let me feel how abrasive the bottom surface of the foliage was. He showed me the possumhaw (*Ilex decidua*, a deciduous holly) in the midst of a clump of coral bean (*Erythrina herbacea*)—it was another volunteer and so pleased Wilbur especially.

That would have been reason enough to love the flocks of bluebonnets that have settled in the Bermuda grass of his backyard —if Wilbur didn't already prize them as the state flower. These were at peak bloom at the time of our tour, and Wilbur ceremoniously picked a stem to present to my eighteen-month-old Yankee son, who had come along to explore with us.

Beyond Wilbur's artificial creek bed, his property trailed off into a wild area of uncut grass, Mexican hat (*Ratibida columnaris*—a red-and-yellow-petaled relative of the black-eyed Susan with a center as tall as the crown of a sombrero), and horsemint. We picked our way out to a little sapling. "That's a native mesquite. . . . I dearly love mesquite." Had I really heard a Texan say that?

Wilbur has become a missionary, and an effective one too, despite a uniquely low-pressure sales technique. In 1987 he joined with several other Austin gardeners to form the nation's first xeriscape garden club, and as an officer and a past president Wilbur has helped to produce the monthly programs by which the membership shares information. He shared some with me, insisting that I visit next the garden of a fellow club member, Nancy Waggoner.

Wilbur spoke of this landscape with something close to envy. Nancy and her husband Duke had had their house custom built. What that meant, Wilbur explained, was that they had been able to preserve the natural vegetation on the site. Wilbur made the Waggoners' property sound like a down-home Garden of Eden. So I rushed off to see what the Hill Country had looked like before the fall.

How did the neighbors react when Nancy Waggoner smothered her front lawn with old newspapers? She smiled slightly, remembering that summer of 1987. "I didn't notice a smell," she mused. Then a grin: "But they all walked on the other side of the street."

Landscaping the yard was not as effortless for the Waggoners as Wilbur Davis had led me to believe. In their case, the builder had left many of the native trees—cedars, for the most part. He had also scraped out an area for turf, though, right across the front of the property. Since the Waggoners' house faces west, that lawn became unbearably hot most afternoons; the same cedars that protected the house from the sun trapped and reradiated heat back onto the lawn. Then, too, the house sat downslope from the street, so that Nancy had to haul hoses uphill every time the St. Augustine grass called for water.

"It was an absolute chore to water, dragging the water sprinkler out there three times a week. And I couldn't keep the weeds out of the front." Nancy doesn't hold with chemical herbicides. "Duke always waited till the heat of the day to mow and edge, and then *he* was mad. So in 1987, July of 1987, I decided, this is enough. Take the grass off!"

That's a motto for a horticultural revolutionary, though with her tailored dress and neatly coifed hair Nancy Waggoner may not look the part. Still her tactics did have an organic, 1960s flavor to them.

"I saved newspapers," she explained, "because I didn't want to use poisons. I put down real thick layers of newspapers. . . . It's nice to have the lizards and the ladybugs. You know, they're doing their things too. You've got to take the bad with the good. Anyway, I put all these newspapers down and I went around and got everybody's grass clippings—scoured the neighborhood. I dumped them on, too." This is a fine way to recycle old newspapers, Nancy noted, "specially if you don't like what's in the news."

"Then, after another two weeks I put another real thick layer of —I wanted to be sure that the St. Augustine, the weeds, and the Bermuda grass were dead, so I put another layer of newspaper and more grass clippings. [A few days later] I couldn't stand it any longer, I had to go out there and start planting. I pocket-planted crape myrtle (*Lagerstroemia indica*), and verbena, and Asiatic jasmine." Two months later she won second place in Austin's annual xeriscape competition.

She deserved it, for she had achieved a remarkable reduction in water use. Instead of irrigating three times a week, she was watering once every ten days. Now, since she has installed a drip irrigation system, she waters even less, only when the plants show signs of flagging and don't recover by the following morning.* Because the drip system delivers water right to the roots, Nancy can wait now until her plants are right at the point of distress before opening the faucet. Besides saving herself water, Nancy accomplished something else with her relandscaping: she created a display area for the flowers she can plant for customers.

Nancy Waggoner is a professional landscape designer, who at any given time is involved with a half a dozen different projects. Her educational background is in architecture and commercial art; she never has taken a class in gardening. "Learning plants is just something . . . you go out there and you plant them and you get to know them." Gardening books for the most part don't apply to

---

* Frequently, in weather as hot as Austin experiences in summertime, plant roots cannot deliver water rapidly enough to leaves to prevent wilting, even if there is an abundant supply of moisture in the soil (see Chapter One, page 26). An expert gardener such as Nancy Waggoner knows that in such a case, the leaves will recover their crispness by morning—a sign that the plant does not need watering.

her part of the world. Written generally by northeasterners, mid-westerners, or Californians, they offer little information relevant to the Texas hill country.*

Books will tell you, for instance, that you can cultivate acid-loving azaleas in areas like Austin where the soil is alkaline. All you have to do, according to the authors, is dig in lots of leaf mold or pine bark or sulfur to lower the soil's pH. Maybe that would work in some places, Nancy grants, but not where the water from the tap or well is also alkaline, as it is in the hill country. There, you poison the azaleas every time you water.

Really (to borrow a phrase from the politicians), all gardening is local. Nancy learned this through the life as a "corporate gypsy" she led with her husband Duke. Both are native Texans—she's from Beaumont and he's from Plainview—but Duke's career took them to Houston, Detroit, and St. Louis before they moved back to Austin. Nancy gardened everywhere along the way, finding that what she learned would work in one spot might not in the next.

Xeriscaping is working for Nancy in northwest Austin. It has trimmed her front yard with a broad border of self-sufficient color: I recognized the bearded irises in full bloom. Nancy told me that those came from a cemetery. "Anything that grows in the cemetery is an ideal xeriscape plant," Nancy explained, pointing out that graveside plantings get no care and no irrigation. I told her that I had spent a good deal of time in central Texas cemeteries looking for old-fashioned types of roses. One of my motives was a desire to find survivors from pioneer days, such as 'Old Blush', that could endure the prolonged central Texan droughts. Nancy nodded, and told me she likes the old-fashioned roses for the same reason.

Nancy has no particular prejudice in favor of Texas natives, but she grows many because they work. She cultivates bunches of what she called "goldeneye" in the front border—I suspect it is what my wildflower guide calls "sleepy eye" (*Xanthisma texanum* var. *drummon-dii*), a tooth-leaved annual that reaches one to three feet into the air and does indeed (as the common name suggests) sleep in, not opening its lemon-yellow, daisy-like flowers before noon. This blooms in May and again after the first fall rain, matching its

---

* Nancy excepts from this criticism one book, William Welch's *Perennial Garden Color for Texas and the South* (Dallas: Taylor Publishing Company, 1989). That she refers to as her bible.

schedule to the migrations of the monarch butterflies, for whom, according to Nancy, it is a principal food.

Evening primroses (*Oenothera biennis*) and knots of ox-eye daisies contributed more splashes of color. The yellow trumpet flower (*Tecoma stans*) would be spectacular in another month, I was told; last year the five-foot-tall explosions of two-inch yolk-yellow trumpets had bumped pedestrians off the sidewalk.

The collection of sages Nancy showed me was truly astonishing —twenty different species in all. Her *Salvia guarinitica* bore flowers of the clearest blue I've ever seen, though they were closely rivaled by the two-foot-tall stalks of canyon sage (*S. lycioides*). Her lyre-leaf sage made pale violet blossoms, and she keeps varieties of Salvia greggii that flower white, pink, and tangerine, as well as red. She even has shrubby species, like the mountain sage (*S. regla*), a west Texas plant that can raise its branching stems and crimson-lipped flowers to a height of five feet.

A customer looking around this yard might decide to let Nancy plant them a garden entirely of her sages—especially when they learned how self-sufficient these plants are. Not only is their thirst for irrigation slight, but so is their appetite for fertilizer. Nancy has found that a key to success with xeriscaping is keeping growth compact and tough, so she feeds only with a liquid seaweed extract (to supply minerals and micronutrients) and a bioactivator that enhances microbial activity in the soil. For the rest, her plants depend on nutrients released by composting mulch.

Had I thought about the different ways to use fragrance? Nancy places aromatic plants so that you brush up against them as you walk through her yard. Picking a leaf of lemon balm and one of chocolate mint, she handed them to me to sniff. Nancy likes to put a sprig of one or the other in her buttonhole when she sets out into the garden.

Nancy describes herself as "a compulsive rooter." Even when a plant is available commercially, she prefers to start it herself, taking a sprig and slipping it into the soil to see if it will "do." Starting from the beginning and watching a plant as it develops through the seasons is how you really get to know it.

She told me, for instance, that the terrible freeze of 1989, when temperatures went down to 5°F, taught her that the older varieties of crape myrtles were the ones most tolerant to cold. The newer kinds are resistant to mildew (a serious pest in the humid central Texas summers), but Nancy suspects that in breeding for this nurserymen had eliminated some of the plants' original toughness. At any rate, it was the old-fashioned kinds that survived in her garden.

This ability to observe and to remember is what makes Nancy a successful xeriscaper. Every site is different, and you have to meet each one on its own terms if you want to develop a garden design that will survive there without a lot of interference.

"Even the people across the street have different requirements than we have," Nancy added, "just in where the sun is, and the location of their house, and the house next to it."

This flexibility, though, is what brings her customers. They want a garden that is self-sufficient, and they like what they see in hers. Especially if they visit in September. That's the month when Nancy's kind of landscape is at its peak. "After you go through this really hot summer and everybody's yard—traditional yards—look so bad, xeriscape yards stand out." As far as I was concerned, it looked good in the springtime, too. The truth is, I believe Nancy Waggoner's yard would stand out anytime, anyplace.

Personally, my experience of central Texas xeriscaping was that plants are more adaptable than gardeners. Because for all their success at acclimatizing new species of trees, shrubs, and flowers, the xeriscapers never succeeded in naturalizing me. At least, not permanently. After four years, I headed north and home. But Jay Cody isn't returning to Kansas. Central Texas is home now, and gardening is the reason why.

Jay's first job was a water conservationist's nightmare. Armed with a degree in horticulture from Kansas State, he took over management of a golf course set amid a thirsty expanse of sand hills in western Kansas. With annual precipitation averaging only fifteen inches locally, maintaining any sort of turf required pumping water by the tens of millions of gallons from the fast-disappearing Oglalla Aquifer. Hydrologists worry that this underground lake of Ice Age water, the sole irrigation source for many farmers from Nebraska to the Texas Panhandle, may dry up entirely within a generation. Nevertheless, Jay's employers decided to court notoriety by planting their golf course with bent grass (*Agrostis tenuis*), a classic European turf that in hot weather demands watering *daily*.

How could they do this? I wanted to know. They had the money, was Jay's reply. But they didn't have Jay long, and this experience seems to have colored his thinking ever since.

The lanky young man with a lurid fishing hat and the name of a famous western scout headed south, and eventually found himself in a job where water was once again the central issue. Settling in San Marcos (a town thirty miles south and west of Austin) in 1985, he took over supervision of landscaping at a local resort and landmark: Aquarena Springs.

A hotel-cum-amusement park, this resort surrounds the spot where the San Marcos River springs full-grown out of the ground. This enormous spring is famous for its purity—the water has been filtered through 175 miles of Edwards Aquifer limestone—and for its volume. The flow averages 155 cubic feet per second—about 100 million gallons a day.

Populations of endemic species—a wild rice, a giant shrimp, and several insects found nowhere else—testify that Aquarena Spring has also been superbly dependable. Not once during the evolution of these endemics could the spring have run dry. But that may be changing.

Jay worries because he knows that other springs dependent on the Edwards Aquifer, springs near the town of New Braunfels only twenty miles away, have dried up temporarily in recent years. Explosive growth in San Antonio, the city to the south, and the commercial development of the Edwards Plateau have created a thirst which now threatens to drain the entire aquifer any year in which rainfall is at all below normal.

Jay noticed a definite waning of the flow at Aquarena Springs during the abnormally dry summer of 1990, a year before my visit. That was when San Antonio was forced to impose water rationing. The next day seven inches of rain fell from the sky.

"We were lucky; we were real, real lucky." Yet even so, the following spring Jay noticed that the water level in wells at the resort was still way below normal, despite abundant rainfall. Water in the resort's wells was ten feet below what it should be at that time of year.

The health of the springs determines the job security of everyone at the resort, from Ralph the swimming pig to the staff of the submarine theater, but no one more than Jay. From the first, he was determined to do what he could to protect the water supply.

The tool he has adopted is the same one Wilbur Davis favors: native Texan plants. Jay, however, is using them in a significantly different way.

That is partly because Jay Cody most definitely *is* a gardener. When I asked him how he got involved in this work, he replied that as far as he could tell his interest was "God sent"—inborn. For Jay, landscaping with Texas natives is not an exploration of roots (his own, that is), as it has been for Wilbur Davis. Coming to terms with local flora was a way to integrate himself with a new home.

As far as Jay's clients are concerned, he has only been doing his duty by planting natives. Most of Aquarena Springs' clients come from in-state, and as Texans they are enthusiastic about wildflowers. It's easy to admire wildflowers in Texas, since the displays in springtime are spectacular—pointillist sheets of blue, orange, rose, and yellow that stretch away to the horizon. Using highway shoulders as wildflower preserves was proposed in Texas as early as the 1940s, and since Lady Bird Johnson's founding of the National Wildflower Research Center outside Austin in 1982, many miles have been replanted to natives. Wildflowers are as Texan as chicken-fried steak, and introducing the wild stuff into the Aquarena Springs landscape was a patriotic mission.

Most of that landscape has grown wilder with the flowers. Wherever practical, Jay is replacing turf with meadows. But he has also found ways to use natives in a more artful fashion, and that's what interested me.

For example, Jay has used wildflowers to punctuate Aquarena Springs' parking lots with stylish bursts of color. From one island in the blacktop, mealy cup and autumn sage poked their blue and scarlet spires up above billowing springs of Muhly grass and red yucca. Mingling at the center of another green space were Texas mountain laurels and birds of paradise (*Caesalpinia gilliesii*), the latter a shrub that technically is not a native but that was introduced from South America so long ago that most Texans accept it as such. Later that spring the two shrubs would juxtapose purple blossoms with yellow, but at the moment the show was the surrounding swath of bluebonnets. It's not just Wilbur Davis who treasures this symbol of Texas—and since bluebonnets are a legume, Jay noted that they were fixing nitrogen from the atmosphere to feed the lantana that would replace them in the bed.

For me, the most exciting display was unquestionably the beds that flanked the resort's front entrance. There hadn't been any flowers there when Jay arrived, just a few of the conventional shrubs: "some eleagnus, a few pittosporum, the usual stuff that you'd see around institutions. I knew we could do better than that."

Indeed they could. Jay said he designed these plantings to look like English perennial borders. In fact, though, the result was more exuberant than anything I've seen in Great Britain. To begin with, Jay's were real Texas-sized borders—a hundred fifty feet long and fifty feet wide, and a full ten feet deep. What's more, the flowers' colors were hotter, their boldness emphasized by the fineness of the foliage, which was more delicate and subdued than its British counterpart. English plants couldn't have stood the Texan sun without lots of irrigation, and Jay gives his border almost none. He hand waters new additions for a few weeks after transplanting, but after that the plants are on their own.

What Jay found most difficult in creating this border was the lack of precedent. "You know, I didn't have anything to look at when I started. There were no gardens that showed combinations of plants. That's what I wanted to work on more than anything, to show combinations, what looks good with what.

"I started throwin' things together, whether they clashed or not. It didn't make any difference to me, if they had pretty flowers throughout most of the summer months, when our tourists come through. That's what we needed.

"I did some wrong things. I had some salvia plants that got four foot tall right in the front of the border. So I yanked 'em out and slapped 'em at the back." Gradually he assembled a number of combinations he does find satisfactory.

He admires the contrast that the yellow, daisy-like flowers of the coreopsis make when interplanted among the purple spikes of *Salvia farinacea*. Then, too, he's pleased by the effect he's gotten by mixing different selections of *Salvia gregii*, the knots of red, pink, and white. He's used that as a repeated theme down the length of the borders. The desert willow's (*Chilopsis linearis*) pink-and-white, orchid-like blossoms look all the more delicate when juxtaposed, as they are here, with the mountain laurel's lurid bloom. Closer in color to the desert willow are the yarrows (*Achillea millefolium*) that spread out in a pool of pink-and-white saucers around the bases of these shrubs.

To tie the taller, clump-forming plants together and clothe the front of the border, Jay relies not only on yarrows but also on Texas bluebells and *Zexmenia hispida*, a yellow flower like a stubby-petaled daisy that blooms right through the heat of the summer and into fall. Heart-leaf hibiscus (*Hibiscus cardiophyllus*), which raises its valentines of heart-shaped leaves and wine red flowers only a foot and a half high, also figures at the front. "They flower all summer for us." And he's proud of the *Salvia penstemonoides*, with its three-foot-tall spikes of reddish-fuschia flowers; this species was listed as threatened in Texas at one time, but Jay was given some seedlings by a man in San Marcos and they have thrived. "Pretty neat plants."

Other plants Jay used like a spice, mixing them in where the borders' flavor needed adjustment. Hummingbird flower (*Aniscanthus wrightii*) turns up the heat with its two-inch-long fire-engine-red flowers (these are also a favorite drinking spot for the plant's tiny jeweled namesake). Jay has handled this "kinda like confetti, you know, mixed through there." Fine-textured, blue-green bursts of Lindheimer's Muhly grass (*Muhlenbergia lindheimeri*) cool the border, blooming in autumn when they suddenly sprout gracefully tenuous seed stalks.

Jay grew many of these plants from seed or cuttings himself, since he too has had difficulty in finding commercial sources for the species he wanted. Establishing the border has been a lot of work, but the labor, he says, is decreasing as the border matures. "Hopefully I'll get it to where we don't have to do a thing with it, just set back and enjoy it. Weed it ever' now and then."

At present the border is still evolving. Jay had noticed during the winter before my visit that it looked bleak in wintertime. That's not surprising, given that he had designed it for a May-through-October bloom. Now, though, he's inserting a backbone of evergreens—mountain laurels, wax myrtles, possum haws, which drop their leaves but retain their bright red berries, and red yuccas (*Hesperaloe parviflora*)—sunbursts of reddish brown leaves that sometime in late spring send up an improbably tall stalk of tubular red flowers.

Because Aquarena Springs lies in a flood plain, the soil there is a deep, black loam. That's good, but Jay continually adds organic material to further increase the soil's moisture-holding capacity. Every fall, after he has cut back the perennials, he spreads a layer of compost a couple of inches deep and then covers that with a two-inch-deep mulch of shredded bark. Saving water is important to Jay Cody: "If those springs go kaput, I'll have to mosey on down the road and find me another garden." But it's more than self-interest that motivates him.

"It's a moral issue to me. Water's going to be the next big problem for us [on the Edwards Plateau]. It already is. It's something that's going to hit ever' single household. . . . Water conservation has to be implemented *every* single day of *every* single year. It's something that you don't just try to do at certain times. It ought to be practiced day and night. That's what we try to do here. It's something I believe in."

Patrons of Aquarena Springs can be glad that he does. For Jay's belief not only protects their playground; it has surrounded them with a beauty that is, as one local bumper sticker proclaims, "Texan by Choice."

Three

Native or Naturalized?

No issue starts more arguments among water-wise gardeners than this: What is the origin of your plants—local or exotic?

Those who favor the native species claim that their plants *must* be less dependent on irrigation. After all, the natives have been fine-tuned to the local climate by a million years of evolution. Before man disturbed the natural order, these plants *never* got watered, and they flourished just the same. Clearly, they are the water-wise choice.

That's simplistic, reply the internationalists, the plant connoisseurs who want to cultivate the best of the whole world's flora. If a plant comes from a similar climatic region, albeit on another continent, and it approves of your soil, then there's no reason why it shouldn't prove as self-sufficient in your garden as any native. Maybe more so, for as internationalists point out, they have a vastly greater fund of plants from which to choose. Besides, many of their plants have naturalized—though foreign by origin, they grow and reproduce in various areas of the United States without man's help now. Clearly, natives are no more self-reliant than these.

In truth, there is something of value water-wise gardeners can learn from either camp. But before moving on to that, it's necessary to define what a native plant is. That might seem simple—but take care.

Wilbur Davis, for example, presented most of the plants in his Austin garden to me as natives. Yet according to most botanists, many would not qualify—not on his site. Wilbur's coral bean, for example, may indeed be indigenous to Texas, but it's native to the Gulf Coast, not to the Hill Country. Its presence in Wilbur's yard would not occur without human intervention. That makes his Texan coral bean as exotic as a banana tree to a botanist.

Actually, the real native-plants purists would disqualify many others of Wilbur's plants as well, even though they do belong to species which occur naturally in the Austin area. From the strict nativist point of view, the problem is that though the species may grow in the neighborhood (or at least, it did at one time), the specimens Wilbur planted came from somewhere else.

Purists insist that only the local *ecotypes* of these species—forms of the plants that evolved in the immediate area—are true natives. They insist that if you choose to grow natives, you must collect seed or stock from within a narrow radius of your garden: twenty miles is a common limit, but some extreme nativists will not venture farther than a mile. In buying his plants from a nursery, Wilbur ended up with specimens shipped in from fields dozens or hundreds of miles away.

I mention this extreme point of view because the purists are aggressive and have seized positions of influence within the native plants movement. Sooner or later any water-wise gardener will be confronted with these arguments, and if the gardener hasn't thought them through, he or she may be intimidated and discouraged from growing natives at all.

So Wilbur's natives may not be natives, depending on your point of view. What's more, the purists insist that his plants pose a serious threat to the genuinely local populations. By interbreeding, the imported specimens will (according to the purists) "contaminate the local gene pool," overwhelming indigenous ecotypes in a host of mongrels. That's why one naturalist at a prairie restoration conference told me bitterly that gardeners like me are the worst threat to native plants.

At that point I decided I needed a more rational perspective. So I consulted Dr. David Northington, executive director of Austin's National Wildflower Research Center. Founded by Lady Bird Johnson, this organization has been a leader in promoting wildflower conservation through roadside plantings. Its approach to the preservation of native plants is unusual in that it combines exceptional expertise in ecology with a commitment to exploring through methodical research the poorly understood science of wildflower cultivation.

Northington defines a native as a plant that grew in a particular location before human settlement,* and that grows and reproduces there without human intervention. He acknowledges the existence of distinct local ecotypes, but notes that there is little scientific data to support the contamination theory. In cases where mixing does occur, producing what are known to botanists as "hybrid swarms," the natural tendency seems to be a gradual working out of the population back toward the parent types.

Actually, Northington believes that the "contamination" (he prefers to call it "gene mixing") which results from the activities of gardeners may be beneficial. Such intermarriage used to occur naturally before man separated and isolated the different populations with such barriers as highways, cities, and plowed fields. Interbreeding's effect is to increase genetic variability within a species, and so to enhance the plants' resilience and adaptability. In effect, gardeners have become midwives for what was once a spontaneous process.

Still, ecotypes are important, he believes, because they do represent a superior adaptation to local conditions. If you want a plant that will flourish on the local budget of precipitation, Northington recommends you use local ecotypes if possible, or else an ecotype from a relatively more severe climate. If you are planting a wildflower meadow in Oklahoma, you could conceivably get seed of appropriate prairie species from as far east as Ohio—but you'd be wiser to shop closer to home, or even farther west, where rainfall is less than your own.

Once you have decided what you are going to call natives, will you really find them less demanding in the matter of water? Some-

* Early herbarium specimens are the best tool for determining a species' prehistoric range. Botanists are an intrepid lot, and throughout the United States have commonly arrived with or on the heels of the first explorers, when a region's vegetation was still relatively pristine. Since these collectors routinely recorded the site of each specimen's collection, the sheets of dried plants they have left behind furnish a reliable, if rudimentary, map of aboriginal plant distribution.

times. Deep-rooted native trees such as the Texas persimmon, which sprang up beside Wilbur Davis's foundation, are better equipped to deal with Austin's recurring droughts than some imports from a temperate northeastern forest. A transplant from the desert would shrug those off the dry spells just as easily, but probably couldn't cope with the central Texas humidity and the fungi and bacteria it breeds. Natives have had to learn how to cope with those, too.

But a superior adaptation to local conditions doesn't always make for a superior garden plant. The fact is that many natives are overly adapted for a gardener's purposes; these plants used their long period of local evolution to adapt to very specialized ecological niches. Such natives require conditions that they are unlikely to find in the highly disturbed habitat of your backyard, where the forest or prairie has been stripped away, the drainage patterns have been changed, and the soil has been dug up and moved around.

A classic case is the pink lady's slipper orchid (*Cypripedium acaule*), a delicately erotic flower that no gardener could see without feeling an itch to take it home. Yet though it may flourish in the woods around your house, it will almost certainly die if transplanted to your garden. As best the botanists are able to determine, this species grows only in association with certain kinds of soil fungi, and the flower will not find them in garden soils. Without them, its roots do not function effectively.

So natives do not always make good garden plants. What's more, the experience of some Californian gardeners in the current drought has been that exotics from regions of dry climate, especially plants from the Mediterranean basin, outperformed most California natives in the matter of water conservation. The reason for the exotic plants' superior performance in those gardens may be that the exotics came from cultivated stock, from strains that have been selected as good garden plants. Or it may be that the exotics came from regions where the standard climate resembles what is a drought in California. There is no telling if they will continue to perform so well once the climate returns to normal. But they will have one advantage.

When you remove species from their native habitat, you help them to escape their natural enemies. It may be many generations before either the former predators succeed in following their prey or a predator in the new home develops a taste for the transplant.

In either case, there is usually a grace period when the transplant flourishes without the usual checks and balances.

This can make the exotic a pest—purple loosestrife (*Lythrum salicaria*), a European wildflower popular with many American perennial growers, has escaped the garden to choke huge areas of North American wetlands. More commonly, the transplant behaves as a mannerly garden plant—but a plant which (at least for the present) is almost entirely free from pests and diseases.

This is why so many agricultural crops grow better *away* from their land of origin. It's why cacao is cultivated commercially in Ghana rather than in its native South America, why coffee is cultivated in South America rather than Abyssinia (where it originated), and why rubber is grown in Malaysia, not the Amazon. If moved to a land geographically distant from their homes but climatically similar, transplants can provide remarkably carefree material for the gardener, too, and plants whose extraordinary vigor helps them cope with any environmental stress—including drought.

In the end, the critical factor in choosing water-conserving plants, I believe, is not place of origin but adaptation to your garden environment. In fact, "adaptive plant" is the term many water-wise gardeners prefer, since it allows them to landscape without taking sides. How do you identify adaptive plants? The message I get from the experts is that there is no single foolproof method. But they have provided me with a number of tips.

In spite of all my caveats about native plants, I would certainly recommend consulting your local flora. While all natives may not flourish in your garden, many undoubtedly will. At the very least, such research should give you an idea of what type of vegetation the local conditions favor. The National Wildflower Research Center's information clearinghouse* can furnish information about trees, shrubs, and wildflowers native to your state, as well as general tips on their cultivation. Local chapters of native plant and wildflower societies (instructions on how to contact these will be found in the bibliography) can supplement this with more specific advice, and insights about your particular type of site.

An obvious approach to selecting adapted exotic plants is to experiment with plants from a region that is climatically similar to your own. For example, plants from Japan and Korea tend to prove

* Address: National Wildflower Research Center, 2600 FM 973 North, Austin, TX 78725.

well adapted to the northeastern United States, since those Asian countries share a similar pattern of precipitation with the Northeast, and experience winters of similar severity.

How do you determine which areas of the world share your climate? In the library of the nearest university you will find atlases of climate maps which will provide answers to that question. I recently checked *World Maps of Climatology*,* which confirmed that my area, Connecticut, is most similar in climate to northern Japan and Korea. My dip into this book also confirmed a suspicion I had developed in College Station, Texas.

I had noticed, when I was gardening there, the frequency with which "China" popped up in the names of the old-timers' plants. Chinaberry (*Melia azedarach*), Chinese tallow tree (*Sapium sebiferum*), and China roses had been the pioneer landscapers' standbys in the College Station area. What I found in turning through the atlas the other day was that College Station does correspond climatologically to China's humid, southeastern plain. I should have looked to the plants of that region for other materials with which to experiment. I also learned something unexpected: the southern coast of Australia and the eastern half of South Africa would probably have been good sources, too.

For lists of plants native to regions of interest, you can consult the floras (regional plant lists) you'll find in the libraries of botanical gardens and agricultural universities. However, while sifting through these substantial volumes may fascinate the plant connoisseur, it is a tedious way to identify the handful of plants the average gardener needs. He or she should go straight to the botanical garden personnel. Introducing plants from other regions is a traditional part of the botanical garden's mission, and the horticulturists and botanists there will know which ones have proved best adapted to local conditions. Just as important, they can steer you away from those exotics, like the purple loosestrife, which succeed too well.

Even if you never consult a flora, it is still worthwhile to determine which geographical regions are similar to your own. Once armed with this knowledge, you'll have a means of checking any plant recommendations you receive. Find out where each plant originated; if it is native to a region substantially wetter than your own, treat the recommendation with caution.

* H. E. Landsberg, H. Lippmann, K. H. Paffen, and C. Troll, (New York: Springer-Verlag, 1965).

Another caveat: identifying a species, like my Chinaberry, that is locally adapted provides a clue to a climatic region that should prove a profitable hunting ground for more. But in making this search it is important to select plants that share not only the same climate, but also the same habitat. A plant native to regions of dry grasslands may not, after all, prove drought resistant, for it may grow wild only on the banks of its homeland's occasional streams.

Inevitably, identifying adapted plants will involve a certain amount of trial and error.

In areas of chronic water shortage, it's always worth calling the local water department, since it will quite likely have lists of adapted, irrigation-free plants. Your local Cooperative Extension (its number should be listed with the county offices in the telephone book) may have further information.

Sadly, information about adapted plants is not as plentiful as it should be, since most horticulturists pride themselves on growing what is rare and difficult rather than what is practical. Even your local nurseryman is of questionable value as an authority. After all, he must grow what sells, and what sells generally has more to do with fashion than with what is adapted to the local environment.

Native or naturalized, which shall it be? For certain design effects, exotic plants are the only answer. The northeastern United States, where I garden now, is naturally deficient in broad-leaved evergreen shrubs. It has a fine array of needled evergreens, and a superb selection of deciduous trees and shrubs, thicket-forming plants, and herbaceous plants, but no broad-leaved evergreen shrubs aside from wild rhododendrons and the mountain laurel (*Kalmia latifolia*). So if your design calls for those, you have to turn to China, Japan, and the Himalayas.

Personally, I garden with both exotic and native plants. Whichever I am using, I try, as the Texas xeriscapers taught me, to fit the plants together into communities rather than leaving them as assemblies of specimens. This predisposes me toward native plants, because with them nature has worked out much of the design— within walking distance of my house I can find models of how to fit together native plants.

Yet even this argument against exotics seems to be losing its force.

In an article he wrote for *Horticulture* magazine some years ago, [*] Roger Swain, the science editor of that publication and a Harvard-educated biologist, explored what he called the "nouvelle tropics" of Dade County, Florida. Originally, pine scrub had covered the whole of the Miami area, but the developers bulldozed that away to plant exotic flora: Canary Island palms, African tulip trees, Queensland umbrella trees—a host of plants as colorful as their names. The new arrivals not only please human immigrants, they provide habitats for escaped tropical pets.

The most significant, of these, from a gardener's point of view, are the birds. One bird watcher in Coconut Grove has reported sightings of eighteen species of parrots, twelve of them nesting; another reported a pair of nesting macaws. These birds would have starved, Swain noted, when Miami was still pine scrub, but now they find appropriate fruits on the landscape plants. In turn, they are spreading the plants' seeds about, helping them to naturalize around the city. What is arising as a result is a natural community that is entirely new, like nothing that has ever existed before.

Similar if less flashy transformations have occurred and are occurring in every place I have lived. That doesn't change my commitment to preserving native flora wherever possible. But I'm enough of a realist to recognize that like those Christophers who left northern Ireland a couple of centuries ago, the African tulip trees are here to stay. Native or naturalized—the division eventually blurs.

Florida

I met Bruce Adams at a town meeting in Gulf Stream. He's the water conservation coordinator of the South Florida Water Management District, the man charged with promoting xeriscaping throughout the southern half of Florida; he'd come to Gulf Stream to try and curb its thirst. It's one of the wealthiest towns on Florida's Gold Coast. Gulf Stream may not be as big or as famous as Palm Beach—even in season, its population doesn't exceed a well-bred

[*] "Palms and Parrots," *Horticulture*, July 1988.

RECOGNIZING DROUGHT-TOLERANT PLANTS

The first impulse of a novice water-wise gardener is to plant only xerophytes—plants of dry land and desert. After all, nothing conserves water like a cactus. But unless you live in a desert, you'll find that true xerophytes may not be the answer for you. In central Texas I learned (the hard way) that cacti could not cope with the oppressive humidity that accompanied the heat of the summertime droughts. Still, anywhere you garden, it pays to learn how to identify drought-tolerant plants. The clues are simple and clear.

1. Look for thick, fleshy leaves and stems, or thick, fleshy roots—these are reservoirs in which the plant can store water to see it through periods of drought. Succulents such as cacti are the most familiar examples of this group, but it also includes other, less extreme members that are suitable for nondesert situations.

   In Texas, for example, I found the fleshy-rooted irises notably self-sufficient, especially the white-flowered *Iris x albicans*, a plant the country people call the "cemetery white" because of its persistence on old gravesites. Paperwhite narcissuses (*Narcissus tazetta*), the type of narcissus that florists force into bloom for winter sales, also proved unexpectedly durable. Native originally to the Anatolian plateau, a place of regular seasonal drought, these sprouted and flourished through the mild, wet winters and spring, then as the summer drought set in retreated underground to subsist off the moisture stored in the bulb.

   Amaryllis, a bulb native to South Africa (another region of alternating wet and dry seasons) and another florist's standby, also flourished virtually unirrigated in Texas. Later, during visits to southern California, I was to find South African bulbs in virtually every water-wise garden.

2. Look for light-colored, reflective foliage. Gray or silver foliage in particular is a common feature of drought-tol-

erant plants. By reflecting (rather than absorbing) much of the solar radiation that strikes them, such plants protect themselves from the effects of intense sunlight. Reflective plants heat up less during periods of intense sunshine than do darker-hued absorptive plants; as a result, the reflective plants transpire less water. In College Station I learned that a gray-green mound of Texas sage (*Leucophyllum frutescens*) needed far less irrigation than a forest-green rose bush; and though the sage's small lavender blooms were less spectacular than the rose's gaudy blossoms, they came at much less environmental cost.

3. Look for foliage with a nap of fine hairs or down. This coat works like sunscreen to stop sunlight before it strikes the plant, and it also protects it from dehydrating breezes. By trapping air, the down also helps create a zone of higher humidity right around the leaves, in this way decreasing the rate of transpiration.

4. Plants with small leaves or finely cut foliage are, in general, less vulnerable to drought than broad-leaved plants. The finer the foliage, the less surface area is exposed to dehydration.

5. Leathery, glossy leaves may also be a clue to a water-conserving plant. The leaves' tough skin and the wax that gives them their shine both help to seal the foliage against dehydration. The Texas mountain laurel (*Sophora secundiflora*) I found in Wilbur Davis's front yard (see page 73) was a fine example of this kind of water-conserving plant.

6. Smell the foliage, not the flowers: an aromatic foliage is often a clue to a drought-tolerant plant. The familiar herbs such as lavender, sage, and oregano, are familiar examples of this. Native to the parched slopes of the Mediterranean, these plants are practically invulnerable to drought. Many plants from North American drylands and deserts also share this characteristic.

The connection between drought tolerance and fragrance isn't entirely clear, but it seems to lie in the protective role that the fragrance plays. The volatile oils that give the foliage its smell is pleasing to the human nose but distasteful to the palate of herbivores. Botanists speculate the fragrance is a device that evolved in areas of chronic drought, and that it helps protect the plants against overgrazing in times when fodder is in short supply. Whatever the reason, I have found scented foliage a common sign of a water-conserving plant.

twelve hundred or so—but it's there that George Bush has stayed in recent winters when he has taken a Florida vacation.

I hadn't been able to see much as I drove up George Bush Boulevard—I had no problem with the vision thing, but tall masonry walls and hedges screening the yards hid everything from view but the tops of the palm trees. A mere glance at the inside of Town Hall, however, its creamy cypress-wood paneling hung with photos of polo players, suggested how comfortable a place Gulf Stream could be, if only you had the money. A letter of introduction, too. And unlimited fresh water, of course.

But by March of 1991, even a presidential endorsement couldn't protect this town from its neighbors' disapproval. During the previous four years, annual precipitation had ranged from 10 to 26 percent below normal. The state had declared a drought emergency, and Bruce, a past president of the National Xeriscape Council, had spent over a year awakening Floridians to the need for conservation. Residents of Gulf Stream needed more awakening than most.

Floridians, on average, use 175 gallons of water per capita each day (in Connecticut, the average is 75 gallons, and that's typical of most eastern states). Residents of Boca Raton, the next city south of Gulf Stream, had reduced their consumption by about 15 percent in response to the calls for conservation. In truth, the sacrifices required to achieve this hadn't been too painful. The state hadn't forbidden car washing, for instance. It had just requested that residents park cars on the lawn before opening the tap. That way, the water got double usage, since it irrigated the turf, too. Still, changing old habits is annoying—especially when you know that up the road in Gulf Stream, water still ran free, with the average household consuming 1,000 gallons daily.

By 10:00 A.M., the meeting room had filled with a silver-haired crowd—men in chinos and topsiders, women with long, lacquered nails and gold bracelets heavy as shackles. Bruce Adams strode in looking spruce in a crisp linen jacket and neatly clipped mustache and beard. The violet and pistachio shirt open to the third button, the gold chain round his neck served as reminders that this was, after all, the land of "Miami Vice." He announced in friendly but measured tones that he had seen eleven sprinklers working in the course of his drive down from Delray Beach that morning. The owners of those sprinklers, he remarked, pausing one beat for effect, were criminals.

They were, of course, watering outside the legal hours. As part of the emergency measures, the state had mandated that all sprinklers must be turned off between the hours of 9:00 A.M. and 5:00 P.M. Having grabbed his audience's attention, Bruce went on to reassure and admonish by turns, to tell the citizens how they would cut their water usage in half over the next twenty years. South Florida wasn't going to follow California's lead—there wouldn't be any water rationing in south Florida. Instead, people would change their behavior. He knew they would do this, because they would have to. Every city along this coast would have to conform to the new water-use regulations if it wanted the South Florida Water Management District to continue to supply it with water.

Changing patterns of landscape irrigation would be the key for residential water users. Hand in pocket, Bruce stepped forward and confided to the audience that this area of Florida's Atlantic coast, Palm Beach County, uses more water per capita than does Phoenix, Arizona—and in Phoenix they have to irrigate year-round, whereas a Gulf Stream lawn didn't need any supplemental water at all at this time of year. The average south Floridian, Bruce continued, waters his or her lawn 180 times annually, even though studies have proved that a mere twenty times would be adequate. Fifty-five inches of rain fall on South Florida in the typical year; to this gardeners habitually add another *seven feet* from the tap.

In sum, the daily water consumption on the south Florida coast runs around 750 million gallons. Compliance with the new water-use guidelines—installing low-flow shower heads, screwing a pistol-grip nozzle onto the hose when car washing so that the water doesn't flow continuously—by an estimated 80 percent of the population during this drought had brought daily usage down to 650 million gallons. A general adoption of xeriscaping would reduce the flow to 500 million gallons, and then there'd be no need for other methods of conservation. Xeriscaping alone could save the south Florida coast from its water deficit.

Bruce then briefly outlined the seven principles of xeriscaping, and for a few minutes the town meeting took on the self-conciously upbeat, formulaic air of an Alcoholics Anonymous meeting. Though here, of course, it wasn't the booze to which this crowd was addicted, it was the water chaser.

Afterward a town policeman joined in, to show everyone in a courteous manner the mailed fist that was the alternative to Bruce's velvet glove. The rule against watering out of hours would be enforced; a first infraction would be met with a warning, the cop explained, adding that he expected everyone would want to cooperate. But hardened water wasters would find that starting with the second offense, the police would issue summonses, and fines would swiftly escalate from $50 to $250.

A woman asked nervously how she was going to replace the water that evaporated out of her pool; Bruce soothed her with the information that topping up a pool was still legal, but advised her to cap the pool with a floating cover when it was not in use. What impact could one person's sacrifices have? a man demanded; he just wanted to make sure, he remarked in a plaintive voice, that his efforts would be cost effective. A study of Boca Raton, Bruce replied, had found that twelve households had consumed 5 percent of all the water supplied to the town's 100,000 customers.

Someone raised the subject of golf courses, provoking a groundswell of resentment. In fact, Palm Beach County, where golf is more of a creed than a game, offers 140 courses, all emerald green—an irresistible target for water wasters in the throes of withdrawal. Why should homeowners have to conserve, the audience demanded, while greens keepers still sprinkle at will? The average south Florida homeowner, Bruce replied firmly, applies three to five times as much water per acre of landscape as a golf course does. And what about the farmers up around Lake Okeechobee? yet another man demanded. They had voluntarily reduced their water consumption by 50 percent this year, Bruce explained, and they had been willing to do so only because of the conservation measures adopted by residential users to the south.

Gradually the audience drifted out of the room, and though there was no way of telling if Bruce had made any converts to xeriscaping, still he had spread the word. On the whole the audience had seemed resigned, all except for one middle-aged couple who cornered Bruce after his talk. The man, a picture of conservative splendor in a sober, charcoal-striped suit and black tasseled loafers, proved to be the town mortician; I supposed he couldn't afford the levity of sports clothes. He had been disturbed, he said, when the town sent him a notice that his household numbered among the top 15 percent of water-users. Yes, they were using 35,000 gallons a month, but he had just had the property relandscaped. Bruce explained that the new regulations allowed for daily watering during the first month after the planting of new trees, shrubs, and turf. The man seemed somewhat mollified, but not so his wife.

What were they supposed to do? she demanded. Had they tried the water-conserving shower heads? She'd rather not take showers at all, she insisted, than stand in that miserable dribble. And no, she wasn't going to park the car on the lawn before washing it— there wasn't enough turf anywhere on their lot. She *could* tell her landscaper to enroll in a xeriscaping course, she supposed. Where should she send him? Florida Agricultural University, Bruce said; he was teaching a course that would begin next Tuesday. Impossible, the woman said with obvious satisfaction; she wouldn't be able to get in touch with her landscaper by then.

Later I asked Bruce what the answer was to such stubborn holdouts. Well, he noted, there are legal penalties. Sheriff Nick Navarro, the Broward County law enforcement officer who had won nationwide attention with his arrest for obscenity of the rap group 2 Live Crew, had also been cracking down on water wasters. He'd issued more than 1,000 arrest warrants for violations of the water-use restrictions.

But communication, taking the time to listen to people's problems and to work out solutions with them, remains Bruce's tool of choice. He never anticipated working for a water authority when he was studying labor relations and conflict resolution in college. But it has proved to be the perfect opportunity to practice what he'd studied.

Florida's environmental catastrophes receive a great deal of attention from the press, and the state's diversion of water *has* crippled both the Everglades and Florida Bay. There's a horrible irony in the fact that landscaping should threaten the landscape itself. Part of the solution to the crisis surely lies in the enlightened legislation the state legislature is backing now. Section 255.259, Florida Statutes (enacted in late 1991) mandates the use of xeriscaping on public properties. It also calls on municipal governments to develop codes that would oblige local businesses and residents to incorporate xeriscape principles into their landscapes.

When change comes, though, it has been largely a matter of gardener talking to gardener, of convincing people there is a better way. Bruce Adams recalled that when he covered his former lawn with a mulch of wood chips, someone sneaked in the following night to post a sign: "The Dump." Nevertheless, his message of green but not greedy seems to be getting through. Months later, I learned from William Koch, Jr., Gulf Stream's mayor, that the town had cut its water consumption by 30 percent.

Betty Jean Stewart

When Bruce Adams and I had parted, he had told me that one person I must talk to lived no more than a ten-minute drive from our lunch site. Her name was Betty Jean Stewart, and she had made her town, Highland Beach, the first community east of the Mississippi to enact a xeriscape code. I had made an appointment to meet with this revolutionary, and following her directions had found the cryptic sign: "Nova Kancee."*

Turning into the driveway was like pulling into a cave: the parking area and the house behind it were almost completely hidden by a dense canopy of tropical trees—gray-barked, sprawling banyans dangling festoons of aerial roots, and a native gumbo limbo; the peeling red trunk of this "tourist tree" truly looking like a sunburnt nose. The house is small. A low bungalow of silvered

---

* It took me two hours to figure out the significance of this name. I'll pass along only the hint that Betty Jean gave me: the original builder had relatives up north and had purposely limited the house to three rooms.

cypress wood, it sits atop the low bluff (a "highland" in flat Florida) that edges the beach here, and faces away from the town to embrace the Atlantic. The view is its main attraction, the sea impossibly turquoise blue, the strand of white sand seemingly endless. The garden, though tiny, offers a well-planned space to sit and soak it in.

Betty Jean's tiny freshwater swimming pool, for example, has been turned into an ornament by capping it with an arched wooden bridge. Betty Jean copied that from the one she saw in Monet's garden at Giverny. In the same miniature scale is the gnarled sea grape (*Coccoloba univera*) to one side—dwarfed by ocean winds and salt sprays, this tree with its tough, leathery leaves had the look of a bonsai, though it may have been as much as ten feet tall. The pittosporum by the kitchen door Betty Jean grew from a cutting "borrowed" during her tour of Ostia Antica outside Rome. She also borrowed the wooden staircase that twists down to the beach; it was inspired by the boardwalks she saw in the Everglades.

Florida natives bind together the sea side of the bluff. More sea grapes thread their roots through the abrupt sand bank—these she keeps pruned low, though technically a state law prohibits cutting this guardian of the beach at all. But it has been Betty's observation that heading back the sea grapes helps them resist the storms that eat away at their roots, and anyway, "for ten thousand a year in taxes, I really want to see the ocean." At the bank's foot, the sea oats (*Uniola paniculata*) Betty Jean planted trap windblown sand, helping to restore what the ocean steals.

Both the tree and the grass are natives, as are the aptly named spider lilies (*Hymenocalis keyensis*) that the tides washed in to bear bouquets of fragrant white, "spidery" flowers at spring's end. She's no purist, though; she admires just as much the gracefully curved trunks of her coconut palms (*Cocos nucifera*).

Simple, but exactly right. Besides, to maintain this landscape, Betty Jean need hardly ever turn on her irrigation system (she won't use a timer). She had watered only once during the month before my visit, and then only to wet the beach side of her yard for about half an hour. If all the yards in town were like hers, Betty Jean pointed out, the town wouldn't have a water shortage. Where her water bill averages ten to fifteen dollars a month, her next-door neighbor—whose lawn is all sod—pays a hundred.

Betty Jean blames some of the water wastage in her town on its transient population, but notes that the housing—condominiums for the most part—greatly aggravates the situation. How can you teach conservation, she asks, when everyone in the building draws their water through a single meter? One person is careful and the man next door lets the tap run all day, and who can tell the difference? It's because of this that Betty Jean long ago decided that only through political action could a gardener like her make an impact.

Her involvement began in 1972, eight years after she and her husband moved down from the Brandywine Valley of Pennsylvania. By that time Betty Jean realized that Nova Kancee was caught between the developers and the deep blue sea. "The whole place was being bulldozed . . . all you heard was the rumbling of trucks and the churning of saws." Betty decided that unless something was done, the builders were going to cut down every tree and pave the whole town.

She began with a petition drive to bring sidewalks to Ocean Boulevard, the town's main thoroughfare. Her reasoning was that if people started walking instead of driving everywhere, they would meet neighbors and maybe develop a sense of community. Her success in this venture emboldened her to push for the establishment of a community appearance board, a body that would enforce certain minimum aesthetic standards in landscaping, and that would preserve as much as possible the native trees. Naturally enough, Betty was assigned the task of writing landscaping codes. That kept taking her over to the building department, and before she knew it she was its commissioner. Then mayor.

That final promotion changed her understanding of landscaping. Now she was responsible for all the town's resources, and as Highland Beach increased its population by 300 percent, from under two thousand to more than six, Mayor Stewart found her green spaces competing with people for a very finite supply of fresh water.

Highland Beach has no wells of its own. It draws its water from a field in neighboring Boca Raton, and the aquifer there was showing signs of exhaustion. When the South Florida Water Management District announced that Highland Beach had to cut its usage by 15 percent, Betty knew the town faced a choice between conservation and building a ruinously expensive desalinization plant. *

* Desalinization is increasingly popular along the Florida coast, though to my surprise I learned that the installations aren't generally used to treat seawater. Instead, they are used to purify well water, as the sea increasingly infiltrates and salinates overdrawn coastal aquifers.

Telling me about her discovery of xeriscaping, she said, "We were pioneers because we had to be."

There's a wealth of technical expertise in the retired community of Highland Beach, former engineers and administrators, and they all told Betty there was no way that conservation could make a significant impact on the town's situation. But she forged ahead anyway. In November 1987 the town relandscaped the town hall according to xeriscape principles. Then, two years later it mandated that *all* new or significantly remodeled landscaping must follow that example. The regulations that the town adopted were based on a "Model Landscape Code" circulated by the South Florida Water Management District, and like the model, the Highland Beach code stuck closely to the principles of the National Xeriscape Council.

There are a couple of significant differences between the model and Highland Beach's code, however. The Highland Beach code is mercifully short (twenty-nine pages, versus the code's sixty-three). Besides, I can understand the Highland Beach version. That's because when Betty Jean put it together, she rewrote or eliminated anything she couldn't understand. She reasoned that if she couldn't understand it, it would probably be unintelligible to her neighbors too.

Her simplification doesn't seem to have diminished the regulations' effectiveness, however. The exact gallons the new code saves for the town are impossible to establish, since their effect is combined with that of other conservation measures such as the gradual phasing out of water-cooled air conditioners. But one condominium reported a savings of 21.9 percent (roughly 4 million gallons a year), largely due to reduced lawn watering, and the town hall's water consumption has dropped by two-thirds.

We strolled down there to view the results. The maintenance crew had applied their shears to the streetside dry zone, an area that Betty Jean intended to be a billowing tide of shrubbery, and she was a bit piqued. Even so, she was delighted by the evidence of lush good health. What we found was a cheerful hodgepodge, a collage of fruits and flowers as diverse as the town residents. As long as a plant behaved itself (and Highland Beach's xeriscape code includes a list of forbidden plants, species that, though drought tolerant, are too aggressive to be allowed within town limits), no one was asking about country of origin.

I found in the dry zone pigeon plums (*Coccoloba diversifolia*) from the Florida Keys—they would bear their greenish white flowers in March, I was told, following these with bunches of grapelike berries. There were dwarf carrissas from South Africa, too, and ixoras —called "jungle geraniums" but actually related to gardenias—from southeast Asia. The dwarf oleanders reminded me of southern Italy, while the gigantic, fingered leaves of Philodendron 'Seloum' sheltering in the shade of a huge sea grape gave the "mini-oasis" next to the building the tropical look that most Floridians mistakenly associate with their state. Carpeting the oasis around the attached police station was mondo grass (*Ophiopogon japonicus*—from Japan) and Moses in the bulrushes (*Rhoeo spathacea*—Central American). There was artillery plant (*Pilea microphylla*—tropical America) here too, and primitive-looking cycads (cone-bearing palm-like contemporaries of the dinosaurs). Across a breezeway, up against the library, was perfumed, waxy flowered Kopsia (*Ochrosia parviflorum*), an Australian shrub from which I picked plump red fruits.

This sort of smorgasbord landscape is as close as Florida comes to tradition. Nearly everyone I spoke to there described their adopted state as "a paradise"—and yet no one seemed satisfied to let the Garden of Eden alone. Every gardener to come to Florida since Ponce de León has introduced a few more of his or her favorite plants (Ponce de León planted oranges). But though many ingredients of the town hall landscape were foreign, at least in assembling them the landscapers had for once consulted the local climate. That might seem a minor thing, but in fact it was a radical departure, and the result was something genuinely Floridian. A celebration of the brilliant sunshine and nurturing warmth, the landscape around the town hall presented a collection too miscellaneous, maybe, for a person of chastely classical tastes—but what would such an individual be doing here anyway?

Betty Jean had retired from public service briefly before we met; she said that she'd get back to cultivating her own garden now. She hasn't yet read the inscription on the bronze plaque set into a boulder in front of town hall, the official memorial to the achievements of her eighteen years in office. I think that's because she knows the real memorial is the tax rate—conservation has, so far, saved this little community from the crushing expense of developing new water sources. It has left it greener, pleasanter, more colorful too.

A Piece of the Real Story

Tell Dan Boyar that his yard looks like a jungle, and he'll thank you kindly. Because that's more or less what he set out to create in 1988 when he started relandscaping his one-sixth-acre suburban plot. He remembers the Palm Beach County of thirty years ago, when there were still long stretches of tropical hammock vegetation lining the coast, and when the area his development occupies was all virgin sand scrub.

For the most part, the native growth is gone now. It was a shipwreck that began this process. When a Spanish brig broke up off the coast, local residents rescued its cargo of coconuts and planted them up and down the beach. This gave the area a sort of South Seas look that in 1893 enchanted Henry Flagler, an oil baron in flight from the northern winter. He spent millions trying to complete Palm Beach's transformation, and though "lethal yellowing," a microbial epidemic, has eliminated most of the original coconuts, enough remains of Flagler's dream that its need for irrigation drains the modern city of fresh water.

Dan Boyar dismisses it all as "tutti-frutti exotics." He hasn't a thousandth of Flagler's resources, but that doesn't stop him from pursuing a dream far grander. What he's hoping to accomplish is to reverse a century of history; to persuade his neighbors to plant their yards back to the original flora. What Dan Boyar has created around his own house he calls "a piece of the real story," and there's a lot to be said for it. It's an oasis for wildlife—butterflies, birds, lizards, and the smaller mammals—and a very pleasant, practical place for human residents, too.

It was Richard Moyroud, a local nurseryman and one of the most expert growers of Florida natives, who had brought me to see this do-it-yourself wilderness. Richard and Dan made quite a contrast. Richard—sandy-haired and wiry, with an outdoorsman's long springing stride—was dressed farmer style in khakis and work boots. In his Bermuda shorts, sandals, and dark glasses, Dan looked ready for the beach, and where Richard's face was mobile, intense, and expressive, Dan's was deadpan and deliberately relaxed. Their agreement on matters of landscaping, however, was absolute.

Or almost absolute. They agreed that irrigation is not only unnecessary, but a positive evil. Richard told me of cases where home builders had left the native vegetation intact but then sentenced it to a slow death by installing an automatic irrigation system—laying the pipe involved cutting too many roots. Besides, the extra moisture the irrigation system supplied fostered diseases and insects that over a period of years claimed all the native trees and shrubs. As a water-quality officer for the state's Department of Environmental Protection (D.E.P.), Dan had seen plenty of that, too. But he still insists on a little hand watering once a week or so, for new plantings and to help out plants obviously stressed by drought.

Unnecessary, replied Richard, if you've matched the plant to the site properly. Just a little water to perk them up, was Dan's rejoinder. Richard shook his head, but let the matter drop. Really, there wasn't much point in quibbling over an amount of water that the meter would hardly register.

As Dan pointed out, he'd broken one of landscaping's primary rules when he put his yard together. To give a landscape unity and coherence, it's common practice to limit the selection of plants to a handful of species. Yet Dan had crammed more than 100 into his yard. It worked, too, at least for me; despite the diversity, all the plants seemed to harmonize easily.

According to Dan, that's because they are all from a couple of closely related habitats; they are natural associates that are products of the same evolutionary conditions. Besides, Richard pointed out, Dan had arranged the plants just as you would find them in the wild, setting each species into the appropriate niche, right beside its natural neighbor. As Richard put it later, when he was describing his own business, what he sells isn't just plants; the product, really, is a complete ecosystem.

Out of consideration for his neighbors, Dan designed his front yard along conventional lines, though he planted only natives. There's a white indigo berry (*Randia aculeata*) hedge across the front. This replaced an existing hedge of ixoras, Asian shrubs whose yellow, red, or purple blossoms are far showier than the small white flowers of the indigo berry. Dan explained the substitution perfectly by showing me a lingering shoot of the original. It was weak, the leaves sparse and yellow—for the most part, Richard broke in to explain, the exotic species can't deal with this area's dry, sandy soil unless you give them lots of fertilizer and irrigation.* The indigo berry, I noticed, looked fine: rounded and glossy, evergreen leaves, a three-foot-tall file of sturdy, dense shrubs whose white berries, when Richard crushed one, stained the fingers as deep purply-blue as the dye for which they were named.

Behind the hedge there was a tiny patch of Bermuda grass—more a gesture than a lawn, and Dan is planning to reduce it further. By the front door to the house he had planted a red iron-wood (*Reynosia septentrionalis*), a small evergreen tree of the Florida Keys whose bark is as scaly as an alligator's hide; and then a cinnamon bark (*Canella winterana*), a tree not only of aromatic bark but also with a neat rounded head of broad evergreen leaves. The mastic tree (*Mastichodendron foetidissimum*) beyond was yet another evergreen, a cautious one with a neat, slow habit of growth and stabilizing buttresses of roots at the trunk's bottom. It had a virtue I had never heard ascribed to any other landscape plant: Dan recommended it as making a nice noise when the wind blows through it. Overhanging the driveway were a gnarled sea grape and a gumbo limbo. They shade the car, Dan noted, so that he doesn't cook when he sets off for work in the morning.

Along the fence line dividing Dan's property from that of his neighbor was a screen of shrubs—cocoplums (*Chrysobalanus icaco*); and compact trees—willow-leaved bustics (*Dipholis salicifolia*). I found the contrast of foliages pleasing; the bustics were evergreen doubles for the willows we grow up north, while the cocoplums' glossy leaves were too broad and thick to be anything but subtropical. Pushing them aside, Dan showed me the reddish fruit for which the cocoplum is named. "I don't like living in a sterile environment," he remarked. There's an opossum in the neighborhood that feels the same way, apparently, for Dan took us around to the backyard to see the path that critter has worn through the wildflowers there.

Dan left a belt of open space carpeted with wood chips right

* Florida's well-drained soil has also left its shallow aquifers terribly vulnerable to the state's gardeners. Typically, the water table lies just ten to twenty feet underground, so that when a proud homeowner floods his lawn with water, all the pesticides and fertilizers wash right down into the groundwater. There they stay, too. In several areas of Florida now, dangerous levels of nitrates are turning up in the well water; nitrates are an essential nutrient to plants, but when ingested by humans they may cause birth defects and cancer. In 1990, a study by the Institute for Southern Studies found that residential landscaping was the second-worst source of pollutants in Florida's water supply, exceeded in this only by agriculture. Sixty-seven percent of Floridians, the institute warned, draw their drinking water from sources liable to this sort of contamination.

next to the house—the only thing growing there was a volunteer pawpaw (*Asimina triloba*) he hasn't the heart to uproot. The gap serves to keep wildlife away from the house, and it protects the structure from insects, too, since watering next to the foundation encourages colonization by termites.

Just across the mulch began a dense island of subtropical trees, shrubs, ground covers, and wildflowers. One after another, Dan identified these in matter-of-fact tones as "one of the five best native trees [or shrubs, or ground covers, wildflowers, etc.]." That kept me scribbling frantically, filling pages of my notebook, until I caught Richard's chuckle, and realized that Dan was telling me, in a roundabout way, that he plays no favorites.

Still, his catholic taste left me with a colorful list: wild coffee (*Psychotria nervosa*), with its emerald, quilted leaves; and wing-leaf soapberry (*Sapindus saponaria*), whose wings are carried on the leaf stems; and from the Florida Keys, a geiger tree (*Cordia sebestena*—with its tubular, scarlet-orange flowers a year-round hummingbird feeder), wild dilly (*Manilkara bahamensis*), and joewood (*Jacquinia keyensis*). The Keys plants are particularly drought-hardy, since evaporation is rapid in those sunny, exposed islands, and the rocky soils are particularly well drained. Whereas in many parts of Palm Beach County, plants too can tap groundwater a few feet below the soil's surface, on the Keys they must depend entirely on precipitation, no matter how long the dry spell.

More typical of the scrub forest that formerly covered the site of Dan's development was the gopher apple (*Licania michauxii*) he showed me nearby, a creeping shrub whose whitish, plum-like fruits are a mainstay of the gopher tortoise. Shiny blueberry (*Vaccinium myrsinites*) was staging a comeback on its own, as were three other relics: sand pine (*Pinus clausa*) and slash pine (*P. elliottii*), and the cool-looking fans of bluestem palmetto (*Sabal minor*). "All traditionally bulldozed," Dan noted. Nearby, a wild passionflower was weaving up into the branches of a simpson stopper (*Mycianthes fragrans*), a large flaky-barked shrub whose leaves smell of nutmeg, and whose fruit is a red berry.

"A lot of stuff," Dan remarked absentmindedly as he moved about, stroking the smooth bark of a blolly (*Guapira discolor*), crushing the leathery leaf of a redbay (*Persea borbonia*) to inhale its bay leaf odor. The diversity of this landscape gives its plants a synergistic effect, Richard explained. It's a common conceit to plant flowers attractive to butterflies. But how many gardeners think, as Dan has, to provide the plants on which their caterpillars feed, too, so that the butterflies can complete their life cycle? Besides, Richard has found that clustering the plants together seems to protect them from south Florida's occasional freezes.

When I remarked that too close a planting prevents trees and shrubs from developing their best shape (that's a bit of wisdom I absorbed during my student days), Richard laughed. What is the "best" shape? he asked. He believes you have to know the conditions in which a plant grows naturally to use it well in the landscape, and if it naturally occurs in a thicket, in the shelter of its fellows, then to isolate it out in the sun is doing it no favor. That's why he may deliberately cluster several stems of the same tree or shrub in a single container back at his nursery. Any other nurserymen I know do that only by accident, and probably consign the results to the compost heap.

We set out on a tour—I drove, while Dan challenged me to play a variant of a game I remembered from childhood car trips. Then the goal was to call out each Volkswagen Beetle we saw; now, as we wheeled down the grid of long, straight streets, I must spot a native plant. "You see?" Dan grumbled. "Not even one." In fact, the vistas were all of yellowed, anemic-looking date palms and ficuses. "Exotics"—my passenger shook his head sorrowfully, pronouncing the town a "biological desert."

That's what Ray Miller had, too; he recognized this fact right away when, back in 1988, he read an article Dan had written for the local newspaper. Ray also works at D.E.P. (he's in wetlands regulation), so he came to Dan at the office. He confessed, then asked for help.

When we stopped by his house, Ray showed me a "before" photograph: it pictured a bleak sea of lawn; an area devoid of life, the owner recalled, except for schools of little lizards, immigrant Cuban anoles, "leaping through the grass like porpoises." Most of the lawn is gone now, and Dan was exhilarated to find a native (and much more uncommon) *green* anole emerging from one of the new cabbage palms. Ray's yard was still meticulously groomed when I saw it, though now almost entirely replanted with natives. Yet in some ways it is even more of an affront to conventional suburban sensibilities for that very reason. Any passerby can tell he's deliberately breaking the rules.

Take the brush pile in the backyard. It's barely visible through the fence and shrubbery, but the neighborhood association still took issue with it, reproving Ray for his "unsightly compost heap." Ray was incensed—his brush pile is no dump, it's an artful shelter for wildlife. To build it, he loosely crisscrossed larger branches (that's the den), then clothed these with a thatch of smaller twigs. Still, he admitted that the neighborhood association wouldn't be any happier if it knew of the brush pile's success. So far, it has attracted a garter snake and a pair of elegant black racers.

There was also a hammock in Ray's backyard, a copy of the mounds of tropical vegetation that still dot the Everglades, and an area of scrub. In full view of the back porch was a pool of wetland plants: leather ferns (*Acrostichum danaeifolium*), the underside of whose fronds were the color and texture of suede, bulrushes (*Scirpus*), arrowhead (*Sagittaria*), and lemon Bacopa (*Bacopa caroliniana*). Here an artificial trickle springs out from a cluster of rocks to feed first the pool, then spills over into a miniature slough.

For a water conservationist this feature would have been an unpardonable extravagance—except that Ray uses only rainwater for this, runoff from his roof which he catches and stores in a plastic barrel. Other areas he waters once every few weeks in dry weather, using a timer-controlled irrigation system he installed himself. ("Completely unnecessary," Richard muttered.)

A merlin, a perfect miniature falcon, swooped in to settle briefly in a tree, then left, seemingly annoyed by our intrusion into his yard. We left, too, soon afterward.

Rounding out Richard and Dan's tour was a stop at an insurance office in downtown Delray Beach. Dan had landscaped this building three years ago; previously, the area around it and the parking lot had been nothing but grass. Now it offered shade, some relief from the noise of the highway, and a feast of textures and various shades of green.

Dan had given this client a much more structured, conventional kind of planting. He'd limited himself to just thirty species, and set them out in the types of arrangements insurance customers expected to see in such a setting. There were lots of hedges (all carefully clipped): cocoplum, wild olive, wax myrtle (*Myrica cerifera* —which I recognized at sight as a close relative to our northern

Bayberry), and silver buttonwood (*Conocarpus erectus* var. *sericeus*), a shrub or small tree that grows equally well in standing water or dry sand. All native, all evergreen, and all in lush foliage in the middle of this, the dry season—Dan told me that the fine-looking blocks of cocoplum alongside the building are *never* watered.

Flanking the entrance to the court at the office building's entrance was a pair of crabwoods (*Gymnanthes lucida*), fastidious, broad-leaved evergreens as glossy as holly and with an additional attraction: their new foliage emerges with a warm, reddish tint. These trees stood perhaps fifteen feet tall, and would probably add another five to this height as they matured. They'd never need pruning, according to Dan; nor would the gumbo limbo, the fiddlewood (*Cytharexylum fruticosum*), and the paradise tree (*Simarouba glauca*) he'd spaced around the parking lot. All of these top out at thirty feet or so, the perfect height to shade the typical one-story Florida ranch-style house or office. The reason for the trees' uniform stature, Richard explained, is that they evolved in a land of hurricanes, so they have developed the habit of keeping their heads down.

As someone who has spent many days hanging from a rope barbering trees, I could admire these species' conformity. Dan and Richard, though, true anarchists at heart, hooted with a fine subversive joy when they found a seedling of fiddlewood springing up spontaneously from a gap in the pavement. Wild Florida resurgent.

Xeriscaping is not a movement Dan and Richard support, particularly, though their kind of landscaping does lend itself to water conservation. As Richard made clear, xeriscapers don't go far enough; he believes they have been sidetracked by technological tricks. Soil amendment, for example—"improving" the soil with huge injections of organic matter—is unnecessary, even a mistake in Palm Beach County if you are planting natives. Irrigation systems, no matter how efficient, discourage self-reliance; plants that depend on a flow from a nozzle or emitter, Richard calls "water junkies." "Why, *why* must you water?" he replied in an agonized tone when I persisted in my questions about irrigation techniques. What we need, he maintained, is not an adjustment but a revolution.

I had caught a glimpse of where that might take us that morning, in the swamp that lies just beyond Richard's nursery yard. He took me there down a zigzag of half-floating planks, a walk we negotiated at a crouch through the tunnel of greenery. At the path's end lay a stand of head-high leather fern framed by the rough-barked columns of pond cypress trunks, and smoother gray palms. This scene wasn't natural, strictly speaking. It had emerged over a period of ten years as Richard cleared away a tangle of weedy invaders—exotic trees—and he has enriched the remaining vegetation with royal (*Roystonea elata*) and needle palm (*Rhapidophyllum hystrix*), two handsome but increasingly rare natives that he grows for sale. Still, to me, the scene looked positively prehistoric (and it's no accident that Richard named his business "Mesozoic Landscapes, Inc.").

Clearly, Richard was pleased that I shared his admiration for this dramatic spot. He quoted Henry David Thoreau to the effect that any fool can see the beauty in mountain scenery, but it takes real sophistication to appreciate a swamp. Or, he might have added, scrub forest and tropical hammock. Evidently, though, the population of Palm Beach County is already quite sophisticated. In March of 1991, the residents of this one county allocated $100 *million* for the preservation of natural areas. But if Richard, Dan, and Ray have their way, their neighbors won't be just preserving; they'll reclaim the whole county, from Jupiter to Boca Raton, lot by lot.

Bonita Bay

The long-legged fisherman looked up, then leaped into the air and flew away. "Wood stork," Jerry McPherson remarked matter-of-factly as our jeep pulled up to the pond. The sighting stopped my pen dead; as intent as I was on recording the stream of information Jerry was directing my way, I was even more interested in the bird. Half as tall as a man, this species is easy to recognize, with its bald, black knob of a head and its ten-inch-long wedge of a beak. These storks used to prowl south Florida by the tens of thousands, but in 1990 no more than 115 pairs nested in all the Everglades. Yet here was one in the middle of a housing development. I'd already seen enough of Bonita Bay to know that an endangered bird's presence was no freak; it was a fundamental part of the builders' plan.

"Nature still flourishes on these 2,400 acres," the video at the visitor's center had promised. David Shakarian, the entrepreneur who assembled this tract on Florida's southeast coast in 1979, had gotten his start managing a yogurt factory. He'd become a crusader for good nutrition and preventative medicine; that was exactly what he intended to practice in landscaping Bonita Bay.

Central to his plan was a commitment to leaving more than a third of the property, much of it wetlands, untouched. The conservation ethic extends throughout the community. In the past, Florida developers' gardening tool of choice has been the bulldozer. In Bonita Bay, by contrast, a concerted effort has been made to work within the natural framework.

So the slash pines that covered the sandy ridges have been preserved wherever possible, and in landscaping the public areas, the clubhouses on the golf courses, the community center, and the marina, an effort has been made to re-create natural plant communities as much as possible. The sea wall along the bay, for example, was assembled from a concrete block perforated with holes so that the mangroves could reestablish themselves—and continue to scatter over the water the leaves that feed the microorganisms that in turn nourish shrimp and fish.

This was all explained by Jerry McPherson, the field coordinator for landscaping at Bonita Bay, who had taken charge of my tour. A large, blond man who looked far more at ease in a four-wheel-drive vehicle than in his air-conditioned office, Jerry volunteered very little about himself except that he had studied horticulture at Virginia Tech and that he had lived in Florida for fourteen years. Still, his satisfaction was obvious when he showed me the tracts of palms and palmettos that had been preserved when the area around them was developed, and the kink in the road where a center island suddenly widened to embrace a string of especially fine live oaks.

The trees he was planting along Bonita Bay's streets, he told me, were native mahoganies, hollies, and cabbage palms, as well as slash pines. Using these indigenous species helped keep the local ecosystem intact, of course, but it also makes sense financially, since he rarely has to buy a tree. Instead, he transplants them from areas slated for construction. Working within the natural vegetation also saves water. What's more, it simplifies aesthetic decisions by providing a context into which individual landscapes are easily fitted. With its canopy of slash pines regularly punctuated by palmetto jungle and uplifted hardwood hammocks, Bonita Bay has a homogenous, coordinated look very unlike the jarring juxtapositions of the average suburb.

One way that Bonita Bay's planners ensured that the land would retain a relatively undisturbed character was to divide the tract into many distinct "neighborhoods," clusters of architecturally related houses, and setting each within a buffer of natural vegetation. Almost every individual yard, too, includes a natural area. Jerry marks off these wild zones with tape before construction of a house can begin, and homeowners must post a deposit that is used to restore the natural area if they disturb it. Finally, before new homeowners can landscape their lot, they must submit a plan for Jerry's approval. What if that plan violates the site's natural character?

"They come in with some wild stuff," Jerry admitted, "and we flat-out reject it." Does that make them angry? "Sure it does. But we try to work with them, it's an education process. People moan and groan at first, but after they get used to it [the Bonita Bay landscaping concept] they're our best allies."

One inflexible rule that Jerry follows when reviewing residential landscape plans is that there shall be no watering system run into a natural area. He agrees with Richard Moyroud that such assistance is detrimental to the native flora. On the contrary, it favors the spread of exotic invaders, especially Florida's three great arboreal weeds: the cajeput tree (*Melaleuca leucadendra*) from Australia, the Australian pine (*Casuarina equisetifolia*), and the Brazilian pepper (*Schinus terebinthifolius*). All three grow at a feverish rate in Florida's benevolent climate, and succeed better than natives where the natural balance has been disrupted. Together they have forced natives off thousands of acres in south Florida.

Jerry cuts these weeds down wherever he finds them, and paints their stumps with a systemic herbicide. Then, with a rough sort of justice, he tosses the branches into a chipper and the shredded remains are used to surface nature paths through "the Slough," the wetland that cuts across Bonita Bay from the Imperial River on its southern border to its northwest corner at Estero Bay.

As I soon learned, Bonita Bay's brand of preservation is an active process. To protect the wetlands and adjacent areas, the development channels all its runoff into two ponds near the front gate. From there, a system of mains distribute it for use in irrigating lawns and gardens. Actually, the need for such water is limited, since both private and public spaces have been landscaped in accordance with xeriscape principles. In addition, homeowners are required to install a rain switch in their irrigation system, a simple device that centers around a series of absorbent wafers. Humidity from rainfall causes the wafers to swell, an action that trips the switch and shuts down the irrigation system until the wafers dry again.

Much of the equipment Bonita Bay employs in its pursuit of water savings the staff has had to devise itself. Jerry showed me a pop-up sprinkler head that hid inside a bed of shrubs—he'd modified this device so that it distributed water in a flat rather than arching spray. In this way, he explained, the droplets stay underneath the shrubs' canopy of foliage and far less water is lost to evaporation.

Besides water conservation, there are other benefits that derive from Bonita Bay's style of development. Use of indigenous plants creates a more stable landscape, one that requires less trimming, spraying, and feeding to maintain. Pat and Gene Fry, for example, whose house lies in the River Ridge neighborhood, told me they spend maybe fifteen hours every month on yard care; and that for two-thirds of an acre that is as heavily planted, and as luxuriantly appealing, as any I have ever seen.

I didn't meet them until a year after my tour with Jerry—I'd returned to take photographs of Bonita Bay. One January morning, about 8:30, I rang the doorbell to find Gene in white shorts and sweatshirt, headed out for a game of tennis, while Pat prepared to feed the crowd of squirrels who clung, complaining, to the porch screens.

The scene took me aback, since as an apprentice at the New York Botanical Garden I'd come to regard squirrels as little more than rats with bushy tails, creatures that grew fat on a diet of buds nipped from prized shade trees and bulbs dug out of flower beds. Certainly, Pat didn't look at all like the befuddled squirrel feeders I'd seen in the Bronx. Of medium height, crisp in dress, speech, and manner, she was very much in command of herself and the situation. But the Frys are turning their yard into a wildlife refuge —they plan to register it with the National Wildlife Federation. They are planting shrubs and trees that will furnish wild visitors with food. In the meantime, Pat told me, she's got three pregnant females out in the yard, and they need help.

We went out onto the deck and stood by one of the two feeding stations as Pat handed out the nuts one by one. She pointed to something that looked like a birdhouse but wasn't—it was a nesting box for squirrels—and a low, hut-like structure set on a patch of sand amid the saw palmetto fronds. That proved to be a feeding station for rabbits, a structure that struck me as entirely unnecessary since in my experience rabbits have always been too adept at feeding themselves. For Pat this was just playing fair, since she and Gene have also installed four different bird feeders, several birdhouses, and a birdbath carved out of a chunk of coral rock.

I had missed the gopher tortoise by a couple of weeks, apparently; he had disappeared from his burrow. Pat warned me, too, that this was a poor season for birding (though I'd already seen a blue heron that morning in the pond beside their house, and a red-tailed hawk with entourage of scolding crows in a tall dead pine across the road). I'd have to come back at night if I wanted to see the armadillo—he's Pat's answer to insecticides. When neighbors told her that she and Gene would lose their tiny remnant of turf to grubs if they didn't spread the appropriate poison, she'd replied that if grubs hatched in *her* yard, the armadillo would dig them up.

She calls it her "wild yard." Yet the landscape was carefully planned. The Frys had hired a landscape architect, instructing her to make the planting drought proof. Pat has continued amending the plan after installation, replacing plants that demanded extra water too insistently with something hardier, generally something she'd noticed in the woods nearby.

The landscape's frame was the natural vegetation of the surrounding pine flatland/scrub forest habitat: slash pine, sand live oak (*Quercus geminata*), with an understory of scrub palmetto (*Sabal etonia*, a tree that has adapted to life in dry terrain by keeping most of its trunk underground), saw palmetto (*Serenoa repens*), and wax myrtle. The Frys had left this more or less untouched in the backyard, intervening only by removing deadwood and dead palmetto fronds (though they make sure to let the palmettos leaf all the way to the ground, since the cover is essential to the wildlife). On the north side of the house, they'd carved out a space for a cluster of citrus trees—grapefruits, oranges, and a calamondin. Throughout I found no formal paths to follow, just meandering passages created by Pat's careful clipping.

The front Pat and Gene had unobtrusively civilized. Flocks of bromeliads—"air plants" that take their nourishment from rainwater and dust and never send roots to the ground—perched in naturally dwarfed oaks, but otherwise the view through the pine trunks had been kept open and inviting. Along the street was a ground-hugging band of yellow, daisy-flowered wedelia, and the driveway was set in a tufted carpet of grasses—dwarf and regular Fakahatchee grass (actually two distinct species, *Tripsicum floridanum* and *T. dactylliodes*, both natives of Florida's once-extensive dry prairies), and behind them the plumed seedheads of a pennisetum.

Banked up to the right of the drive was a billow of shrubbery. The native "rosemary" (*Ceratiola ericoides*) there was a doppelgänger for its namesake the herb in everything except size, since it made a six-foot-tall mound of fine-needled silver. There were buttonwoods, too, both green and silver (*Conocarpus erectus* and *Conocarpus erectus* var. *sericea*), trees of the mangrove swamp that make surprisingly drought-tolerant shrubs on terra firma. Crouched behind a drift of dwarf bougainvillea (a Brazilian native that understands south Florida's cycle of wet and dry seasons) was a familiar sight: the neat, gray-green mounds of Texas sage (*Leucophyllum frutescens*).

A foundation planting of liriopes mulched with pine cones and three queen palms (*Arecastrum romanzoffianum*) in a raised bed on the north side of the door were the Frys' concession to conventional landscaping; the potted mangrove shoot in the roofed entranceway struck the more authentic note. When I commented on the lack of flowers, Pat said that the rabbits had made that decision. They ate them all.

Pat told me that they hadn't gardened much, either one of them, before moving to Bonita Bay four years ago. The previous fourteen years they had spent on Key Largo, where water was too expensive, in their view, to give any to plants. The neighbor who kept a lawn had paid five hundred dollars a month to irrigate it, Pat told me in scandalized tones. What did the Frys' bills run now? The last one totaled nineteen dollars.

Because their yard is so heavily given over to natives, they have only installed an irrigation system in the about half of it, in the front and side, and they never run it more than once a week, giving the plants from three quarters of an inch to one inch of water, even in the driest weather. That can be very dry, too, on the Gulf Coast.

Pat keeps not one but two rain gauges, since she measures rainfall for a local radio station. So she knew for a fact that it had rained only .45 inch in the last ten weeks.

Pat was born out of state and has lived longer in Punxatawney, Pennsylvania, than anywhere else. Still, both her parents were natives of Florida, and she visited several times each year. Florida has always been her center, and she understands that when it comes to climate, the figures of average annual rainfall tell only part of the story.

Florida has a true monsoon climate: rain, when it comes, falls intensely and runs away. Because of the sandy soils, little moisture remains to see plants through the subsequent drought. That's one reason why the Frys fertilize so sparingly—no more than once a year, and then at half the recommended rate, with a relatively weak 6-6-6. The spartan diet encourages compact, hardy, drought-resistant growth.

The Frys left Key Largo because intense, thoughtless development had destroyed its natural beauty. They worry now that the same thing is happening to the Gulf Coast, that it could happen to Bonita Bay. When, at my urging, Pat recited the list of birds they have spotted, I thought it had the sound almost of a mantra, a spell to keep destruction at bay. I admit that I found it reassuring when that evening as I left, a wild turkey swooped low, looming big as a zeppelin overhead.

Still, what seems more likely to protect this 2,400 acres of "environmentally responsible community" is the profit motive. At the time of my visit in March of 1991, Florida was in the middle of an economic downturn. In stark contrast to the surrounding communities, though, business was good at Bonita Bay; $47 million worth of homes had sold in the previous year. Apparently, there is a market for wood storks and sloughs.

Producing this product isn't easy, though. Jerry McPherson is keenly aware that he and his colleagues must walk a fine line to preserve something of the natural vegetation without antagonizing the human residents. Landscaping at Bonita Bay is a balancing act. It's one well worth studying.

Four

Earthworks

top dismissing it as "dirt." Think of it as a reservoir, a sponge. Virtually all garden plants collect their water through their roots, and that means what matters to them is only the moisture actually in the soil. So the composition of your soil, how you handle it, and what you add to it have a critical effect on the availability of water to your plantings. Really, it doesn't matter how carefully you handle the hose. It doesn't matter how much money you spend on improved sprinklers and irrigation systems. If you don't know your soil, if you haven't made it your partner, you cannot water accurately.

The reason for this is that soils differ dramatically in the amount of water they can absorb and retain. A quantity of water may be extravagant if applied to one patch of earth—you may be trying to force an eight-ounce cup to hold a quart of liquid, with the result that most of what you apply runs or drains away. Yet the very same amount may not wet another soil sufficiently that any moisture is available to the plants growing there.

Primarily, it is texture that determines how much water a given soil can absorb and hold. A clue to the importance of texture is that this is the characteristic by which farmers have always classified soils. What determines a soil's texture is the sizes of its mineral (rock) particles.

Coarse sand is the name applied to the largest particles, *sand* the next coarsest, then *silt*, and finally *clay*. The exact sizes of the various particles are not important to the average gardener; it's enough to understand how they differ and how that affects the soil's efficiency as a reservoir. So keep in mind two facts.

First, that the moisture a soil retains, the water gravity can't pull down to the water table, is the fine film that wraps itself around each soil particle. It follows from this that a soil's water-holding capacity relates directly to the total surface area of its particles. This in turn is determined by the number of particles per unit, which brings us to the second fact: that the size of the particles varies enormously. A fine clay soil has about a billion times more particles per ounce than does a coarse sand, so that the clay offers 800,000 times more surface area to any water sprinkled on it. Clearly, a clay soil must be a far more capacious reservoir than a sand.

That isn't always an advantage. In a region of regular, abundant rainfall such as south Florida, a clay soil may remain so continually sodden that plants drown. Where the interval between rains is longer, however, finer-particled soils are generally desirable, especially if your goal is to limit your irrigation.

Even where rainfall is irregular, however, too fine a texture is problematic. Roots may have trouble threading their way between the densely packed tiny particles, and the innumerable particles may bind the water so strongly to themselves that roots cannot extract it. Generally, what the gardener wants is a compromise suited to his or her region; in Connecticut, where the rain is ample but may not fall for several weeks at a time, I aim for what is called a *clay loam*, a soil composed of almost equal parts of each particle: 35 percent clay, 35 percent silt, and 30 percent sand (approximately). If managed intelligently, this absorbs a great deal of rain or irrigation water, holds it for a prolonged period, and surrenders it readily to my plants.

Before you mutter "Numbers again!" and flip to another section, understand this, too: working with your soil is somewhat like cooking. Like a sauce or a salad, garden soils are confections. Just as you must spice, dress, and toss the lettuce leaves, and blend them with other ingredients before you serve them, it's rare that you find

Infiltration Rate:*
How fast does your soil absorb water?
(Rate varies with type of plant cover and condition of soil.)

Soil Type	Inches per hour
Sand—with plant cover	2.0
Sand—bare soil	1.0
Loamy sand—with plant cover	1.8
Loamy sand—bare soil	0.9
Loam—with plant cover	1.5
Loam—bare soil	0.75
Silt or clay loam—with plant cover	0.5
Silt or clay loam—bare soil	0.25
Clay—with plant cover	0.2
Clay—bare soil	0.1

* Adapted from Oscar A. Lorenz and Donald N. Maynard, *Knott's Handbook for Vegetable Growers*, third edition, New York: John Wiley and Sons, 1988.

a soil that can be gardened satisfactorily as is. Now a gifted, experienced chef can mix ingredients successfully by eye or intuition, but an everyday cook (such as myself) needs the guidance of a recipe. What will follow are recipes. You needn't follow them to the digit, but they are worth consulting before you start to pour and stir.

You shouldn't do anything to your soil, however, until you know what you are starting with—this is especially true with regard to irrigation, where a soil's composition, its texture in particular, determines not only the amount of water you should apply but also

The Soil Reservoir*

Type of Soil	Water Available to Plant When Soil Is at Field Capacity†
Sandy	½ gal. per cubic ft. = ¾ in. of water per ft. of soil
Loamy	1 gal. per cubic ft. = 1½ in. of water per ft. of soil
Clayey	1½ gal. per cubic ft. = 2¼ in. of water per ft. of soil

* Adapted from Oscar A. Lorenz and Donald N. Maynard, *Knott's Handbook for Vegetable Growers*, third edition, New York: John Wiley and Sons, 1988.
† For explanation of term see Chapter 4, page 173.

How deep?*

How deep does 1 inch of irrigation wet the soil if applied when half the available moisture has been depleted?

Soil Type	Depth of penetration
Sandy	24 inches
Loamy	16 inches
Clayey	11 inches

* Adapted from Oscar A. Lorenz and Donald N. Maynard, *Knott's Handbook for Vegetable Growers*, third edition, New York: John Wiley and Sons, 1988.

How much?*

How much irrigation does it take to wet your soil to the plants' root zones?

Amount of water required (in inches of irrigation) to rewet a soil half depleted of available moisture

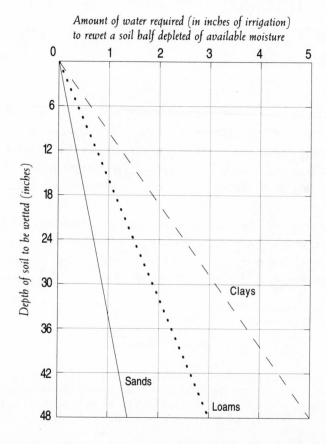

* Adapted from Oscar A. Lorenz and Donald N. Maynard, *Knott's Handbook for Vegetable Growers*, third edition, New York: John Wiley and Sons, 1988.

the schedule of application. The table on page 121 lists the water capacities of different kinds off soils; consult this before watering to gain idea of how much water you can administer before the irrigation becomes sheer waste.

It will tell you, for example, that a layer of sand a foot deep has the capacity to absorb and retain for plants' use something like ¾ of an inch of irrigation; whereas a similar layer of clay will absorb and retain 2¼ inches. Obviously, if your soil is clay you'll need almost three times as much water to thoroughly moisten it than if it were sand. But you'll also have to administer the water more slowly. As the same table indicates, water soaks ("infiltrates" is the technical term) into sand much more quickly than into clay, so that in less than half an hour your patch of plant-covered sand will absorb all of that ¾ inch of water it can hold. If you apply water at the same rate to your clay bed (that is, about 1½ inches in one hour), you'll find it pouring out over the ground much faster than the soil can absorb it, so that most of the water will run away and be lost.

Check this table and set your irrigation system accordingly. If your sprinkler or drip system applies water faster than your soil can accept it (and you can determine the application rate through the calibration systems included in Chapter Five), try running the system until it has applied half the water your soil needs, then turn it off. Wait two hours, then turn the irrigation system back on to apply the remainder of the water. This should eliminate your runoff problem.

Fortunately, determining the texture of your soil is a fairly simple matter. You can check with the nearest office of the Soil Conservation Service (your county Cooperative Extension agent should be able to direct you to this) for a soil survey of your area. This will give you an idea of what soils are typical locally. Such a survey may be of limited help in analyzing your exact site, however, since the chances are good that your soil was disturbed during the construction of your house.

If that is the case, you should have a sample of your soil analyzed. You can do this by sending a sample (or samples, for often a yard will include a couple of different types of soil) away to the soil laboratory at your state agricultural university; your county Cooperative Extension office can supply the necessary address and information about fees. Generally, the cost is nominal—in Connecticut it costs twelve dollars per sample—but make sure you specify a comprehensive soil test, since otherwise the lab will test only for your soil's nutrient content and acidity. If you are really thrifty, or merely curious, however, you can analyze your soil yourself.

Actually, you can tell a good deal about your soil just by its feel —even soil scientists use this for making a quick appraisal. Dig down at least three to five inches to collect your sample. What interests you, after all, is the soil encountered by your plants' roots. Take a pinch from the sample and rub it between your fingers. If it feels gritty, you've got a sandy soil. If it feels floury when dry, then your soil is principally silt, and if it's sticky when wet, then it's a clay. Next, take a handful of soil, moisten it, and knead it to a putty-like consistency. Then squeeze it between your thumb and the crook of your forefinger; if it takes a good cast, a clear impression and thumbprint, you can be sure it's a silt. Roll a bit between your palms, and if it makes a long, flexible string, it's a clay. If the string is brittle, then your soil is something between clay and silt —say, a clay loam.

There's still another test, one that's simple enough for the amateur to undertake.

Take a one-quart canning jar, fill it half full of water, and mix in until dissolved a teaspoon of some dishwasher detergent such as Calgon. Next add a cup of your soil sample, screw the lid onto the jar, and shake it vigorously until the soil particles are thoroughly dispersed and about evenly distributed. Set the jar down, wait one minute, and then with a grease pencil mark on the jar the sediment that has settled out of suspension. This first fraction to settle out is the sand. Wait one hour and mark the level again; this fraction is the silt. Wait a full day and mark one last time; this last fraction is the clay. Finally, measure carefully with a ruler the depth of each of the fractions and the total depth of soil at the jar's bottom.

To determine the percentages of sand, silt, and clay, divide the depth of that fraction by the total depth of the soil. If the sand fraction measures half an inch thick, for example, and the total depth of the soil is three inches, then you divide .5 by 3 to arrive at an answer of 0.17—and that means your soil is 17 percent sand. Once you've determined the percentages of sand, silt, and clay, you can plug these figures into the soil-type identifier on page 125 to determine what kind of soil you have.

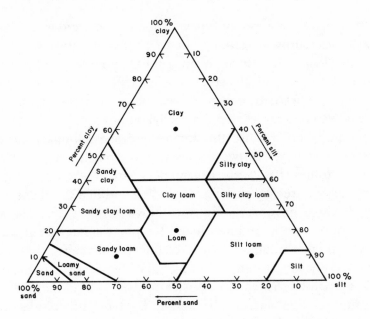

Every soil is a complex of three basic classes of particles—clays, silts, and sands. Each corner of this triangle represents a soil composed entirely of one class of particle; that's why they are marked "100% clay," "100% silt," and "100% sand." Ordinary soils lie somewhere in between these extremes, and this diagram will help you find where your soil falls and so identify it by type. To do this, follow these steps:

1. First use the test on page 124 to evaluate your soil's fractions of clay, silt, and sand. It may tell you, for example, that your soil is composed of 50% clay, 25% silt, and 25% sand.

2. Draw a line from the top corner of this diagram (the one marked 100% clay) to the middle of the line below it (bisect the angle). This is the clay line and represents the range of clay from 100% (the top of the line) to 0% (the bottom of the line). Measure halfway down the line from the top to the midpoint—that's the 50% mark. Draw a line there across the triangle, making it perpendicular to the clay line (and parallel to the base of the triangle).

3. Repeat the process with silt. That is, draw a line from the corner marked 100% silt to the middle of the opposite line (the left-hand side of the triangle). This time measure three quarters of the way from the beginning of the line ("100% silt") to the bottom of the line (which again equals 0%). The point you reach will be the 25% mark—a value equal to the amount of silt in your soil. At this point draw another perpendicular line (this one should be parallel to the triangle's left-hand side).

4. Repeat the process once again, this time starting from the corner marked "100% sand," measuring down to the 25% mark (your test revealed a soil content of 25% sand), and drawing a third perpendicular line (this one will parallel the triangle's right-hand side).

5. Your three perpendicular lines should intersect within the area marked "clay"—so this hypothetical soil classifies as a clay soil and you should treat it accordingly. Of course, your real soil will most likely contain different proportions of clay, silt, and sand and so may well test out as belonging to another soil type: sandy clay, loam, silt loam, etc.

Identifying the type (or types) of soil in your yard is critical not only to regulating irrigation, but to choosing plants adapted to your site. Generally a given plant will tolerate a range of soils, but most prefer one type. If you choose plants best suited to the soil, you will be rewarded with healthier, more vigorous growth, and you will also find far less need for irrigation.

Naturally, the reverse also applies: a careless choice may result in plants that never thrive, no matter how much you water. The inkberry hollies (*Ilex glabra*) I planted as part of a screen along the perimeter of a treeless parking lot all died within a couple of years. Though these grow naturally from Nova Scotia to Florida, they prefer a loose, cool, and moist soil. Despite the buckets of water I brought them through the first couple of summers, they never thrived in my sun-heated curbside of gravelly, sandy clay loam.

Yet when I revisited that spot yesterday, I found that the wild-type rugosa roses and the bayberries I set on either side of the hollies have spread into satisfyingly impenetrable thickets—and I haven't watered them in ten years. Almost certainly, as I noted before, you will want to moderate the texture of your soil. It's only common sense, though, to match the planting to the existing soil type as much as possible. In that way, you keep the changes you must make in the soil modest.

Before going on to prescriptions for soil "amendment," you should analyze your soil for one more characteristic: its structure. Texture may determine a soil's capacity for water, but structure is what determines drainage—how easily the soil absorbs water, and how quickly it allows an excess to leak away.

If texture depends on the size of soil particles, structure is the way in which they are arranged. Ideally, the individual particles should be clumped together in crumbs; the description most often used is that a slightly moist clod should crumble between your fingers like rich cake. Such a loose (or "friable") soil is easy for roots to penetrate, and offers them an abundant supply of oxygen. A loose soil also moistens easily, yet its porousness ensures that excess water can pass through so that the garden doesn't waterlog.

Unfortunately, soil of this quality is rare, especially in suburban areas. There, where the landscape has been pushed around by construction equipment, and then pounded by pedestrian traffic (how many times do you plant each foot with every lawn mowing?), soils are typically compacted. Pressure, especially when the soil was wet, has collapsed the larger pores, forcing out the air and jamming soil particles together. This creates an impermeable layer through which neither water nor roots penetrate readily, and a soil which, once wet, is slow to drain.

Sometimes the problem of surface compaction is compounded by the presence of another compacted layer, what farmers call a "pan," underneath what's left of the topsoil. This not only further inhibits root growth, but also stops the movement of water downward so that moisture backs up into an artificially high, or "perched," water table. That guarantees waterlogged soil after every irrigation or rain, and it encourages fertilizers, or any other chemicals dissolved in the irrigation water, to collect in the plants' root zone. Since too many nutrients are as bad as too few, gardeners with a subsurface pan commonly find that a level of fertilization that would be fine on a well-drained soil proves fatal to the plants in their yards.

Pans, by the way, are a particularly common problem in the arid soils of the West, where heavy rains don't come often enough to flush salts away. In a region of limestone, the halfhearted sprinklings wash calcium (from the limestone) a few inches down into the soil, where it is stranded when the water is sucked back up into the sky by evaporation. Irrigation water adds its own quota of dissolved lime, and eventually enough accumulates to bond together like mortar, making the subfloor of crumbly, gray caliche that afflicts gardeners like Wilbur Davis.

Crumbling a moist handful from one of your soil samples should reveal if your soil is properly loose and friable. Watch your soil, too, as you turn it with a fork or spade, for compacted soil shatters into block-like, hard clods. Once again, a local soil survey may furnish insights about structure and warn you of the probability of pans. You should add to this an inspection of your own, however.

Dig a pit three feet deep, and cut one wall smoothly vertical. That way, you can read the natural layering of the soil as easily as you'd run your finger down a page. Check the uppermost layer, the topsoil, to make sure that it is loose, not compacted. Ideally, it should be eight inches thick or more (the thicker the better) and darker in color than the layers below, since a dark hue reveals the presence of humus.

You'll find anywhere from two to half a dozen distinct layers below the topsoil. Check for pans. If you find one, you face the arduous task of digging down to fracture it wherever you plant. A post hole digger can make that chore easier—use it to punch drainage holes down through the pan just as you'd punch drainage holes in the bottom of a flowerpot. Watch not only for compacted layers, though; watch also for gray layers. That color betrays a subsoil that is continually wet. Bad drainage is what horticulturists call that and it stunts root development, creating a plant that's easy prey for even a modest drought.

If digging a proper inspection pit sounds like too much trouble, at least excavate a hole one foot deep and six inches across and fill it with water. After the water drains away, refill the hole and watch: if the second dose of water takes more than eight hours to soak in, your drainage needs improvement.

How does the gardener do that? Older gardening books recommend installing a network of drainage tile, but I've never been willing to undertake that kind of backbreaking labor. If I've deduced that the problem is a pan or waterlogged subsoil, then I plant high and dry in raised beds. I prefer to frame my beds with timber, but you can achieve the same effect by simply raking soil up into leveled heaps and leaving the depressed areas in between to drain excess water away. More commonly, though, I find that the problem is not a pan but the texture and structure of the soil's upper layers—the soil in which my plants actually root.

How do you adjust a soil's texture or structure? *Cultivation*— turning the soil with a fork, tiller or plow—will loosen and aerate it temporarily. I prefer to cultivate deeply, generally two lengths of the spade's blade deep ("double-digging" is what the old-time gardeners called this). The reach of a plant's root system is partly dictated by genetics, but by loosening the soil deeply you encourage each plant to extend its root system to the maximum. This, in turn gives the plant a greater reservoir on which to draw for moisture.

But unless combined with other measures, cultivation has only a short-lived effect, since the soil immediately begins settling back into compaction. The most permanent measure you can take is to adjust the soil's mineral content—that is, to add rock particles of a larger or smaller size.

For example, if you garden in the northeastern or south-central parts of the United States, the two regions in which I have experience, what you will likely find in your yard is a clay. One of the measures I have taken to lighten a clay soil has been to mix it with a coarse sand—what masonry supply dealers refer to as a "sharp" sand.

Spreading a layer two inches thick and then digging it in can transform the topmost foot of such a sticky, soggy soil into a more satisfactory clay loam (depending on how pure the clay was to begin with—a really heavy clay might need several more inches of sand to accomplish as much). I've read of Chinese peasants dredging silt from canals to add body to eroded, sandy soils. Either way, this is hard labor—too hard to extend to anything more than a compact vegetable bed or flower border.

Luckily, there is a far less arduous fix. It isn't quite as permanent, but it provides an almost magical cure for either compacted clay or thirsty sand. It's humus.

That is the gardener's term for a soil's organic constituent. The decayed remains of plants and animals, *humus* is the familiar carbohydrates, proteins, and fats, as well as all the other materials of life, digested by microorganisms into an amorphous black or brown acidic matter. It may not look like much, but it has a number of remarkable abilities.

Humus bonds readily to mineral particles, so that it serves as a catalyst in promoting a light, crumby structure in practically any type of soil. As it decays further, humus slowly releases a moderate stream of nutrients into the soil, which makes it the ideal nourishment for a xeriscape. If you wish to limit irrigation, you must avoid heavy doses of fertilizers, since they will incite your plants to extravagant bursts of insupportable growth, but at the same time you'll find it counterproductive to starve your plants. Because plants take their nutrients from the water they absorb from the soil, they must draw far more water when they are growing in a nutrient-poor soil. So a complete, but not too rich, diet such as humus furnishes will promote water conservation.

The most direct effect humus has on water use in the garden, however, lies in its tremendous absorptive power; each particle will absorb many times its own weight in water. Fine-particled but purely mineral silts and clays may absorb and hold as much as 45 percent of their total weight in water—but a really humus-rich soil, like the black, crumbly material you scrape up from the forest floor, will retain roughly six to ten times that much. Compost, the semi-decayed organic matter which is humus in the making, can absorb as much as nine times its own weight in water. That is why "improving" the soil with massive quantities of organic matter is one of the basic tenets of the xeriscapers.

You will probably need to do this too, since the soil in your yard is almost certainly deficient in humus/organic matter. If you live on former cropland, you can thank the farmers for this, for American-style agriculture depletes the soil's humus at a rapid rate, using up as much as a quarter or a third in the first twenty years of cultivation. And if your property was never cropped, that was probably because the soil in its virgin state was too humus-poor to interest a farmer.

Anyway, whatever humus remained when the land was developed for housing was almost surely taken by the contractor. It is standard practice to strip each lot of topsoil and then sell a fraction of it back to the new homeowners when they pay to have a lawn installed. The rest of that humus goes, for a price, to someone else's landscape; it is the farm's last harvest.

A check of your topsoil's color can tip you off to its organic content. Black or brown commonly indicates a soil with a good organic content, while yellow or gray generally means your soil is humus-deficient. A precise reading of your soil's organic content should have been part of the soil test the soil laboratory performed for you. But how much humus is enough?

Organic gardeners, the greatest devotees of humus, recommend a humus content of 5 percent (by weight) as a goal, and this is quoted as ideal in various guides to xeriscaping. But before accepting it as the standard, it's worth noting how the figure originated. Five percent is the average humus level of virgin prairie soil of the upper Midwest. Organic gardening began, at least in the United States, with J. I. Rodale's vision of a return to that particular version of a rural utopia: the Midwest when the sod was just busted, when the earth was still rich and it belonged to homesteaders and not agribusinesses. Not a bad dream—but the organic gardeners ought to warn us that it's a will-o'-the-wisp through much of this country.

For as I learned in Texas, nature is going to take a hand in determining the humus content of your soil. It had been easy keeping a soil humus-rich in the Northeast, the place where I learned to garden (just a few hours' drive from Emmaus, Pennsylvania, the birthplace of the American organic gardening movement). Whenever I dug a new bed, I covered the soil with three or four inches of compost, and then turned it in, double-digging as usual. In the relatively cool northeastern climate, the humus that compost creates is relatively stable. In Texas, though, I found to my amazement that by the end of the first growing season the soil retained no hint of my therapy. Within a couple of months, all evidence of the compost had vanished.

Apparently, the United States Department of Agriculture had noticed the same thing more than a half-century before. In the studies it conducted, soil scientists found a direct correlation between climate and humus content. The hotter the climate, the faster and more completely the humus decomposed. After studying soils along a line drawn from Canada to Florida, one researcher[*] found that while farm soils around Syracuse, New York, averaged almost 3 percent humus, those in Florida, Alabama, and Georgia tested at less than 1 percent. Virgin soils in Arizona, a farmers' bulletin from the University of Arizona notes, may run as low as 0.1 percent organic matter. It's *really* hot there, and there's little vegetation at the surface to replenish the supply.

There are a number of theories as to why hot-weather areas support soils lower in humus, but all agree that an increased rate of decomposition plays a role. I can only surmise that the tons of compost I dug into my gray, humus-poor topsoil in College Station incited a population explosion among the microorganisms. As the temperature rose to 105°F and I made sure the garden stayed adequately moist, the various fungi and bacteria went wild, devouring the organic matter to the last crumb.

I found two ways of dealing with this situation. The plants that demanded a genuinely humus-rich (i.e., light and perpetually moist) soil—my lettuce and tomatoes, for instance—I treated like potted plants. I confined them to four raised beds which I re-enriched with compost every spring, double-digging every time. Through the rest of the garden, I prepared the soil before planting with shredded pine bark, counting on this being slower to decompose than the compost. The bark, though organic, didn't provide all the benefits of actual humus, but it helped lighten the soil and

---

* Hans Jenny, "Soil Organic Matter–Temperature Relationship in the Eastern United States," *Soil Science,* April 1931, pp. 247–52.

increase its moisture-holding capacity.* On that soil I landscaped with plants adapted to clay.

As I discovered later, I also inadvertently adopted the practice best calculated to protect the soil's humus, and therefore its water-holding capacity. I always kept the garden covered with an organic mulch.

I tucked in my plants with mulch because I had been told by the xeriscapers that it conserved water. How much, they couldn't say. A Californian claimed that a two-inch-deep layer of an organic mulch (shredded bark, cocoa bean hulls, etc.) would reduce a planting's need for irrigation by a half. It seemed sure to me that climate and soil must influence the effectiveness of mulch as a water saver; unfortunately, I can find no investigation of this. Maybe that is because mulch has been a gardener's commonplace for so long—everybody knows (or think they know) how beneficial it is, so why waste time proving the obvious?

Whatever the reason for this oversight, the only hard data I have found concerning the effectiveness of mulch as a water con-servator came from cool, moist Madison, Wisconsin, a place where the evaporation of water from the soil's surface would be relatively low. Even so, researchers at the University of Wisconsin found that a layer of shredded hardwood bark five centimeters (approximately two inches) deep kept soil moisture 5 percent higher (when mea-sured by weight) than in an adjacent uncovered plot.

That may not seem like much, but consider: the field capacity (the maximum amount of water a soil will hold under normal con-ditions) of an ordinary loam is 19.6 percent. That means that this soil, a good average garden soil, will, even after the heaviest rain-storm, ordinarily retain just 19.6 percent of its own weight in water. Not all of this water is available to the plants, either, since the attraction of water to soil particles increases as the moisture level drops. Actually, for this same soil the *wilting point*—the level of moisture at which most plant roots can no longer extract water —is 10 percent. That leaves just a 9.6 percent window in which the soil moisture must remain if plants are to survive—and 5 per-cent, the quantity of water conserved by the mulch, is more than half of this.

---

* Weathered sawdust would have been another durable choice. Even peat would have lasted longer than compost, since peat is virtually nutrient free and so relatively unattractive to decomposers.

Mulch, however, as I have since learned, also conserves water by conserving humus. It does this partly by keeping the soil cooler and so moderating the activity of microorganisms. I was pleased to learn that a study down the road from me at the Connecticut Agricultural Experiment Station found the soil 18°F cooler under a three-inch-thick mulch of leaves than on an unprotected site; that's the mulch I use. An organic mulch also moderates the access of air to the topsoil, and that, too, slows the decomposition of humus. A correlary of this is the fact that cultivation—digging, rototilling, or even hoeing—by aerating the soil helps *speed* the decomposition. Luckily mulch, by suppressing weeds and keeping the surface from crusting over, eliminates most of the need for this stirring.

As I've already noted in Chapter Two (see pages 65–66) none of the synthetic or inorganic mulches offers all the benefits of a layer of natural organics. Besides, if you use a little imagination, the natural organics can be had for free. I've used weathered sawdust as a mulch, composted horse manure when there was a stable nearby, and spent mushroom compost—that wasn't actually free, since it cost me ten dollars to persuade the backhoe operator at the mushroom farm near to College Station to fill a pickup bed. In Connecticut I celebrate autumn by collecting the bags of leaves the neighbors set out on the curb. After running these through an inexpensive electric leaf shredder, I spread them over the garden, where they make a most attractive as well as water-conserving undergarment for flowers, shrubs, and vegetables.

There are a number of other effective devices for increasing the moisture level of your soil. Terracing a slope so that it presents level surfaces will reduce runoff and so increase the amount of rainwater the landscape absorbs. In areas of salinity, heaping up the soil—building raised beds—may, by improving the soil's drainage, increase the supply available to the plants while also reducing the need for irrigation.

This seeming contradiction (less is more) derives from the way in which salts affect plant roots: by reducing the relative concentration of water in the soil, they reduce the roots' effectiveness as pumps (see page 23). The source of the salts may be, as in caliche-prone areas, salts such as calcium already in the soil, or it may actually be the irrigation water that you apply. In College Station,

Texas, for example, the municipal water contained an average of 274 milligrams of sodium chloride per liter. If I forgot a pot on the stove and boiled away a gallon of tap water, I found an eighth of a tablespoon of table salt in the bottom of the empty pot.

The source of the salt in College Station was a subsurface deposit that underlay the wells. In many other areas of the West, the salt derives from the recycling of irrigation water; each time the water drains through the fields, it picks up a load of salts from the soil which it brings back with it to the river. But whatever the source, if you use this kind of polluted water to irrigate your garden, salt will build up into the soil, and eventually your plants will start to show symptoms of salt poisoning: typically, a browning at the leaf tips. The plants will wilt, too, in hot weather, because the roots cannot extract moisture effectively from the salty soil. Increasing your irrigation only worsens the problem, of course.

Heaping the soil in raised beds eases this condition by increasing the effect of whatever rain you do receive. By enhancing the soil's drainage, a raised bed helps the purer rainwater to wash salts down through the soil and away. I never ran a controlled, scientific experiment in my Texas garden, but the symptoms of salt poisoning did disappear once I began raising all my planting beds.

Finally, there are the wonder drugs.

Every decade or so, some new laboratory concoction bursts onto the market with promises to solve your watering problems in a single application. Thirty years ago there was "Krillium," which would cause your clay soil to reassemble itself in crumbs. A decade later there were wetteners which, by reducing surface tension of soil moisture, were supposed to help water infiltrate more quickly. And now, there are "soil polymers."

These are water-absorbent gels of the kind used in disposable diapers. Sow them into your soil (at considerable expense) and (supposedly) you transform it instantly into a xeriscaper's dream. According to a brochure provided by the manufacturers, at least one of these polymers can absorb up to 400 *times* its own weight in water as it swells from salt-like crystals to a clear flubber.

In theory, the presence of polymers should reduce the need for irrigation. The gels, because they are so absorbent, greatly increase the water-holding capacity of the soil as a whole, so that rainwater which would otherwise run off or drain away and be lost is retained. In this way, gels are supposed to help your landscape become more self-sufficient. But it's not clear how much of the water the gels will re-release to plant roots.

Manufacturers claim that this ranges from 60 to 95 percent, depending on the polymer. A number of university-sponsored tests, however, have found that the presence of polymers in the soil provided no apparent benefits to the plants and did not decrease the need for watering. It seems likely that the polymer particles bind water so tightly to themselves that roots cannot pry most of it loose. Consequently, your plants may wilt even while your polymerized soil is awash with water.

As best I can tell, the jury is still out on the soil polymers. I do know that my own experience with them, while slight, was unhappy. Outside our kitchen there is a window box of herbs that, by midsummer, I have to water every day. Last spring I thought I'd eliminate this annoying chore by inoculating it with a polymer sample I had received through the mail. So I mixed the granules into the potting mix. The next rainstorm floated gel up to the surface, where it lay gleaming like a sheet of out-of-season ice. Though I scraped that off, every rainstorm that followed brought another slick. Nor did I notice any change in the need for irrigation.

I don't believe you will find the answer to your watering problems in such shortcuts. You will find them, though, at least some of them, right underneath your feet—if you take the time to make the soil your partner.

Rules of Thumb

Before landscaping, dig and amend soil as deeply as possible; double-digging (cultivating to a depth of two spade blades) is ideal. A deep, well aerated, and humus-rich soil encourages deep rooting, giving plants a greater reservoir on which to draw.

Such a deeply prepared soil requires more water with each irrigation—all other things being equal, it takes twice as much water to moisten a two-foot-deep bed as a one-foot-deep bed.

A deeply dug bed requires irrigation far less often, however, and is greatly superior at storing natural precipitation.

Mechanical cultivation should always be supplemented with occasional hand digging. A garden rototilled repeatedly to the same depth will form a pan just below the machine's reach.

A back-saving way to improve your subsoil is to raise an occasional crop of some deep-rooted plant such as crown vetch or sweet clover. These legumes' penetrating roots will force their way into all but the most compacted soil and after death will decay to leave the soil riddled with air channels and organic material.

Use color as a clue to your soil's water-holding capacity.
- Black or dark brown is usually an indication of a soil rich in organic matter; the color results from the organic matter's staining of the soil's mineral particles. Such a soil furnishes a good reservoir.
- Red and yellow soils may be fertile, but tend to be low in humus; common to warm, humid climates, they are evidence that organic matter is decomposing before it can stain.
- Gray topsoil (such as I had in College Station) is typically humus-deficient. Gray subsoil is evidence of waterlogging.
- White soils, common in the arid West, are mostly composed of rock particles; they may be fertile and are generally well drained. Where limestone is common, however, white soil may be a warning that caliche lurks below.

Tucson, Arizona

I had thought that the arrival of the first aqueduct would be cause for rejoicing in a desert community. And in fact, the gardeners of Tucson were relieved that the Central Arizona Project was slated for completion in slightly less than two years' time. Yet most of the ones to whom I spoke were also glad that the easy water wasn't arriving any sooner.

The irony is that water had been abundant here, once upon a time. *Stjukshon* means "dark spring" in the language of the Tohono O'odham Indians, and springs at the foot of Sentinel Peak had fed a lush oasis of wetlands when Anglo settlers began arriving in the nineteenth century. Mosquitoes were the most dangerous threat to pioneers then; their grim joke was that malaria killed settlers faster than the railroad could replace them.

By 1990 nobody was worrying about mosquitoes. The springs were long gone; in many places the water table had dropped five hundred feet, thanks to the pumps of Tucson's modern residents. Rainfall averages 11.14 inches a year—this was the first place I had been where the weathermen measured the day's precipitation in hundredths of an inch. For half a century the city had been operating at a deficit, and it had used up in a couple of generations water that had taken thousands of years to accumulate. This situation should change once the aqueduct arrived—there were even plans to replenish the aquifer by injecting Central Arizona Project water into the ground. Tucson's gardeners agreed, though, that the years of water emergency had been a very good thing.

They said this because they knew it was the water shortage that had made Tucson embrace its environment. The average Tucsonian uses nearly one hundred gallons less water per day than his fellow in nearby Phoenix, and the savings is mostly made outdoors. Despite the 350-plus days of sunshine each year and an ET rate that may reach three quarters of an inch per day, Phoenix remains a piecework of emerald lawns, palms, and citrus trees. In the miles of subdivisions that ring Tucson's city center, by contrast, you're hard put to find turf at all. Instead, the cholla and prickly pears sweep right up to the houses. Tucson's gardeners have invited the desert in.

This is partly the result of official action. Tucson's water managers have worked hard to educate the city's gardeners, and as of this writing were continuing to do so, hoping to reduce residential usage even further, by another twenty or so gallons per person per day. But it's a measure of Tucson's gardeners that they find this new challenge exciting.

In no other place have I found gardeners testing so many different methods of water conservation. Certainly, nowhere else are the gardens more distinctive or lovelier. I must admit, though, that the garden at Native Seeds/SEARCH* was more thought-provoking than beautiful on the morning that I stopped by.

There had been a plague of beetles and grubs, and the desert crops the Native Seeds/SEARCH gardeners were growing are not used to that; generally, their environment isolates these plants from such predators. But Native Seeds/SEARCH's headquarters is located in the Tucson Botanical Garden, a compact (five-acre) but diverse collection of plants that undoubtedly hosts an equally outstanding collection of pests. Besides, it was fall, past the end of the harvest produced by summer rains, and the Native Seed/SEARCH garden is by design a very seasonal one.

But I'd been sent by friends who'd seen it at its peaks—in late spring when the first corn, beans, and squash ripen; again in late summer, when the monsoons bring a respite from the heat; and throughout the cool, relatively moist winter. These eyewitnesses assured me that the garden was as astonishingly luxuriant then as the fields of wildflowers that follow a desert rain.

Kevin Dahl, the organization's assistant director, while showing me around, took me to the edge of what looked like a huge earthen waffle. I am a native person of the Northeast—Christophers have been tending the rocky farms of central Connecticut as long as anyone there can remember—and our horticultural tradition dictates *raising* the beds, so that rainwater runs away. That, Kevin Dahl explained, is appropriate to an area of generous precipitation. But in Tucson, and throughout the surrounding Sonoran Desert, water from the sky is not to be squandered, and so beds there are sunk into the ground.

Under the direction of staff member Daniela Soleri (an anthropologist who specializes in traditional aridland horticulture and who has written extensively on the gardening techniques of southwestern peoples), the Native Seed/SEARCH staff dug eighteen to twenty-four inches down, excavating shallow rectangular pits that measured roughly four feet by five. The first five inches or so of what the gardeners removed was topsoil, and they set this aside. Below this came a layer of dense adobe clay, which they dug out

* SEARCH here is an acronym signifying Southwestern Endangered Aridlands Resource Clearing House.

and packed around the new beds' perimeters in a grid of low walls. Below the clay was caliche, so that the gardeners had to excavate the last foot of each bed with iron bars. Then they mixed the topsoil with compost and manure and shoveled it back into the holes.

Based on the traditional terrace gardens of the Hopi, this arrangement has in an arid region several advantages over my style of planting. Of course, the improved soil within the bed absorbs and holds water more efficiently than the native desert soil. In addition, the walls ensure that no irrigation water is lost through runoff. Finally, by blocking the wind the walls also create a dead air space over each bed; the stagnant air within this absorbs some water from plant leaves, but as it becomes more humid (significantly more humid than the air in the windblown area outside the bed) it cuts the plant's ET rate. This, of course, reduces the need for watering.

The Native Seeds/SEARCHers do irrigate. Using a bubbler at the end of a hose, they pour an inch of water into one bed after another. But whereas gardeners in the Anglo tradition may sprinkle three times a day in the hot, rainless months of May and June (and still may lose their vegetables to drought), gardeners at Native Seeds/SEARCH water no more than once a week then, and often not for weeks at a time in winter. They enjoy generous harvests, too.

Not all their water comes from the tap. With a shallow swale, the Native Seeds/SEARCH gardeners collect the water that runs off a nearby slope during the winter monsoons, and they channel this down to another garden patch just as the Tohono O'odham Indians used to do. This runoff, incidentally, furnishes crops with food as well as drink; in its career down the slope, the runoff sweeps up bits of organic matter and soluble nutrients.

This is important, since Sonoran desert soils typically are poor, with an organic content of less than ½ percent.* Native gardeners are extremely resourceful in the matter of fertilizers; Gary Nabhan, the ethnobotanist who founded Native Seeds/SEARCH in 1983, has observed Tohono O'odham Indians collecting bat guano from churches and desert caves to spread on their fields. But they depend

---

* Gary P. Nabhan, *The Desert Smells like Rain: A Naturalist in Papago Indian Country* (San Francisco: North Point Press, 1982).

on floodwater above all else—in tests by Nabhan, the water itself yielded a modest amount of nitrogen, but its cargo of debris was the really valuable stuff. "The cream of the stream," he has called it, * noting that it has fifty times the nutrient value of the water.

I recognized most of the crops in the Native Seeds/SEARCH garden, at least by family. There were the yet-to-be harvested remnants of corn, beans, squashes, and sunflowers, and Kevin pointed out to me where in a few weeks they would plant the winter crops of wheat, fava beans, lentils, garbanzos, peas, garlic, and onions. Daniela Soleri explained to me later that summer crops tend to be native American species, while winter crops generally originated in the Old World and came to the desert with the Spanish. This is because the pre-Columbian southwestern peoples gardened only in the summer; in wintertime they gathered wild greens that the cooler, moister weather brought. Desert dwellers are opportunists, though, and the Indians were quick to adopt the best-adapted European crops.

A coarse-leaved, sprawling bush provoked a feeling of déjà vu, and it proved to be a wild tomato (*Lycopersicon esculentum* var. *cerisforme*) from southern Mexico. According to Kevin, it bears well right though the southwestern summer, and the fruit tasted good, tart yet sweet, to me. Was that okra? Yes! But that's a native of tropical Asia. Kevin explained that it too had arrived with the Spanish centuries ago, and had found the intense desert heat and sunlight to its liking. Along with a new home, it found a new use, for the Indians call it "nescafe," because they roast and grind the seeds to make a coffee substitute. The sorghum nearby I learned is called "sugar cane" here; it's a treat for Indian children, who chew its sweet stems.

Even the most familiar crops here—the corn, say, or the tomato—looked very different from any varieties I had seen before, and that's not surprising. These were all heirlooms, cultivars that had, like the people that grew them, adapted over many generations to life in the dry lands. Anglo settlers, intent on adjusting the environment to suit their lifestyle, dismissed them as mere curiosities. When the pumps threatened to run dry, though, the settlers' descendants began looking with more interest at the Indians' legacy.

* Ibid.

This reversal occurred just in time. Since World War II the native peoples of the Southwest have mostly abandoned their traditional agriculture (the Tohona O'odham had abandoned all but one hundred acres of their fields by the late 1980s), and in the process discarded the heirloom seeds that had fed them faithfully for a thousand, maybe two thousand years. A number of factors contributed to this. The poverty of reservation life and the government's program of "Americanization" had chipped away at all aspects of the traditional cultures. Then, in this century, flood control projects either drowned or parched most of the old flood-nourished fields. Lastly, government relief efforts introduced Indians to white bread, fatty meats, and processed sugar; the spread of automobiles and paved highways made it easy for them to gratify new appetites. The net result has been a diet almost devoid of fresh fruits and vegetables, and an abnormally high rate of obesity and diabetes—the Pima Indians, for example, suffer the highest incidence of diabetes in the world, with more than half the women over thirty-five affected.

It was an attempt to address this problem that led to the birth of Native Seeds/SEARCH in 1983. At that time there wasn't a single grocery selling fresh produce on Arizona's Tohono O'odham reservation, the second-largest Indian reservation in the United States. A foundation called "Meals for Millions/Freedom from Hunger" decided to encourage the Tohono O'odham to grow their own vegetables, and sent Gary Nabhan to pass out seeds and seedlings of such undeniably healthy, but (to the Indians) unfamiliar fare as broccoli and cauliflower. The response was generally a thank-you, followed by a question: "Do you have seeds of that corn my grandfather used to grow?" "What about the melon we used to call *geli baasho*—'old man's chest'? That was the best melon we ever had."

Nabhan realized that he didn't have to teach these people how to garden; on the contrary, they had a lot to teach him. What he could do was to make it possible for them to resume their traditional ways. This, he speculated, might be the solution to their health problems too. Nabhan believed that even a partial return to traditional foods, with their higher fiber and complex carbohydrates, might curb the epidemic of obesity and diabetes.

As he traveled around the reservation, he asked the remaining gardeners for seeds of traditional varieties so that he could pass them on to other would-be gardeners. Gradually he wandered farther and farther from home, ranging deep into Mexico. What he found was the remains of a tremendous diversity.

Different native groups grew different varieties, not just because their cultures differed but also because their homelands were each unique. The Mohave Indians, for example, live along the Colorado River on Arizona's western border in what is, aside from Death Valley, the hottest, driest region of North America. In this low desert, rainfall usually totals from two to four inches a year, and the temperature rises above 100°F almost every day in summertime. Before the arrival of the white man's pumps, the growing season in the riverside fields lasted from the ebbing of the Colorado's flood-waters in May or June to the moment a few weeks later when the desert sun sucked the last drop of available moisture from the soil. As a result, Mohave corn is fast-growing, sprouted from seed, grown, tasseled, and ready to pick in fifty-five days.

Hopi farmers, on the other hand, who live in the higher, cooler desert of the northern Arizona mesas, depend on water left in the ground by winter rains to nourish their summer crop. To tap this moisture they grow a type of corn which tolerates being sown eight inches down into the sandy soil. Native corns also show an amazing tolerance for temperature fluctuation, a characteristic of desert lands where searing heat during the day may be followed by a near-frost at night. The hardy southwestern varieties thrive even as the thermometer swings from 120°F to almost freezing and back.

Not only are the native seeds adapted to the natural water budget, they thrive in the Southwest's very distinctive soil types. Saline soils, such as I encountered in central Texas, are common in the homelands of the Hopi and Pima. My solution was to enhance the soil's rate of drainage so that salt would leach away. The Indians, by contrast, accepted things as they found them and sowed salt-tolerant crops. Hopi and the Pima lima beans, for instance, flourish in saline soils.

Some of these crops Nabhan had brought back almost literally from the dead. There was Sonoran panicgrass, for instance. This millet-like wild grain bears a seed that is 13 percent protein, and it had been a staple of the Cocopah Indians of the Colorado River delta before the construction of dams upriver killed the native stands. Botanists had pronounced the plant extinct and the Indians had despaired of reintroducing it. But after packing by burro into the Sierra Madre of Mexico, Nabhan found a stand still growing at a remote Guarihio Indian settlement.

Besides collecting seed, Native Seeds/SEARCH distributes rare varieties to trustworthy local gardeners to grow on, so that their harvests may increase the supply. Native Seeds/SEARCH distributes seed without charge to native gardeners; any surplus is available to the public at a modest price and can be ordered through the catalogue that Native Seeds/SEARCH distributes to members twice a year.

Kevin Dahl told me this as he showed me around the Native Seeds/SEARCH's adobe-walled offices. We passed through a room filled with racks of drying seeds; sealed plastic tubs of corn seed, kernels of every color from white to plum, orange, maroon and blue; a white enamel basin of long, thin fire-red "Rooster's Beak" chilies. Dried and splitting okra pods were heaped in a basket of bear-grass fashioned by Tarahumara Indians in Mexico. The loosely woven sides were *not* the result of sloppy workmanship; Kevin gave the basket a shake to show me how the seeds dropped through holes to leave the trash behind. Native Seed/SEARCH packers rely on this homemade sieve just as much as its makers do. Why not? "It works," Kevin pointed out, and that simple remark could serve as this organization's motto.

Back in the front office, we found an airy room where tables covered with brightly striped weavings held trays of multi-hued beans like casual mosaics, and displays of gourds—the ones from which Apaches fashion dippers, and those the Hopis turn into ceremonial rattles. As I put my nose into a tiny, sweet-scented basket double-woven from pine needles (this sits on *my* desk now), Kevin explained that these artifacts serve as more than decoration. Southwestern Indians maintained no written records, instead preserving knowledge in dances and songs. Studying native horticulture requires developing a familiarity with these other aspects of the culture.

As to Anglo gardeners, they are very welcome as paying customers. The Native Seeds/SEARCH catalogue goes out to 20,000, and this clientele grows by 30 percent each year. What's the attraction? Partly intellectual, according to Kevin. "We have some real unusual crops, but we also have some interesting folklore that comes along with them. You're not just growing a yellow-meated watermelon, you're growing a Hopi yellow-meated watermelon that has to do with a certain Kachina [an ancestral spirit]"; a benevolent Kachina, apparently, one who feeds people fruit.

"Gardeners are also responding to our crops," he continued, "because they can grow under some pretty harsh conditions—different conditions; none of our seeds are designed to work everywhere." Yet some have proved surprisingly adaptable. Hopi blue corn grows just four feet tall on the mesas of northeastern Arizona, but Kevin had heard from a gardener in northern California that there it soared to eight feet, attracting to his garden flocks of curious Drug Enforcement Administration helicopters.

Many of the desert crops, though, like certain wines, don't travel well. Tepary beans (Native Seeds/SEARCH offers sixteen cultivars) are a low-desert standby, a quick-maturing crop that doesn't mind short growing seasons, alkaline soils, or drought—in fact, too generous watering will promote leaf growth at the expense of seed production. The Indian cultivars often carry a virus that is relatively harmless in arid lands, but that may cause crop failure in humid regions.

Still, tepary beans flourish in Tucson. A switch to these unthirsty native crops would please Tucson Water, no doubt. Anyway, that's not all Native Seeds/SEARCH has to offer. Even Anglo gardeners who don't care to abandon *their* traditional diet can benefit from the Native Americans' horticultural skill.

At home, Daniela Soleri grows the full range of conventional vegetables and greens, but she plants them in sunken beds and sows according to a Native American schedule: corn, string beans and squash she plants in March, as soon as the danger of frost is past; at the same time, she sets out seedlings of long-season crops such as watermelons, eggplants, chilies, and basil. Mid-July, the beginning of the summer wet season, is the time for planting another crop of corn and beans, cowpeas, squash and okra, and in late October and November, as the temperature drops, she plants lettuce, greens, peas, carrots, and other cool-weather crops. She was eating salads every night, she told me. When I asked her how her harvests compared with those of a conventional Anglo garden, she replied that she couldn't say. Because if she insisted on planting her garden in that inappropriate style, it would have died by midsummer.

Santa Barbara, California

"Californians for drought" has been Owen Dell's watchword as he redesigns Santa Barbara's public and private spaces.

A rosy mist of *Achillea* 'Cerise Queen' wraps around the bench Owen set in a quiet corner of the ARCO Conference Center.

1

Nearby, a cascade of fountains lends the sound of water to what is now a very dry landscape.

2

Flowering spikes of blue hair grass (*Koeleria glauca*) rise from a wave of purple catmint (*Nepeta x faassenii*); behind stretches a foam of white *Achillea millefolium*.

3

The secret of ARCO's dramatic cuts in water use?
Replacing the monotony of lawns with a sea of flowers.

4

A Southwestern meadow spreads out at the foot of a gazebo: Mexican bush sage (*Salvia leucantha*) furnishes the swathes of indigo, Mexican marigold (*Tagetes lucida*) the yellow, while Mexican evening primrose (*Oeneothera berlandieri*) supplies the distant touch of pink.

5 The red fountain grasses (*Pennisetum setaceum* 'Rubrum') which frame Russell and Jane Polan's house are as carefree as these two travelers could wish; each clump is cut back hard just once a year.

6 Illuminated by the early morning light, the grass fountains seem to reach out to passersby.

Each of Owen's residential designs reflects the client's personality.
No two are the same, but all are unthirsty.

(TOP) Dr. Jerry Griffith counts the gallons he gives this rocky hillside. Lighting up the foreground is the yellow of *Aurinia saxatilis*—basket of gold—tempered by the bold glossy foliage of sea lavender (*Limonium perezii*); against the house stand the pink blossoms of an Australian blue hibiscus, *Alyogyne heugelii* 'Santa Cruz'.
(BOTTOM) The silver foliage of *Achillea* 'Moonshine' gives a Mediterranean tone to the garden of classics professor Howard Clarke; swordlike leaves of fortnightly lilies (*Dietes bicolor*) ward off Vandals—and Huns and Visigoths, too.

Wilbur Davis was surprised to learn he is a "xeriscaper"—he only knew that conventional landscaping didn't work in the Texas hill country.

9

Turning off his sprinklers has turned the Davis landscape into an island of fertility amid the green desert of clipped turf.

10

Cypress mulch traces a path in Wilbur's front yard. To the left is an informal hedge of dwarf yaupon (*Ilex vomitoria*); to the right an evergreen mound of coral honeysuckle (*Lonicera sempervirens*); and at the rear a border of white-flowered autumn sage (*Salvia greggii*).

The smooth, crooked trunk of a Texas persimmon (*Diospyros texana*) rises through a cluster of more dwarf yaupons; at their foot nestle the white flowers of blackfoot daisies (*Melampodium leucanthum*) and the yellow blossoms and aromatic foliage of damianita (*Chrysactinia mexicana*).

11

Native stone and native plants combine in a garden that is (as the Texan bumper sticker proclaims) "Texan by Choice."

12

The mason's work didn't satisfy Wilbur Davis, so he relaid the paths and walls of local limestone himself. Here the grandchildren's swing stands guard over a path of Texas' state flower, bluebonnets (*Lupinus texensis*).

Duke Waggoner hated mowing the front lawn—
so Nancy buried it under newspapers, mulch, and sheets of flowers.

13

A spring scene in the Waggoners' front yard: (front to rear) Tahoka daisy (*Machaeranthera tanacetifolia*), blue sage (*Salvia farinacea* 'Victoria'), white sweet alyssum (*Lobularia maritima*), bluebonnets, and damianita.

14

Though this hybrid clematis is *not* a drought-tolerant plant, the cool note it lends to the Waggoners' deck makes the extra irrigation a sound investment.

J*ay Cody aspired to an "English-style" garden, but the plantings he has given the Aquarena Springs resort are too exuberant and too tough by far.*

At Aquarena Spring's entrance, coral honeysuckle serves as backdrop to a desert willow (*Chilopsis linearis*), *Achillea millefolium* and yellow coreopsis.

Hot red and cool gray—only a plant as tough as the west Texan *Salvia greggii* could survive a summer perched atop this stone wall.

A visit to Monet's garden in Giverny inspired Betty Jean Stewart
to build this bridge. Always her garden's centerpiece,
it changes aspect with the time of day and the persepective.

17

Looking out toward the Atlantic past the gnarled trunk of Betty Jean's sea grape
(*Coccoloba univera*).

18

Glowing softly, a bowl of fishing-net floats from the high-tide line adds the only
other touch of color this simple landscape needs.

19

Stepping into Dan Boyar's front yard moves the visitor through an essay in coastal hardwood hammock vegetation, from the orange flowers of firebush (*Hamelia patens*—right foreground), to the flowers of the golden dune sunflower (*Helianthus debilis*—left foreground), then back past saw palmetto (*Serenoa repens*) and beautyberry (*Callicarpa americana*) to the foundation planting of wild coffee (*Psychotria nervosa*), live oak (*Quercus virginiana*), and darling plum (*Reynosa septentrionalis*).

"A *piece of the real story*"—*these Floridians are replanting their state to natives, lot by lot.*

20

Behind Dan's house, a concrete bird considers a live one amid the islands of Keys and tropical hardwood hammock flora. The planting is intentionally, naturally congested here; over the faux heron stands a geiger tree (*Cordia sebestena*) while shading the dove perches just below the compound leaves of the appropriately named paradise tree (*Simarouba glauca*).

*W*ater is always close at hand in Florida, even if often in short supply.

21

(TOP) Ray Miller feeds his pool with water harvested from the downspout. Fragrant white water lily (*Nymphaea odorata*), duck potato (*Sagittaria lancifolia*), soft rush (*Juncus effusus*), and pickerel weed (*Pontederia cordata*) are all local wetland species—framing them are giant leatherleaf fern (*Acrostichum daneifolium*) and royal fern (*Osmunda regalis*). (BOTTOM) Bonita Bay has surrounded its ponds with houses—Pat Fry has made sure that birds still have housing, too, and has confined her gardening here to editing the natural cover of saw palmetto, scrub oak (*Quercus geminata*) and wild grass (*Pennisetum sp.*).

22

23

Slash pines (*P. elliottii*) that the Frys left undisturbed when they built their house now serve as arbors for festoons of silvered Spanish moss (*Tillandsia usneoides*).

Creating a landscape in harmony with it surroundings is difficult if, like Pat and Gene Fry, you begin by preserving the native vegetation.

Pat and Gene made the builder assemble this railing on site, so that they could fit it around this bromeliad-laden scrub oak limb.

24

*"Inviting the desert in," was how Harriet and David Daly described
their landscaping, and their garden has become a means of
exploring a retirement home and an unfamiliar habitat.*

(TOP) Old time 'mission grape', a clump of scarlet sage (*Salvia coccinea*) and a
chiminea—a free-standing clay fireplace from Mexico—combine in a scene that is
at once lush, colorful—and irrigation-free. (BOTTOM) A garland of queen's wreath
(*Antigonon leptopus* 'Baja Red') brings a splash of color to the Dalys' garden wall, color
intense enough to compete even with the desert sunlight.

27

No immigrant lawn encumbers the Hamils' front yard; instead they have left it to desert-proof mesquite (*Prosopis sp.*), blue paloverde (*Cercidium floridum*) and creosote bush (*Larrea tridentata*).

For native Southwesterners Bob and Carol Hamil,
a private oasis is the key to outdoor living in this desert region.

28

Around back and through the gate, though, there is a walled court where trailing indigo bush (*Dalea greggii*) spills over walls, Chilean mesquite (*Prosopis chilensis*) and willow acacia (*Acacia saligna*) filter the light, and Bermuda grass flourishes as a luxuriant and exotic rug.

"Lush desert" is what landscape architect Phil Van Wyck calls the garden he designed for the Hamils; in fact, it could succeed nowhere other than on this Tucson hillside.

A juxtaposition of skull and star jasmine (*Trachelospermum jasminoides*) strikes the authentic Georgia O'Keefe note in this shaded corner of the Hamils' court.

29

30

Bluish pads of Indian fig (*Opuntia ficus-indica*) are the setting for scarlet blossoms of *Bougainvillea* 'Barbara Karst', and strung out below are the expansive rosettes of *Agave vilmoriniana*.

A scrap iron coyote emerges from a clump of autumn sage to dip his muzzle in the
pool behind Margaret's house. Mirrored in the water are the feather-light canopies
of a foothills paloverde (*Cercidium microphyllum*) and Chilean mesquite.

Let the desert dictate the planting, Margaret West explains;
that's why this Tucson landscape architect sets her plants not in
conventional drifts but each one in its own space as nature does here.

By setting boulders into the conrete, Margaret created the illusion of a terrace wedded to this earth; and the jagged lines of the pool she drew from the distant Santa
Catalina peaks.

With proper treatment, this desert land can become equally inviting or austere.

33

Euphorbias (*E. rigida* and *E. antisyphilitica*—known locally as candelilla) spill over the concrete pavers in Margaret West's side yard, softening the hard edges of a shaded seating area.

34

The snakes of stone give another Tucson landscape (a few miles away) an air of druidical mystery; by channeling rainfall they allow shade trees to flourish with no supplemental irrigation.

*For a new generation of Midwesterners, bringing the
prairie back is a matter of pride as well as conservation.*

At Neil Diboll's Prairie Nursery, purple and yellow coneflowers (*Echinacea purpurea*
and *Ratibida pinnata*) tangle in a growing field as handsome as it is productive.

Where does the water go,
Lorrie Otto wanted to know; all that falls on her Milwaukee
"pocket prairie" is quickly absorbed by the head-high grasses and flowers.

37   Summertime lines a path in Lorrie Otto's yard with sunflowers (*Helianthus strumosa*).

Different seasons bring different moods to the prairie, which changes appearance as completely, and nearly as quickly, as a chameleon.

38

Fall turns scarlet the smooth sumac (*Rhus glabra*) nestled against Pat Armstrong's Illinois homestead; tans and russets mark the buffalo grass (*Buchloe dactyloides*) and sideoats grama (*Bouteloua curtipendula*) lawn which requires neither watering nor mowing.

Autumn also brings new rhythms and textures
to Pat Armstrong's suburban grassland.

Twisting spikes of sun-dried purple prairie clover (*Petalostemum purpureum*).

The graceful fountain of a well-ripened
prairie dropseed (*Sporobolus heterolepis*) lasts through until spring,
when Pat Armstrong burns it and the rest of her prairie to the ground.

Steve Olsen lets plants find their own niches
in his serendipitous cottage garden.

41

In the shade of a bur oak (*Quercus macrocarpa*) sprung from a squirrel-planted acorn,
orange and yellow marigolds (*Tagetes*) self-seed along the curb. Each year these
flowers return in a new and unexpected pattern.

42

A yellow-flowered oxlip (*Primula elatior*), a native of northern Iran, has likewise
found a hospitable microclimate beneath a weathered branch of juniper brought
home from the nearby foothills; above, a European maiden pink (*Dianthus deltoides*).

43

Steve Olsen's front garden mixes alliums, chives, a Montgomery blue spruce (*Picea pungens* 'Montgomery') and a dwarf mugo pine (*Pinus mugo* "Compacta') in an unlikely but somehow pleasing mismatch.

U*nder pressure from the Environmental Protection Agency, Denver is moving away from the wasteful tyranny of "clean and green" to self-reliant landscapes as varied as the population.*

Planting in the rain shadow of the Rocky Mountains' Front Range, Gwen Kelaidis stocks her backyard peaks with sedums and sempervivums, alpine succulents.
44

45

A granite-mulched *Yucca harrimaniae* flourishes in the Kelaidises' front-yard range, its fraying leaves posing a dramatic contrast to the soft gray foliage of the partridge feather (*Tanacetum densum amani*)—yet neither plant receives more than a few soakings all through the arid Denver summer.

Gwen Kelaidis saved water by transforming her front yard into a practically self-sufficient essay in mountain scenery; Marc and Barbara Horovitz achieve the same end by gardening in 1:24 scale.

46

An 1880-vintage "Colorado & Southern" steam locomotive pulls a train of wooden boxcars through the Horovitzes' "Ogden Botanical Railway." A white rock jasmine (*Androsace lanuginosa*) blooms in the right foreground, and just behind it a hot magenta Dianthus deltoides 'Zing Rose'. Over the right-hand end of the trestle tumbles Barbara's favorite: Lebanese oregano (*Origanum libanoticum*).

In a landscape where each foot of height or spread has been reduced to ½ inch, irrigation is correspondingly limited; Barbara waters her broad fields and groves with a watering can.

(TOP) The train puffs past a grove of cypress spurge (*Euphorbia cyparissias*) and into the station yard. Once the orange flowers have faded, the row of *Penstemon pinifolius* will be trimmed into a perfect conifer hedge; in the center foreground a clump of blue fescue (*Festuca ovina* 'Glauca') tempers the deep rose of a bloody cranesbill (*Geranium sanguineum*).

(BOTTOM) A turf of woolly thyme (*Thymus pseudolanuginosus*) spills out below Marc's turn-of-the-century railbus. Beyond the track is a shrubbery of *Sedum acre*; to the left a stand of Panayoti Kelaidis' hardy, purple-flowered ice plant (*Delospermum cooperi*).

. . .

The vine that climbs the pillar at the northwest corner of the Dalys' veranda is handsome, but out of place. It's a mission grape, a cutting from a vine that Jesuit father Eusebio Kino brought to this valley in 1700, when he stopped here to found the mission of San Xavier del Bac. Father Kino, who is also credited with having established cattle ranching in the Southwest, was an enthusiastic introducer of European livestock, grains, and fruits. Harriet and David Daly are not. Aside from one or two exotics like that grape, what they've planted are natives. They've had the good sense to embrace the desert, and in response it has surrounded their home with color and life.

Harriet and David Daly are not long-term residents of Tucson; they retired there in 1986. Both are originally from Minnesota, though they've lived in California, Texas, and, years ago, in Phoenix for a period. But they are well settled in Tucson now. They're addicted to desert.

When they arrived in the La Cholla Hills adult community, however, their lot wasn't a desert but a waste—a barren, artificial mesa of sand and rock. Harriet and David had taken care that all the details of their new house should be right. When, in going over the plans with the builder, David discovered that none of the interior doors was wide enough to allow passage of a wheelchair, he insisted that they be widened. That's not morbid, he explained to me, it's just insurance. But David's a neurologist, not a landscape architect, so it didn't occur to him that their greatest problem might lie outside.

Soon after they moved in, a heavy rainstorm washed out the retaining wall that supports the north end of the terrace on which their house sits. The developer gathered up the scattered boulders, re-erected the wall in the same way, and—over the Dalys' protests —edged their terrace with an ugly concrete spillway to channel future downpours. David and Harriet didn't see why this should prevent a recurrence of the collapse. Nor did they see why it should be necessary, in a desert, to route water off-site as fast as possible. It seemed to them that if the landscape was planned properly, there wouldn't be runoff.

They began attending the conferences and classes sponsored

by the city and by SAWARA (Southern Arizona Water Resources Association) a nonprofit citizens' group founded in 1982 to ensure the area's water supply through education. SAWARA also supplied them with lists of drought-tolerant trees, shrubs, and perennials. From these, David extracted a list of true desert natives. What he was looking for was nonallergenic plants, and nearly all species indigenous to the desert fit that description.

Because of their sparse and widely spaced populations, desert plants cannot broadcast their pollen indiscriminately, relying on chance to deposit a grain or two in the right place. Instead, they employ insects to transfer pollen from blossom to blossom, and so they need only produce a modest quantity. It's the immigrants from moister regions—the olive trees, the Bermuda grass, and the mulberries—that fill Arizona's air (in urban areas) with pollen, turning it from a place to which allergy sufferers could come for relief into an allergy hot spot. It's a serious health problem for the retirees, Dr. Daly insisted, and he wasn't adding to it.

All the trees framing the Daly garden shared another characteristic as well: a fine and lacy foliage. The contrast this made—soft greenery against harsh landscape—was pleasing, but the truth is the choice was involuntary. Broad-leaved trees are rare in arid lands, since their greater leaf area gives them an unacceptably high ET rate.

So there was a feathery-leaved Ethiopian acacia (*Acacia abyssinica*), a nonallergenic native of an African desert; and two kinds of pea-leaved palo verdes, the blue and the Sonoran palo verde (*Cercidium floridum* and *Cercidium praecox*). The name "green stick" was given to the trees by early Hispanic settlers because in drought the trees drop their leaves and carry on photosynthesis in their smooth green or (in the case of the blue palo verde) bluish green bark. These spreading little trees reach a height and width of twenty-five feet or so, and are spectacular when they explode into clouds of fragrant yellow bloom in early spring.

Mesquites are about as popular as vegetarians with Arizona ranchers, who blame these thorny little trees for over-running and ruining rangeland (in fact, mesquites only invade grasslands damaged by overgrazing). Like many desert gardeners, however, the Dalys find a rough-hewn beauty in the shaggy bark and gnarled trunks, and they admire the mesquites' ability to withstand the lengthiest drought. They've planted two kinds: the native velvet mesquite (*Prosopis velutina*), a species whose foliage has a soft, knappy appearance from a distance, and the taller, more symmetrical Chilean mesquite (*Prosopis chilensis*). The shade the mesquites provide is welcome in this sun-baked land, but the Dalys prize even more the contribution of their roots. Those are famous for their tenacity and penetration, and the Dalys believe it is the mesquites that have bound together their knoll and prevented a recurrence of the landslide.

Originally the Dalys installed two irrigation systems, one for low-water-use plants and another for high-water-use ones, but both systems have been turned off long since. Instead, the Dalys feed the water from the four downspouts into a series of depressions, or catchment basins. A good rain fills these to the brim, but within forty-five minutes the water's gone, soaking down to the roots of trees, shrubs, and perennials.

The growth this has produced is fantastic, so that only three years after planting, trees that went in as saplings are mature specimens (and the spillway is entirely hidden). Ironwood (*Olneya tesota*), a native of Arizona mesas, spreads an umbrella of bluish green, finely divided leaves that in late spring sprouts pale, rose-purple, sweet pea–like flowers. The orange berries that the Palo blanco (*Celtis reticulata*—"white stick") bears in autumn are a favorite food of the local birds, which are in turn favorites of the Dalys.

They told me that Gambel's quails nest under the terra-cotta tiles of their roof, that the chicks leap down onto the terrace as soon as they can walk. We heard quails whistling as we picked our way down through the sage green mounds of salt bush (*Atriplex nummularia*) and the purple-flowered foam of prostrate indigo bush (*Dalea greggii*) with which the Dalys clothed the slopes below the house. Here and there I'd spot a plump, feathered body slipping through the bushes, searching for the bean-like mesquite pods that are their favorite food.

Returning to the house, we explored the ribbons of flowers that lace the edges of the terrace. The blue spikes of mealy-cup sage (*Salvia farinacea*) looked happy enough to me, but Harriet insisted they were suffering from an excess of sun and supposed that she'd have to move them back into the filtered light underneath the trees. A queen's wreath vine (*Antignon leptopus*) had wrapped its shocking pink flowers most of the way up a Chilean mesquite. A humming-bird darted out to drive us away from the red flower spikes of a pineleaf penstemon (*P. pinifolius*).

This desert perennial bore a most curious resemblance to a dwarf pine, except for the colorful bloom which had the yawning mouth of a furry-tongued snapdragon. But this is only one of the penstemons the Dalys grow; there are four spring-blooming species as well. Come April there would be the brilliant red trumpets of the firecracker penstemon (*Penstemon eatonii*) and, just beyond, the pink, two-foot-tall spikes of Parry's penstemon (*P. parryi*). Blue flowers would eddy on the soft billow of the mat penstemon (*P. linarioides*) lurking down among the soft, narrow leaves, and the spikes of *Penstemon superbus* (a species too rare to have earned an English name) would be hung with its blossoms of carmine that, for a gardener, need no introduction. As an easterner I had known penstemons as a rock-garden rarity, but clearly they could be a workhorse in the Southwest garden.

Later, when researching the plants I had seen in the Dalys' garden, I found that many, especially the natives, were not listed in any of my handbooks of cultivated plants. The reason seems to be the disdain with which landscapers used to regard the desert flora. All the older guides to "desert gardening" I consulted, books from the 1950s, exhibited a classically colonial mentality. What they offered was advice on re-creating a familiar suburban land-scape, so that the new Tucsonian might live as if he or she were still in Boston or Peoria. Naturally, the recommended plants were all temperate-region species—and given unlimited irrigation, these broad-leaved exiles *would* survive.

None of this affected the Dalys at all, because as far as I know they never turned to books for guidance. Besides SAWARA's bro-chures, their main source of inspiration has been the staff at the nearby Arizona-Sonora Desert Museum, and the field trips to arid-land ecosystems that institution organizes. They urged me to go there, too.

I folded down the roof of my rented convertible the next morning for my drive across Gates Pass. The wind was in my face as I swooped up and down the hairpin turns; around me jagged red peaks sank their teeth into a sky as vivid as the turquoise in a squash-blossom necklace. The overture from *The Barber of Seville* boomed from the radio, but under the circumstances bel canto seemed almost understated.

Ken Asplund brought me back to earth. As assistant curator of plants at the Desert Museum, he knows the output of every line in the irrigation system, and by checking his computer files he can tell you when that line was last turned on and for how long. He's precise because he has to be. In 1980 the state declared this area an active water-management district, decreeing that withdrawals from groundwater could no longer exceed the rate of recharge. That imposed an absolute limit on the gallons the museum could draw from its wells, and since then, the only way the institution has been able to extend its plantings is by increasing irrigation efficiency.

Yet Ken's first recommendation upon joining the staff two years ago was to increase the allotment of water to certain plants. Since the museum's plan is to display plants and animals from all over the Sonoran region, and to display them in re-creations of their native habitats, there are many plantings that are not adapted to this low desert region. Ken found ashes and cottonwoods, trees that naturally cluster along mountain streams, suffering from drought at the museum; not only were the dead limbs unsightly, they posed a hazard to visitors. To increase these trees' ration, however, Ken had to cut elsewhere.

He achieved this mainly through close supervision. Sitting me down at a computer monitor, Ken called up a spreadsheet that listed every valve in every irrigation zone, what that valve's output is, how long it is run in summer and winter, and on what days of the week. This program lets him track usage, of course, but it also helps him adjust the watering schedule to suit the supply. A day that brings a lot of visitors to the museum—a public holiday, for example—may divert so many gallons to toilets and fountains that Ken can't water then. By consulting his electronic bookkeeper, Ken can determine if the hiatus will put some area in jeopardy, so that he should perhaps move its irrigation to the day before.

Bookkeeping is as much involvement in water management as Ken allows the computer, however. Electronically controlled watering systems don't work well in the desert, he explains. The best systems depend on moisture sensors, instruments that monitor soil moisture and, when it drops below a preset level, turn open the water valves. Desert plants, however, are accustomed to drought, and will rot if the soil remains continually moist. The key to watering these plants effectively is knowing how long each species should go between waterings, how long an interval of drought it needs.

That's why Ken believes the decision of when to irrigate is best left to the plants themselves. One of the studies currently underway at the museum involves growing various species in tubs so that the staff can control precisely the amount of water each plant receives. By observing the plants at different levels of soil moisture, and on different irrigation schedules, the researchers hope to establish each subject's relative tolerance to drought. Once a hierarchy of drought tolerance has been worked out, it will be possible to use plants as moisture meters; the least resistant specimen in any given planting will, when it begins to flag, send a signal to the gardener that its fellows are approaching the critical point.

To my surprise, I learned that drip irrigation isn't much use in plantings of desert natives. Ken explained that while some desert plants, such as the mesquite, send roots down deep to seek out hidden pockets of water, many others spread their roots in broad, shallow nets. The roots of a four-foot-tall saguaro cactus (and this species may reach a height of sixty feet after a century of growth) penetrate only two to four inches deep but spread through an area thirty-five feet across. Such a root system is admirably adapted to capturing every drop of moisture deposited by the occasional desert rainstorm, but cannot cope effectively with a drip irrigation system that leaks water deep into the soil at a pattern of isolated points. So the Desert Museum is condemned to the use of overhead sprinklers. They may lose a lot of water to evaporation in this dry air, but what does reach the soil is delivered in a way that the plants can absorb it.

I had been reading the predictions of various experts that in the future water would become mankind's limiting resource; that future is already here at the Arizona-Sonora Desert Museum. The museum is reaching the limits of what it can do with the water it has. Management is exploring new sources of supply: it's investigating the possibility of "harvesting" rainwater and storing it in cisterns, and it's looking at recycling its wastewater. But in the meantime there's competition among the institution's different departments, and the plants department has drawn fire for the size of its daily ration of 35,000 to 40,000 gallons. But because he knows there's no waste, Ken Asplund is unapologetic. "When they say, 'well, the plants department is using the most,' I say, 'no, no, correction; we manage the water the *plants* are consuming. It's not we who are using the water.' "

The popular image of the desert is an unforgiving place, yet in Phil Van Wyke's hands it can take on an air of whimsy. He keeps a small lawn at his own house for his son P.J.'s benefit, but it's a lawn with a difference. When autumn's cooler weather turns Arizona's Bermuda grass turf brown, the conventional practice is to overseed with annual ryegrass. This keeps the turf green, though it greatly increases the landscape's water use. Phil, however, allows his winter lawn no more water than it takes to dilute a rainbow of dyes. With them he colors the dormant Bermuda grass into a giant child's pinwheel.

Yet even when lighthearted, Phil's landscape design is always practical. The evergreen, ornamental pear he planted in his backyard he set at the bottom of a water-collecting basin; the sand with which he filled the basin serves partly as a water-conserving mulch, but also as P.J.'s sandbox. And P.J.'s excavations keep the mulch loose and root-free.

Phil's landscapes *work*, and that's because he understands the desert. He studied landscape architecture at Tucson's campus of the University of Arizona, but it was countless long rambles that really taught him to understand the desert plants, the special light and sense of space. These taught him to savor the desert water, too, the liquid that comes up absolutely pure from deep underground. This water ran through every one of the designs he shared with me.

At our first stop—a house belonging to a pair of physicians— Phil pointed out to me the ways that desert plants channel water. He showed me the guttered, outreaching leaves of an octopus agave—they collect rainwater and run it down to the roots at the leaves' base. Phil had mimicked this in that very same yard. He'd solved its erosion problem by regrading the soil into a dry wash, an artificial arroyo that he lined with rocks to slow the water's flow and encourage infiltration.

Lessons in water conservation were all around us. Cactus spines

I had thought of as a defense against grazing animals, but I learned that they are far more. They shade the plants and protect them from the hot desert winds by surrounding the stems with a dead air space. Those downward-curving spines on a barrel cactus collect droplets of condensing dew at night, too, and sprinkle it over the roots. Many desert plants, like the *Opuntia violacea* 'Santa Clara' he showed me, a spineless prickly pear developed by Luther Burbank, orient themselves toward the sun, so that as much as possible they hide in their own shadow.

Phil echoes the simple architectural forms of the cacti in his own clean, angular compositions. At each place a shaded terrace, a spa embraced by shrubbery, or a pool provided a vantage point from which to enjoy the horizons Phil loves. Around them he had arranged superior cultivars selected from indigenous plants, a type of planting that gave a feeling of repose while blurring the distinction between man's territory and the wild. "Lush desert" is what he calls the result.

The example of this which impressed me most was at the home of Bob and Carol Hamil; maybe because both of them are south-westerners themselves, so they have an instinctive sympathy for what Phil is trying to achieve.

The house, a stucco in Santa Fe style painted pale "desert rose," sits partway up a steep ridge in the foothills to the north of Tucson. Phil had softened the tumble of rocks in front by piecing together splashes of prostrate indigo bush (*Dalea greggii*) with bigger splashes of *Acacia redolens*, a broad-leaved Australian evergreen that rises only two feet high but spreads some fifteen, exploding puffs of yellow blossoms every spring. The front entryway was properly inviting with its civilized garland of Lady Banks Rose (I knew that would be weighed down with small, violet-scented, yellow blossoms come spring) and the strip of red-blooming autumn sage—*Salvia greggii*. All this was fine, but the real show was back behind.

Under the palo verde tree (in springtime, a cloud of five-petaled little yellow flowers), the visitor slips through a powder-blue gate set in the stucco wall and into the sanctuary. There, in the center of the brick-paved terrace, Phil had planted a lawn for the Hamils: a close-clipped carpet of green nine feet wide and seventeen feet long. This was set at an angle to the house to align it with the route the eye inevitably follows, to the view of the Santa Catalina Mountains' overhanging rampart.

A simple panoramic sweep is too obvious for Phil's taste; that's like gulping the whole treat all at once. What he'd done was to cut away sections from the wall to direct your vision toward choice scenes—a rugged peak, a plunging arroyo—leaving you with the impression that you sat in the middle of a wilderness rather than a housing development. No street sound penetrated here; all I heard was the bubbling of water in the corner fountain. Bob Hamil had turned that into a tiny desert spring, planting the basin with water hyacinth and papyrus and populating it with pupfish and desert leopard frogs.

A cow skull hung against the wall of the house had the genuine flavor of Georgia O'Keeffe. The planting, though, was lush, more like a scene from a Persian rug, with bougainvillea, sand verbena (*Tripterocalyx*, a native wildflower that from spring through fall caps sprawling two-foot-tall stems with parasols of pink flowers), oleanders, blue and red salvias, pink and red penstemons, and Mexican evening primrose all jostling for a space in the zigzagging, stepped planting beds that lined the wall. Mesquite and eucalyptus filtered and tamed the sunlight, purple pansies spilled out of terra-cotta vases, and jasmine climbed a pillar to drug me with its heavy, cloying perfume.

Many of the plants have personal associations for Bob and Carol. I met them both as I wandered their private oasis, and they told me that the hop bush (*Dodonaea viscosa*), its tall, upright stems clothed with bronzed willow-like leaves, was the fellow of any number they'd seen while hiking along the streams of Ventura canyon last weekend. The gray-leaved mats of purple-flowered indigo bush (*Dalea greggii*) recall for Bob the wild ones he saw in Rincon, down near Las Cruces, New Mexico.

The size of this L-shaped space (perhaps twenty feet across and sixty feet long) keeps it intimate in feeling while also minimizing its need for water. According to Bob Hamil, regular irrigation is essential only in May and June and in the latter part of September. In wintertime he waters only occasionally, never giving the garden more than seven minutes' worth of the drip system and pop-up lawn sprinklers. In summer's heat, he may open the taps fifteen minutes every other day.

Maintenance is correspondingly easy. It takes him fifteen minutes now to cut and edge his micro-lawn, an hour or so to cut back the perennials in the spring, and no time at all to sweep up fallen leaves and blossoms. Time once spent tempting sunstroke behind a lawn mower is spent in enjoyment now; this garden with its area rug of turf has come to serve the Hamils as an outdoor room and a gathering place for the extended family. Even Bob's colleagues at the junior high school where he is principal have adopted the garden. Why hold after-hours staff meetings in an echoing class-room when you could be smelling the drought-tolerant flowers behind Bob and Carol's house, and watching for the Ghila wood-pecker?

Romance is the proper way to close a story: man sweeping woman off her feet or vice versa, followed by a fade into the sunset. Unfortunately, that's an ending rarely appropriate to my branch of writing; usually I must content myself with a down-to-earth quote or morsel of wise advice. But this once I *can* end an adventure the right way, and for that I thank Margaret West.

We'd spent most of a day looking at the gardens she's designed and installed for clients all over Tucson. There was one yard whose centerpiece was a small basin set flush with the ground. By keeping it filled with water the owners attract javelinas, roadrunners, even an occasional bobcat down from the mountains for nightime visits. On another property, Margaret had found a natural wash. Rather than regrading to divert the water, she made this the landscape's center. She set in new boulders (some of them artificial, though I couldn't tell which) to create a seating area and a spot for bonfires, and work with red-flowering sages (*Salvia greggii*), penstemons, and brittlebush (*Encelia farinosa*—a fast-growing, spreading native shrub of gray foliage and yellow, daisy-like spring flowers) to turn a gray-tiled spa into a bit of desert geology.

I'd found Margaret every bit as interesting as her work—truly, it was hard to imagine one without the other. She's that rarest of Sonoran species, a native Anglo-Arizonan (third-generation no less) and a former English Lit major who discovered landscape architecture in her own backyard. The developer had given her new home the usual four trees, ten shrubs, and a sprinkling of grass seed; even as a novice she knew she could improve on that. She began taking classes, first in horticulture and later in landscape architecture. She found the latter a wide-open field—at the time she enrolled in the degree program at the University of Arizona (in 1980), there were only two registered landscape architects in the whole state.

Being a pioneer requires imagination, but it also gives scope to creativity. There weren't any models available, except those imported from California and the Midwest, so Margaret and her classmates had to develop their own solutions to the Sonoran desert's challenges. She admits, though, that the municipal water shortage was a potent ally. Besides sharpening her ingenuity, it educated clients.

One difficulty of landscaping in Tucson—it's a problem throughout the Sunbelt—is that nearly everyone is from somewhere else. They come to Tucson looking for jobs, affordable housing, safe neighborhoods, or an easier life. They like the climate, the sunny, not-too-cold winters, and they may even like the dry heat of the summers. But they don't generally like the desert, not right away. People such as the Dalys are the exception; it takes average new arrivals two or three years to acclimatize, Margaret says. Only then do they begin to see the desert as something other than a threat.

A decade ago, immigrants suburbanized their property before they appreciated what they were losing. Today, warnings about punitive water bills make them stop and think. And then maybe call someone like Margaret. Not one in ten of her clients wants a wrap-around lawn now. Instead, they're much more willing to come to terms with nature. Some, like Rick, go much further.

That may be because Rick is no new arrival either. A biochemist at the University of Arizona, he'd been hiking the wilderness here for years, and he made regular visits to the Desert Museum. His instructions when he hired Margaret were quite simple: bring the canyons into my backyard.

This came as close as Margaret could imagine to the ideal job. She and Rick found themselves so much in sympathy that, as Margaret remarked to her father at the time, if she'd been designing this landscape for herself, she would have done it exactly the same way. Which is what she was doing, really, because in the end she and Rick were married and she moved in.

I like to remember this landscape as I saw it not the first time, but one morning the following spring when I returned with *my* wife, the photographer. Dawn was just breaking, and the driving was slow. We had to slalom down the road to avoid the doves who were warming themselves on the blacktop, and pause for the coyote who slunk off into the brush right by the entrance to Margaret's semicircular gravel driveway. Brittlebush, prickly pear, mesquite, and that curious, jointed cactus, the cholla, whose segments grab passersby to hitchike to new ground, ran right up to the jojoba hedge screening the front door. All this simply demonstrated Margaret's powers of restraint. Once again, the real show was in back.

Passing through the house, we came to a simple rectangle walled in with imitation adobe block. For this concept, Margaret acknowledged a debt to the region's first ornamental gardeners, the Spanish padres; an enclosed oasis was a standard part of every mission. However, they had planned their gardens as sanctuaries, places of retreat; Margaret had designed hers (and Rick's) as a vantage point, and a place of translation between man's world and the wild.

What impressed me especially was the use of hardscape here. As a gardener in the moist Northeast, I'd been trained to look upon concrete as an invasion, a necessary evil at best. But as Margaret pointed out, mats of solid greenery aren't common in the desert, while open expanses of pebble and grit are. Concrete, if sensitively handled, can look very much at home here.

Sensitivity hadn't been evident in the landscape as Rick found it; the builder had backed the house with a rectangular pad that overlooked the neighbor's backyard. Margaret had redirected this, swinging the edge of the concrete around thirty degrees to face the Santa Catalina mountains. Then she'd covered it with the same rosy saltillo tiles that served as flooring inside the house, so that the patio became another, open-air room.

Beyond and below was a flowing, irregular expanse of pebble-surfaced concrete, its edges softened by overhanging flowers: verbenas, salvias, globe mallows, and desert marigolds. The boulders that rose up through this level of terrace, their rough peaks emerging like islands, I assumed were aboriginal, stones that had been simply too massive to move. When I remarked on this Margaret was delighted, because that was exactly the effect she had in mind when she installed the stones, just before the concrete was poured.

Besides the look of great age they gave this new landscape, the stones also tied it to the rocky fields beyond its boundary wall.

Enhancing this impression was the pool,* whose bottom Margaret had painted black to turn the water's surface into a mirror. In this I saw reflected the profile of the peaks—and I saw it reflected also in the jagged line Margaret had drawn to divide water from land.

Margaret's planting I found disconcerting at first. I was trained in a European tradition, in which the rule is to spread the plants with a generous hand, in masses, in drifts and sweeps and groves. That's not how it works in the desert, Margaret explained; the vegetation is sparser there, thinned by the competition for water. So Margaret keeps the clusters of shrubs small, and she uses them mainly as the backdrops for "accent plants"—plants of bold form that stand alone as focal points. A fine-textured mound of palo verdes, mesquites, jojobas, or salt bushes made a most effective foil for the skeletal frame of a single cholla, saguaro, or prickly pear cactus, the flamboyant colors of a bird-of-paradise, or the gargantuan, bluish rosette of an agave.

In a more subdued setting the effect of all this might be melodramatic, but here it suited the desert's stark vigor. I particularly admired the spiky exuberance of a red yucca (Hesperaloe parviflora), from whose burst of frayed-edged, narrow leaves rose an impossibly thin, impossibly tall (it stood a full two feet higher than me) stalk of brick red flowers. I'd have been even more impressed had I known that the plant maintains this display from March all the way into September.

Some this garden's effects were calculated, artificial—the wrought-iron lizards who chased each other up a wooden pillar of the porch, the coyote cut from scrap iron who dipped his muzzle to drink from the pool. Others were unstudied. The walk along the concrete pavers to the side yard and the outdoor shower was a matter of picking my way, because the spikes of red penstemons that had seeded themselves there were too perfect to disturb. How should I characterize the tiny garden within a garden, the dwarf grove of sago palms (Cycas circinalis) and heavenly bamboo (Nandina domestica) in a well visible only from the window of the master bathroom? A dry anecdote, perhaps, to add extra zest to a soak in the tub.

---

* A pool can be an extravagant water consumer—if left uncovered. An eighteen-by-thirty-six-foot sheet of water can lose up to three thousand gallons of water a month, depending on the weather. But if the pool is covered when not in use (and this is standard practice in Tucson), water loss is reduced by 90 percent.

Given all the care lavished on this landscape, I was taken aback to learn that Margaret and Rick were already at work on another house. Margaret explained that they want a home that reflects their life as a couple. Then, too, she wants to experiment with a garden even more heavily reliant on hardscape. Anyway, I suspect that like any other artist, Margaret loses interest in the canvas once she has finished it. She wants to get started on another.

Desert, I learned in Tucson, is never deserted. On the contrary, it is one of the biologically richest, most diverse ecosystems. Twenty different species of cacti have been identified at a single site in Sonora; by comparison, an inventory of an eleven-acre sample of one of Ohio's finest unspoiled woodlands (and Ohio's hardwood forests were famous for their lushness before they fell to farmers and loggers) turned up only fifteen species of trees.[*] Besides, cacti are just the beginning of what you would find on that spot of Arizona desert; in addition there would surely be grasses, perennial flowers, shrubs, and trees, and in a wet year perhaps sixty species of annual flowers. Defined as it is by its lack of precipitation, a desert such as this is dry, obviously, but the effect of that may not be as severe as people tend to think.

As the German botanist Heinrich Walter pointed out more than twenty years ago, measuring rainfall not in inches but in the gallons available to each plant puts the desert in a very different light. Suppose that precipitation does deposit five times as much water per square yard annually on a Connecticut Valley woodlot as in some Arizona flat. Still, if the density of vegetation is five times as great in that northern woodland as in the desert (and desert plants do grow at greater intervals, some of them even releasing herbicides from their roots to ward off competition), then each plant in both locations receives the same number of gallons per year. It's true that in the arid desert environment water evaporates more rapidly, but then desert plants have developed far more effective defenses against dehydration. Over all, the Sonoran desert is a superb place to garden; one just has to garden appropriately.

The water company may promote this as conservation, and it

---

[*] Alton A. Lindsey and Linda K. Escobar, *Eastern Deciduous Forest*, vol. 2, Beech Maple Region (Washington, D.C.: National Park Service, U.S. Government Printing Office, 1976.

is that, but it's also something more. Planting a Sonoran front yard to turf is the sign of a person who, however much he appreciates life in Tucson, still thinks of himself as an exile from somewhere more beautiful. Learning how to cultivate mesquite rather than kill it, discovering which flowers provide food for the hummingbirds and quail—this is not only the practical response to life in an arid place, it's the first step on the long path to becoming a native. Because that is as much a matter of attitude as of birthplace: as the Tohono O'odham tribesman corrected one Anglo interviewer, "we don't *survive* in the desert; we live here."*

* Taken from a sign posted along the "Plants and People of the Sonoran Desert" trail at the Desert Botanical Garden in Phoenix.

Five

Technologies Old and New

 suspect nothing so delights an engineer as a genuine shortage. Surely, automotive engineers must have relished the gas crisis of the 1970s. Instead of the tinkering with tail fins Detroit had been calling progress, all of a sudden engineers were allowed to operate on the guts of the car. I assume automotive engineers were happy then; I know that irrigation engineers are now.

American irrigation technology had changed far less than automobiles in the half-century before the current water shortages. Actually, you can find recognizable relatives of our sprinklers, pumps, and hoses in Victorian catalogues—and the technology used to deliver water to the tap was worked out by the ancient Romans. Now, though, because of the need for greater efficiency, we are exploring a tool chest's worth of new devices and approaches. Some of these technologies are new, ingenious confections of electronics, carbon fibers, and plastic. Others are old—so old that they had been forgotten.

Begin with the hose. This irrigation tool is not ancient, nor has it changed substantially over the last couple of decades, but because it is fundamental to every gardener's watering, it deserves a brief examination.

Hoses come in a variety of materials and grades, but I won't deal with those distinctions here since they mainly affect the hose's longevity. Diameter is what determines the efficiency with which a given hose delivers water. You'll find three gauges of hoses at a good hardware store: half-inch, five-eighths-inch, and three-fourths-inch. Obviously, the wider the hose, the more quickly you can deliver water. In point of fact, it takes half again as long to move the same quantity of water through a five-eighths-inch hose as through a three-fourths-inch one, and *three times* as long to move it through a half-inch as through the three-fourths-inch. In one test, engineers found that with a water pressure of 50 psi (pounds per square inch) and fifty-foot-long hoses, it took thirty-nine minutes to deliver the recommended one-inch of water to a 1,000-square-foot-lawn through a three-fourths-inch hose; one hour through the five-eighths-inch; and two hours through the half-inch.

Some irrigation devices, certain kinds of sprinklers in particular, are designed to accommodate higher pressures and a greater volume of water. These probably won't operate well at the end of a half-inch hose. It's worth noting, however, that thinner hoses' slower rates of delivery are not always a disadvantage. Most drip irrigation systems are designed to operate at low pressure, typically at 8 to 15 psi, while normal household water pressure ranges from 40 to 60 psi. In this instance, the constriction of a smaller hose may merely reduce the pressure from the tap to something more acceptable to the irrigation system.

When selecting a hose, you must consider not only the irrigation device but also your soil type, and the rate at which it will absorb water. If your soil is a heavy clay, then the slower delivery of a half-inch hose may suit it better. If it's a thirsty sand loam, then anything less than a three-fourths-inch hose will probably prove an annoying bottleneck.

High Tech: Drip Irrigation

Plastics may be a mixed blessing from a conservationist's point of view, but it is to them that we owe a great advance in irrigation efficiency. Various agriculturalists had experimented with irrigation via leaky pipes: as early as the 1860s, German farmers had tried laying clay pipes a couple of feet below the soil's surface to facilitate deep irrigation of their crops, and somewhat later Australian peach growers began watering their orchards with galvanized iron pipes into which they had cut holes with chisels. It wasn't until an Israeli engineer named Symcha Blass got hold of some plastic tubing in the late 1930s, though, that drip irrigation really came into its own.

The principle behind Blass's invention was the one that underlies all drip irrigation systems today. As I noted in Chapter Two (see pages 60–61), drip irrigation's strength is its slow but precise delivery of water. If operated at the recommended low water pressure (installing an inexpensive pressure regulator at the tap guarantees that), a drip system releases the irrigation right onto the soil surface, ideally at the exact point of need—the base of the plant. This gives drip irrigation a fantastic efficiency in taking water from the faucet to the plant's root zone; as little as 5 percent is lost along the way.

Equally important is drip irrigation's predictable rate of delivery. The flow from each "emitter" or "micropore" may be no more than half a gallon per hour (½ gph, though some emitters release 4 gph, or even more), and if the system has been properly designed, it will be uniform throughout. This makes possible extremely precise watering. It also makes drip irrigation especially useful for a number of problem situations. Clay and fine silt soils, for example, which absorb irrigation only very slowly, are much better watered with drip than with a more lavish sprinkler. Likewise, drip irrigation can eliminate the problem of runoff on a hillside site.

There are three basic types of drip irrigation systems. Drip tapes are sleeves of plastic perforated with built-in emitters or tiny, laser-cut holes; they function somewhat like the old-fashioned soaker hoses, except that the drip tapes release water at a set interval (every eight inches in the kind I tried) and at the same rate all along their length (soaker hoses are notorious for saturating the soil at the beginning of their run and starving it at the end). The second type of system consists of tubes into which the gardener punches "emitters," plastic nozzles with a controlled rate of flow. The third type, "spaghetti tubes," are really just a variation of this, in which the emitters are placed at the end of thin (spaghetti-like) secondary tubes.

Each system adapts to different uses. Spaghetti tubes are the most precise in their placement of water and are ideal for watering trees and shrubs. Lines with emitters punched into them are simpler to install—you just snake them through the areas of the garden you want to irrigate; and because you can insert an emitter anywhere you want, they are a very flexible system of watering.

Emitter-based systems are also best suited to use on sloping terrain. The special difficulty there lies in maintaining even pressure: the weight of the water as it flows downhill increases the pressure in the lower end of the lines. Increased pressure means an increased rate of flow and uneven irrigation, unless you use special pressure-compensating diaphragm emitters. These have built-in pressure regulators and will deliver water at a uniform rate even while the pressure within the lines ranges from 5 to 50 psi.

The liability of emitters is that they clog easily and, in my experience, often. This means that you have to leave the system exposed where you can watch its operation; and a skein of black plastic tubing doesn't add to a garden's appeal. The smaller perforations of a drip tape don't seem to share this problem. Or maybe it's just that they have so many holes that the loss of a few isn't as noticeable. At any rate, drip tapes perform well even when buried under a blanket of mulch, which makes them preferable for a flower border, or any other area that must bear close scrutiny.

One characteristic that all drip systems share, and a secret of their efficiency, is that they don't wet all the soil. Whether the water is coming from a laser-cut perforation or an emitter, it falls drop by drop onto the same spot, and moves mostly downward. There is *some* lateral movement of the water—more on clay or fine silt than on sand—but mostly it just follows gravity. As a result, a bed doesn't become evenly moist; instead, what a drip system creates is a pattern of spindle-shaped plumes of moisture. A soil sampler will help you determine how far the water spreads, but as a rule, spacing the emitters at two-foot intervals on an organic-rich loam will allow continuous planting.

The localized nature of drip irrigation has a marked effect on the growth of plants; they respond by concentrating all their roots in the areas of moisture. Which means that when you turn the water on, you deliver it right to the roots—with a drip system, far less water is sent to areas where the roots aren't. This is efficient, but also dangerous, because if there is an interruption in the water delivery (a break in the line, a failure of a watering clock, a plugged emitter), the plants' confined root systems are not prepared to tap alternative moisture sources. Drip irrigation is addictive. So think about the commitment you are making before you run a spaghetti tube to that newly planted tree or shrub.

Installing a drip system is simple and, for me, pure pleasure. Tubes, elbows, and emitters snap together as easily as Legos, yet it still makes me feel so competent to assemble a plumbing system without the help of a plumber. What makes me feel stupid are the preliminaries: designing the system. This involves a good deal of numbers crunching, since each tube you run out from the faucet will supply only so many emitters or so many feet of drip tape— the exact number will depend on the output of the product you have chosen and the number of gallons per hour your faucet can supply (to calculate that, time how long it takes to fill a fifteen-gallon garbage can, divide that number of minutes into 60 and multiply the result by 15).

Typically, you will find one supply line insufficient to irrigate a whole garden. If that is the case, you'll have to divide the garden into separate irrigation zones that you water in sequence. Mapping out the zones requires that you have some idea of the irrigation needs of the various plants they contain. For example, a feature that is relatively irrigation-intensive such as a bed of annual flowers may make a whole irrigation zone by itself, even though it measures only a couple of hundred square feet. Yet a single line may suffice for the whole bank of shrubs nearby—even though it occupies an area many times larger—because the shrubs are better adapted to your climate.

Usually, drip irrigation works best if you combine plants with similar needs onto the same line. You can allow for the needs of the thirstier plants by giving them more than one emitter, but it's more efficient to segregate them onto their own line, one equipped with higher-volume emitters. As with any irrigation system, though, your design must match the soil type; on a dense, slow-to-absorb clay, higher-volume emitters may serve only to create runoff.

Juggling all these variables struck me as overwhelming, until I discovered that the various drip-irrigation equipment manufacturers supply design manuals, which, remarkably, I found generally easy to understand and use. What I appreciated most, though, were the toll-free numbers that a couple of the companies listed on the product labels. Being able to call the experts for advice was a great convenience. You can also ease into the field, as I did, by buying a kit. With the kit comes a description of the area it will irrigate; all you have to do is snap it together and roll it out. The resulting system may not fit your needs exactly, but nothing could be easier.

Its sensitivity is what makes drip irrigation so efficient, but that quality is also its Achilles' heel. Drip systems demand a fairly high degree of maintenance. In Texas, though I installed a filter (no. 150 mesh) in the water line, I found I still had to remove the plugs from the ends of all the lines every month or so, and run water through them to flush out any accumulated grit. Even so, I was constantly probing with a wire to reopen plugged emitters.

I would have had fewer problems if I'd used self-cleaning emitters. They would have cost me maybe twice as much apiece as the simple orifice emitters I had settled for, but the extra expense would have totaled only forty or fifty dollars, and the payback would have been much less hassle and more consistent irrigation. And while running water lines without the help of a plumber made me feel smart, my work wasn't perfect. Leaks occasionally developed in my do-it-yourself plumbing, and if I didn't spot these and attend to them promptly, my drip systems became water wasters rather than water conservers.

Still, all this work amounted to far less than the labor I had previously invested in dragging hoses and sprinklers, and the results were all that I could wish. Drip irrigation gave me a garden that used far less water yet supplied nearly all our vegetables. Even more pleasing to me as a gardener were the compliments of passersby. Weeding the front garden became a pleasure when it was punctuated with those pleasant, drawled greetings.

The Old Standby: The Sprinkler

Sprinklers have taken a bashing from water conservationists in recent years (myself included), and with good reason. Even a professionally designed and installed in-ground sprinkler system wastes 25 to 35 percent of the water it distributes—too many droplets evaporate before they strike the ground, or before they can be absorbed by the soil. Portable sprinklers, the kind you move from spot to spot around the garden, are even more extravagant. It's impossible to assign an exact figure to them, since the efficiency of a portable sprinkler depends so much on the skill of the operator, but it's common for those devices to waste more water than they actually deliver.

Besides, the way in which conventional sprinklers deliver water is harmful to the soil. Because the droplets are bigger than raindrops, they hit the soil with more force, doing far more damage to its tilth (the structure). Unless the soil is protected with a mulch, a sprinkler will pound the air out of the surface layer so that it dries into an air- and water-resistant crust. An additional problem is the speed with which sprinklers deposit water. In general, they do this much more rapidly than the typical rainstorm. Though that may seem efficient, its effect may be to greatly reduce the total volume a bed will absorb. By immediately slaking the soil's surface—saturating the very topmost layer—such a flood creates a sort of cap, a floating layer over which the succeeding droplets run away.

Nevertheless, as noted in Chapter Two, sprinklers remain the best tool for watering turfs and ground covers: their relatively even water dispersal suits these sheets of plants, with their continuous tissues of roots. As yet, no drip irrigation system has been devised that will do this job well. There are other situations, too, in which sprinklers remain the most cost-effective solution. For instance, when dealing with mass plantings of a single kind of shrub, a drip irrigation system may be too expensive to install, since every plant would require its own emitter. If the planting is substantial, and the individual plants stand less than two or three feet apart, then almost certainly you will end up watering it with sprinklers.

Designing and installing an in-ground sprinkler system is a job for a professional. The sophistication of the hardware makes it too complicated for the do-it-yourselfer, but that is its virtue. For by marrying different types of sprinkler heads, a good contractor can create a spray pattern that evenly irrigates the whole lawn without sending water over its borders. Achieving a similar result with portable sprinklers is much more problematical. Yet in some ways, these more flexible devices are better suited to the needs of the water-conserving gardener.

If your planting is well adapted to the site and climate, then the need for supplemental irrigation should only arise occasionally. That makes an in-ground system an unnecessary extravagance. Portable sprinklers are also better suited to sharpshooting, spot irrigation. That can make these technologically inefficient devices an efficient way to irrigate, in practice.

There are four basic types of portable sprinklers: fixed, rotary, impulse, and oscillating.

Fixed sprinklers—really just high-pressure shower heads—are the least accurate. Since the pattern of droplets never varies as long as the water continues to flow, any gap is sure to leave some area unwatered.

Rotating sprinklers are the familiar "whirlybirds"; their spray heads are mounted at the ends of pivoting arms which the water pressure drives around in circles. The continual shifting of the spray heads means that rotating sprinklers are far less likely to leave gaps in their irrigation, but they do share another flaw with the fixed-head sprinklers: both deposit proportionately more of their water close to the sprinkler. Consequently, to achieve anything like even irrigation with these devices, the gardener must move the device around, overlapping the edges of the spray patterns.

Impulse sprinklers are the ones that sound like an aquatic machine gun. The powerful jet of water they fire is deflected and shattered by a pin, and the repeated shock slowly jumps the head around in an arc. The most powerful impulse sprinklers will irrigate a circle ninety feet across, if your water pressure is sufficient, and because the trajectory of the water is low and straight, their pattern of spray is least affected by wind. The distribution of water is fairly even throughout the area of spray, and most models can be set so that they water just part of the circle before the head reverses its motion.

In oscillating sprinklers the water is forced up through a bowed arm which waves from side to side like a slow-motion metronome. These lay down their water in a rectangular pattern, which is more convenient for watering the typical rectangular lawn. In addition, their distribution of water is the most uniform of any portable type, though the cheaper models tend to dump extra water at either edge of the pattern as the arm hesitates before reversing itself. The drawback of oscillating sprinklers is that they fire droplets out in a lofty parabola, so that on a windy day their performance is particularly erratic.

Even within a type, the rate of water application can vary tremendously from model to model, from as little as three-eighths inch of water per hour to more than three inches. There's an easy way to check the output of your sprinkler, and the consistency of its water distribution. Set a row of cans at two-foot intervals along a radius extending from the sprinkler to the outer edge of its spray. Open the tap and leave the sprinkler running for an hour, turn it off, and with a ruler measure the depth of water in each can. That will give you an idea of the rate of deposition at each point, and at the same time reveal any gaps in the sprinkler's pattern of watering. This is important knowledge, since it can help you compensate for the sprinkler's limitations. For example, it will suggest how far you should overlap the spray patterns of your rotating sprinkler to achieve even deposition.

Another bit of knowledge that can be gleaned from the cans is the sprinkler's approximate total output. Add together the depths of water in each can and divide the sum by the number of cans. With this average, you can easily calculate how long to leave the sprinkler in each spot to give the landscape a desired quantity of water.

There is one more class of sprinkler, and since it represents a new direction in this kind of irrigation, I've left it for last. These are the so-called microsprinklers, miniature spray heads that hook into a drip irrigation supply system. Microsprinklers offer the variety of spray heads found in in-ground sprinkler systems, so that a spray pattern can be designed with the same precision. What sets the microsprinklers apart from the older technology is their flexibility and their ease of installation.

Rather than digging trenches across the lawn, all the gardener has to do to install a microsprinkler system is run in a flexible plastic water supply line of the type used with drip irrigation. The spaghetti-like tubes that feed the microsprinklers themselves attach to plastic nipples you insert into the supply line wherever you want. Usually the sprinkler heads are mounted at the top of short stakes; push the end of this into the soil and the sprinkler is ready to go.

Most of the authorities I checked agreed that microsprinklers' efficiency doesn't match that of a drip system—though I could find no one who had made a systematic comparison. Nevertheless, microsprinklers are a relatively thrifty way to irrigate, since their spray patterns are far more uniform and precise than that of the portables. Besides, because they operate at a lower pressure than conventional sprinklers (typically ten pounds per square inch), the microsprinklers throw larger droplets that are less subject to evaporation in midflight. Because the microsprinklers are designed to water restricted areas, the trajectories are short, so that the droplets actually strike the soil with less force than those lofted by portable sprinklers.

Any potential savings are wasted, of course, if the microsprinklers are operated at water pressures higher than that recommended by the manufacturers—this turns their precision spray into an ineffectual cloud of mist. That's why a reliable pressure regulator is an especially important ingredient of any irrigation system that includes microsprinklers.

Clock-Watching

The convenience of an automatic irrigation system is hard to resist. As soon as I had finished installing my drip system, I plugged it into an electronic water clock. The model I chose operated for a full season on the power from a single nine-volt battery, and it was programmable so that I could schedule a whole week's worth of watering at once. At the end of the week, the clock automatically began the cycle all over again. It was such a relief to punch in the numbers and put irrigation out of my mind—a relief, but it wasn't good gardening.

If a rainstorm soaked the soil and I forgot to override the water clock's schedule, it would pump the raised beds full of water they didn't need and couldn't use, and I'd get a call from the neighbor that I was flooding his backyard.* The convenience encouraged carelessness. As the seasons progressed, the heat increased and the rainfall decreased, I had to reprogram the clock, and too often it took a general wilt to remind me I'd forgotten that task. The plants suffered after I passed off the responsibility for watering.

Opening the tap is the gardener's job; it should involve an informed decision every time. Turning the water off, however, is a job that may be better done by machine. The machine won't get distracted; it won't forget to turn the water off when the job is done. That, by the way, is the use I found for my very expensive clock.

I'd use it like a timer, setting it each time the garden needed water so that it would irrigate for an hour, two hours, whatever time I judged necessary, then turn itself off. That worked better, but I could have achieved the same effect less expensively with a Bermadon valve such as Owen Dell recommended (see page 38).

Even cheaper is a little mechanical timer I recently acquired. Called a Rain Date, it's made by Nelson and it cost me just $14.95. This is not a precision instrument. It measures watering time in increments of half an hour, and allows you to irrigate up to three hours at one setting. Afterward it turns itself, and the water, off.

Because it uses the flow of the water as its power source, this timer won't work with low-flow systems such as drip. And because water flow inevitably varies from house to house and sprinkler to sprinkler, Rain Date's true running time probably won't match that shown on the scale. For example, I found that at a friend's house where the water pressure is exceptionally strong, a half-hour setting drove an impulse sprinkler (with a three-fourths-inch hose) for twenty-seven minutes. At my house, where the outdoor faucet produces little more than a trickle, the same setting drove the same sprinkler and hose for 105 minutes.

The important aspect of this test was that in both cases the timer, when reset and started over, closely reproduced its previous performance. If you use a row of cans to measure the output of

---

* Friends who use more sophisticated clocks, those that draw more current and must be attached to the household power, have experienced the opposite problem. A power outage, even the momentary blink like that caused by a lightning strike somewhere in the system, will erase the clock's programming, putting an end to watering until the clock is reset. If the gardener is away from home, the result can be an artificial but still devastating drought. If you buy such a clock, be sure that it has a backup battery power source.

your sprinkler and time the sprinkler's actual run at different set-
tings, you can use this timer to irrigate reasonably accurately. If
nothing else, it can provide cheap insurance against forgetting the
sprinkler and creating an inadvertent flood.

If you can't bring yourself to take personal responsibility for
watering, there is one way you can at least minimize the wasteful-
ness of your automated system: attach a rain switch to your system's
controller. This simple device suspends irrigation when it is wetted
by a rainstorm, and doesn't let watering resume until it (and hopefully the soil too) has dried out once again. This won't cost much.
The "mini-click" that Bonita Bay obliges its residents to install with
their irrigation systems (see page 115) costs $31.70; residents re-
coup the money within a few months as savings on their water bills.
Similar devices are available from nearly all the major manufacturers
of irrigation equipment. Some depend on moisture-absorbent disks
as their rainfall sensors, while others, like the Rainbird rain switch,
are really rain gauges that activate a switch when precipitation fills
them to a preset level. Neither type measures soil moisture, which
is all that matters to your plants. Still, for less than fifty dollars you
can stop your sprinkler system from turning itself on during a rainstorm.

Clearly the best design for an automatic irrigation system would
be to bury reliable moisture sensors in the soil and let them regulate
the watering. In fact, for less than a hundred dollars you can buy a
stainless steel probe from Rainbird or Toro Manufacturing that
determines the relative moisture of a soil by measuring its electrical
conductivity. Theoretically, this could be the basis of a very accurate irrigation system. But there are some practical difficulties.

To begin with, because every soil is different, the probe must
be calibrated anew by each gardener, and that requires a few weeks
of tinkering. Then, too, the probe only measures the soil moisture
at one spot—and that reading doesn't reflect what you would find
a dozen yards away, where the soil is sandier (and so generally
drier) or perhaps richer in humus (and so more moisture retentive).

Besides, different plants have different irrigation needs: the
moisture level that is acceptable for a xeriphytic shrub might be
insufficient for your turf. Even two plants of the same species may
have different needs, depending on their exposure to sun and wind;
in a more exposed site, the ET will certainly be higher and the

need for irrigation greater. Inevitably, an irrigation system based on a single moisture sensor will either overwater or underwater most of the landscape.

To make a moisture-sensor system really efficient, you would have to divide the garden into distinct watering zones according to plant needs and soil type and then allow a separate watering system and probe for each. Even if the gardener was willing to bear the expense of this, managing the electronics would be daunting to anyone other than types like my brother the computer consultant.

Lest I sound too negative, I should add that I'm sure an irrigation system governed by even a single moisture sensor would prove less wasteful than one that waters strictly by the clock. Neither one, though, will give your plantings the kind of care that will make them really flourish.

A Pair of Classics

No doubt it's because my college degree is in classics, but I take great satisfaction in the fact that two of the most effective new irrigation strategies are really not new at all. Both water harvesting and clay pot irrigation *are* new to American gardeners, at least to the cultivators of our towns and suburbs. But, as I learned in the course of my visit to Tucson, water harvesting has been a mainstay of native farmers of the Southwest for more than a thousand years. Clay pot irrigation is equally old; the California ecologist who brought it to the United States told me he first learned of it in a passage from a Chinese agricultural manual that dates to the first century B.C.

The two strategies are both products of pre-industrial societies, and as such they share a number of virtues. They are simple to implement, and the necessary tools and materials are cheap and common. Since neither water harvesting nor clay pot irrigation includes any moving parts, maintenance is slight; actually, a water harvesting system more or less takes care of itself. Neither one consumes fossil fuels, they don't make noise, and they do make very efficient use of resources: the subsistence farmers who created them couldn't afford waste.

Water harvesting

We'll consider the no-tech strategy first. Though I encountered water harvesting in Arizona, I could equally well have learned of it in the Middle East, since Israeli archaeologists have found evidence of its use in the Negev Desert as early as 1500 B.C. In either place, the principle was the same: with berms and channels, farmers collected the runoff from occasional storms and directed it down onto crops to increase soil moisture in their fields.

In this simplest form, water harvesting cannot provide continuous irrigation, but if combined with the use of deep-rooted plants, it may supply all the extra moisture a crop needs. The skill of the practitioner lay in an ability to read the contours of the land—accurate disposition of the collection system maximized the harvest and minimized the digging—and in knowing what density of planting a given harvest could support. This is still all the knowledge a gardener needs to harvest irrigation water.

To practice water harvesting, a gardener must first develop a new attitude toward topography. Our inclination has been, traditionally, to give every homesite a concave profile, with the house sitting at the high point, so that the yard sheds water as quickly as possible. That keeps the basement dry, but also keeps the soil moisture at a minimum. The water harvester, by contrast, grades the yard to a concave shape. The house is still set at a high point, and water is still drained away from the foundation, but it isn't dumped into the storm drain. Instead, it is led to one or a series of low points. In them is where the water harvester does his or her planting.

Clearly, there are climates in which this treatment will create a bog. That's not necessarily bad. I've known expert gardeners who went to great lengths to create such a feature so that they could cultivate wetland plants. Even if you live in an area of abundant rainfall, though, and don't care for bogs, you may still want to harvest water into a barrel or improvised cistern to serve as insurance against the occasional drought.

If you live where rainfall is low, you will certainly want to harvest all the water you can. The yield of even a small lot may be considerable. W. Gerald Matlock, an agricultural engineer at the University of Arizona, has calculated that in Tucson the yield of a lot eighty by one hundred feet could average as much as 21,000 gallons annually.* Some of this (around 4,000 gallons in the design Matlock proposed) would escape as runoff, unless a cistern or some other form of storage was provided. But the 17,000 gallons or so that soaked into the soil would provide half the water necessary to support a tree to shade the house, a scattering of shrubs and a two-hundred-square-foot hybrid Bermuda grass lawn, and a twelve-hundred-square-foot vegetable garden.

Matlock based his predicted yield on a landscape specially designed for the purposes of water harvesting, one in which runoff would be collected from virtually every surface. My guess is that few homeowners will choose to arrange their entire outdoor environment around the needs of an irrigation system. Fortunately, there is a ready-to-use catchment area built into every residential property: the roof.

Any roof is designed to collect water for disposal—and it's easy to modify a downspout to turn it from a drain into a source. By calculating the area of rainfall your roof intercepts (this roughly equals the square footage of the house's ground floor) and then multiplying this by the average annual rainfall, you can estimate your roof's yearly harvest.

To establish your roof's *monthly* yields (and where rainfall is strictly seasonal, these may be the important figures) you'll need to get a month-by-month breakdown of average rainfall from the nearest weather station (try calling the local airport for directions to that). In any event, by comparing your estimates with the previous year's water bills, you can determine approximately what fraction of your irrigation water the roof will supply. That, in turn, gives you a clue as to how much of the landscape you can plan to support through water harvesting.

In practice, though, trial and error is probably the method you will use to design a water-harvesting system. Dig a couple of shallow catchment basins into the landscape—if broad enough these will be almost imperceptible, though still effective at trapping substantial quantities of water. Link each basin to the next with a spillway, and direct the downspout's end into the uppermost. Then watch through the next rainstorm to see whether your excavations

* W. Gerald Matlock, *Water Harvesting for Urban Landscapes* Agricultural Engineering Department, University of Arizona, (Tucson, Ariz.: 1985), p. 24.

can handle the roof's harvest. A check of your rain gauge and a comparison with the weather records should give you an idea of the storm's relative severity.

If your catchment basins seem inadequate, add another. Naturally, digging humus into the soil around the basins and improving its tilth will enhance their absorptive capacity. Or run part of the harvest over to the vegetable garden; you can divert some of the water by running the downspout into a steel or plastic drum into whose bottom you have tapped one or more hoses. These hoses can irrigate the vegetable garden, and maybe a flower bed, too, while the barrel's overflow continues to feed catchment basins. With a little ingenuity and a supply of PVC pipe and plumbing fixtures, you should be able to set up a system that irrigates several different areas at once.

While I have seen plans for water-harvesting systems involving cisterns and pumps, I can't recommend them. They are too complicated and temperamental for an amateur's use. Take a hint from water harvesting's inventors, and keep your system simple. Let gravity provide the energy. The only hazard you face then is a too-heavy storm and a too-generous harvest. Make sure to leave the water a path to the gutter and drain, should the flow prove more than your garden can contain. However precious water may be, you don't want to collect it in the basement.

Clay pot irrigation

David Bainbridge's professor at the University of California Riverside hadn't time to read the review of an agricultural history book he'd been given during a trip to China. But David was curious. And that was where he learned about a 2,100-year-old agricultural manual, and a technique called "pitcher irrigation."

Could this help his own research into arid-land habitat restoration? He was pursuing low-tech but efficient means of irrigating desert tree plantings in remote and primitive sites. David tracked down a copy of the ancient text, the *Fan Sheng-shih Shu*. He had the relevant passage translated, and found he had stumbled across a genuine breakthrough.

"Bury an earthen jar of six liters capacity in the center of a pit," he read. "Let its mouth be level with the ground. Fill the jar with water. Plant four melon seeds around the jar. Cover the jar with a tile. Always fill jar to the brink if the water level falls."

David tried this in the student garden at U.C. Riverside, substituting eight-inch Italian terra-cotta flowerpots for pitchers (before burying each flowerpot, he plugged its drainage hole with silicone caulk). Instead of tiles, he covered the pots with aluminum pie pans—he found a size in the supermarket that just fit the mouth of the eight-inch pots. Water slowly leaked through the porous walls of the pot to wet the surrounding ring of soil. Germination of his seeds—David planted corn instead of melons—was almost 100 percent, growth was lush, and best of all, water consumption was far less than it would have been even with a drip system.

Indeed, David's preliminary study indicated that the pots were roughly *twice* as efficient as drip (and ten times as efficient as flooding the soil surface). David speculates that the phenomenal economy is a result of the self-regulating nature of the system. The lower concentration of water in dry soil is what draws moisture out of the pots—and as the soil moistens, the water's outward movement naturally slows. But as plant roots absorb water, the soil dries and the flow increases. It's a conservationist's dream: the sunken pots supply water exactly when the plants need it and at the ideal rate, too.

David has since used the pots to irrigate a number of crops besides corn: tomatoes, chilies, mints, and salvias, as well as desert trees such as palo verdes and mesquites. He found that clay pot irrigation worked particularly well with roses. Watering roses in conventional fashion with a hose tends to wet the leaves, and that favors the spread of fungal diseases such as blackspot and mildew. Pot irrigation not only produces lush growth, but, because it wets only soil, healthier growth, too.

Once he knew what to look for, David found contemporary examples of pot irrigation all over the world; the technique is still used in China and Pakistan, India, Mexico, and Brazil. In Egypt it is used to establish young palm trees. Now he has adapted it for use in America.

His pie pan lids, for example, when weighted down with rocks, not only protect the water from thirsty wildlife and keep it from culturing algae and mosquitoes, they also help recharge the pots.

He punches a few holes into the bottom of each pan before setting it upright over a pot's mouth; that way, the pan feeds all the rainfall it catches down into the reservoir below. David has also worked out the spacing at which the pots should be set: six to ten feet apart for vine crops (such as melons), and three to four feet for corn or other upright plants.

He's found this to be a particularly useful form of irrigation on sandy soils, where irrigation water normally drains away almost immediately. Emending the soil around the pots with compost or manure seems to enhance their effectiveness. Before seeding, he recommends filling the pots and letting them wet a band of soil; in that band is where you sow.

For further testing, David enlisted a colleague and friend, Andrea Kaus. She's an anthropologist and co-director of Groundworks International (a research and education organization that promotes the practical management of natural resources), and in 1991 she introduced this style of irrigation to several isolated ranching settlements in the Chihuahuan Desert of Mexico. Residents planted six small gardens, digging pots into the soil at one-meter intervals. The soil there was highly saline—literally off the scale in some cases when David tested it. But the continuous, slow wetting of the pots pushed the salts out to the margin of the moistened soil, so that the gardeners harvested satisfactory crops not only of tomatoes, but also tomatilloes, watermelon, herbs (cilantro, chives, basil, lavender), asparagus, pinto beans, and marigolds.

Andrea herself uses the clay pots to maintain her flower garden in Riverside, California. For that purpose she may use the pots as focal points, planting the flowers around them, about an inch or two out from the lip. She also sets the pots in a row at eight-inch intervals, planting between the pots. Cosmos, salvias, agapanthus, nasturtiums, marigolds, alyssum, and verbena have all flourished, and when I called her in August she was still enjoying a bloom from the pansies she had planted the previous October. She finds that the clay saucers sold to fit under the pots make attractive, secure covers; and anyway, the flowers hide the irrigation system almost completely.

The best feature of this method of irrigation, apart from its effectiveness, is its ease. This involves nothing more than topping up the pots once every week or so—the interval depends on the crop's water use. Pots clog eventually—they may have to be re-placed after three or four years—but until then the system suffers none of the glitches that plague drip systems.

If nothing else, rabbits leave the pots alone. David gave up using drip irrigation altogether after a recent test of rabbit repellents he conducted in the Colorado desert. He had treated transplanted mesquite seedlings with a variety of repellents, figuring that they would be a target for hungry rodents' teeth. What he found instead was that the rabbits had an insatiable appetite for the drip tubes. If he repeats the tests, he confesses, he will apply the repellents to the irrigation system, not the plants. He won't need to do that if he installs pots.

High-tech or low-tech, whatever your preference, there is a better way of watering your garden. The choice is yours, but a gardener of conscience must make some commitment. The greenest ends don't justify the means if the means are as obsolete, inefficient, and environmentally destructive as that leaky old hose nozzle. A better irrigation system will cut the water bill, probably save you time and effort, and certainly promote a healthier landscape. The decision seems clear to me.

Prairie Roots

"In June of '88," Neil Diboll said as he waved his hand toward the lush, waist-high growth of grass and flowers, "those fields were gray. Bluish gray. When you walked on the grass, it *crunched* under your feet." Yet Neil chose that time to sow seed. In the midst of a corn belt drought that was ruining harvests there in central Wisconsin and capturing national headlines, Neil planted a whole field of prairie grass: *Andropogon scoparius*, or little bluestem, as generations of plains people have called it.

"Planted on July 8, and it was dry as a bone. I thought, Well, if it works, they'll call him a genius, and if it doesn't, they'll call him an idiot. Who would plant then?"

Someone who knows prairies. For a prairie is an ecological

community which relies on drought. I had yet to learn about that relationship, but I could see the result. It was the summer of 1991, and Neil and I were looking out over a phalanx of bluish spears. "It's solid," Neil remarked. "It's looking good."

This is a nurseryman with a background as unconventional as his plants. It was at the University of Wisconsin (at Green Bay) that he'd first become intrigued with prairie, in a small restoration that the school maintains. After completing a degree in plant ecology, Neil had supported further research by working for the U.S. Forest Service. Spring through fall, he was on fire watch in Colorado; then he'd migrate back to Wisconsin to resume his studies in prairie ecology. He was, he says, "a Xerox junkie," a compulsive reader who amassed volumes of self-generated bibliographies. Somewhere along the line there was a spell of work as a deck hand on Mississippi riverboats, and a period in the Yucatan where he studied Mayan farming practices. But he settled down when he and a partner bought Prairie Nursery in 1982.

What they got was a few acres of mixed grasses and forbs (the prairie ecologist's term for flowering herbs other than grasses) from which the previous owner had harvested seed and plants to sell to a handful of prairie enthusiasts. This might not seem like much of a spread, but actually, once the planting expanded to cover twenty-eight acres, it became a significant fraction of Wisconsin's grassland remnant.

A century and a half ago prairie covered 2 million acres of Neil Diboll's home state. And Wisconsin isn't even one of the major prairie states—not like Iowa, which was once 85 percent tallgrass prairie, or even Illinois, where grasslands covered more than two-thirds of the land. But virtually all is gone. Because Wisconsin was home to pioneering ecologist Aldo Leopold, that state now has the largest expanse of prairie east of the Mississippi. Located in the southern part of the state, on land that farmers bypassed as too sandy, this remnant was restored by the University of Wisconsin during the 1930s, when the dust bowl was forcing Americans to reassess their management of the former grasslands. Prairie had covered 400,000 square miles of North America. Wisconsin's Curtis Prairie totals just one-half square mile.

Today, however, prairie is returning. The sea of grass and flowers had continued to haunt midwesterners' imaginations, even as they turned the last wild sods to corn and soybeans. Now, however, they are discovering its practical advantages. The prairie plants are resilient in ways that no imported crop is.

Drought is a regular feature of the central United States. In Neil's neighborhood, central Wisconsin, the annual precipitation averages only twenty-eight inches, and prolonged episodes of dry weather come about once a decade. Out toward the Great Plains, drought comes every summer, commonly in combination with withering temperatures of 100°F or more.

For the suburban landscapers' plants (which are, for the most part, immigrants from the East) this weather is fatal, unless the gardener supplies abundant, regular irrigation. To prairie plants, by contrast, the harsh weather is an old friend, their best defense. It's what kept the forest out before man's interference, allowing the grasses and flowers to flourish from Alberta to Mexico, from Ohio to the Rockies.

Yet in most cases water shortage has not been the original motivation for backyard prairie makers. Typically, gardeners first come to prairie in a search for midwestern identity. Restoration begins as a reaction against the homogenization of America; prairie is beautiful—and it isn't bicoastal.

Still, water problems have contributed much of the movement's vitality. In the fast-growing suburbs of cities such as Milwaukee or Chicago, water tables are dropping at an alarming rate as aquifers are drained to keep lawns green. Besides, here as in Florida, over-generous irrigation has washed toxic pollutants such as nitrates down into the groundwater. In Des Moines, Iowa, for example, the television news offers a nightly report on the nitrate level of tap water.

Prairiescaping is even more economical than xeriscaping, according to Neil Diboll. Xeriscapers had boasted to me that their landscapes needed little supplemental irrigation after the first season. Neil's prairie plants, by contrast, are self-sufficient from the day of sowing.

After showing me the little bluestem, he took me to see a patch of showy goldenrod (*Solidago speciosa*) he had planted during the spring of 1988, just before that year's drought. He'd chosen a sandy, naturally dry part of his land, a sand barrens in fact, on which to grow them.

"This had no irrigation on it. The plants came up, they got this tall"—Neil measured a crack with thumb and forefinger—"they came up in April and May and we didn't have any rain for fifty days. They sat there, not even one inch tall, little seedlings, and the sand was blowing over the top of them." They were fine, sturdy plants now, showy indeed.

What of the purple flowers Neil showed me nearby? Those were pale purple coneflowers (*Echinacea pallida*), and if they seemed omnipresent in Neil's fields, there was a reason.

"The wind was so powerful, and everything was so dry, it blew —this was seeded that same spring and it blew all the seed. So you find this trail of pale purple coneflowers all over the place, 'cause the wind just blew 'em around." Not even the wind could reduce the prairie seeds' vitality.

During dry spells, Neil explained, seeds and seedlings make little growth. They just wait the weather out. But when finally toward the end of that terrible summer he decided to irrigate (as a nurseryman he had to have salable plants by fall), running the sprinklers all night to give the fields an inch and a half, two inches of water, the response was nearly instant. The next morning, plants that had been crisp were green and soft again. "In a matter of hours, they were right back like nothing ever happened." In fact, the bloom was unusually fine that year, for the drought had killed all the competing weeds.

Because such horticultural laissez-faire isn't acceptable in a residential landscape, Neil suggests to clients that they water for the first four to six weeks after sowing seed. After that, though, they must stop. Over the long term, extra water encourages the growth of weeds and does the young prairie plants little good, since they pass the first and usually second growing seasons in extending their roots downward. At the end of a full year's growth, the prairie seedlings may stand only one or two inches high. But their roots should stretch down a foot or more.

Eventually, they will reach much farther than that. Mature prairie grass roots can penetrate nine feet into the soil, and those of forbs run even deeper, to fifteen.

"The roots are the power of the prairie," Neil told me. "By the third or fourth year, the prairie plants begin shutting the weeds down by basically occupying the soil environment. That's where the prairie wins the war—at the root level."

As we tramped around his nursery, Neil spoke like a prize-fight promoter. "All this," he explained succinctly, "is basically plant it, let 'em fight it out." So here, evening primroses (*Oenothera spp.*) "fought it out" with spiderworts (*Tradescantia ohiensis*); I admired the look of the pale Oenothera blossoms hovering over the spiderworts' dense, tufted foliage. Neil pointed out the white flowers of daisy fleabane (*Erigeron annuus*) that had invaded a planting of pale blue bergamot (*Monarda fistulosa*); an unplanned contest, but one that Neil calls "a very nice combination." Nearby, columbines (*Aquilegia canadensis*) and golden alexanders (*Zizia aurea*), and a number of other forbs and grasses, all grown for seed, mix it up in "a fight-it-out situation." Baptisia (false indigoes, white and cream) struggled up among grasses—"another fight-it-out experiment."

The talk may be bare-knuckled, but what Neil is really looking for in experiments of this kind are examples of cooperation. Because the fact is that prairie plants have definite preferences in the matter of bedfellows. Neil has learned, for instance, that butterfly weed (*Aesclepias tuberosa*), a blindingly orange-flowered milkweed, grows best in association with certain prairie grasses. It grows better in such circumstances than it will with other companions, better even if cultivated in weed-free, manicured conditions all by itself. When I asked Neil what those special companions were, he laughed, and told me that information was part of his stock-in-trade and not for publication.

He was quick to add that there's nothing mysterious about the plant preferences. To some degree, the determining factor is purely physical. A customer who wants tall prairie grasses such as big bluestem (*Andropogon gerardii*) or Indiangrass (*Sorghastrum nutans*), the grasses that reach eight feet up into the sky, must grow the tallest forbs, or else wildflowers that bloom in early spring before the grasses grow up to bury them. If a customer prefers shorter flowers, then he or she must blend with shorter grasses, such as little blue-stem.

But there are other reasons that dictate the way Neil associates plants, and these derive from the unusual degree of cooperation among prairie species. This is well understood in its broader out-lines. So, for example, while the grasses's fibrous roots hold the topsoil in place and protect the prairie against weeds, the deeper-rooted forbs are drawing minerals up from the subsoil; when the forbs die and decay, the minerals become available to the grasses. The decay of grass roots adds humus to the topsoil; the decay of the forbs' roots opens up channels by which air and moisture can penetrate downward.

One reason for the very specific nature of the partnerships is the seasonality of the species involved. When I visited the nursery, in early August, the spiderworts had just entered a period of dormancy after their spring bloom. Prairie grasses, which are known as "warm-season grasses," would remain active through the summer, and their growth would taper off in the fall when seedlings of the tradescantias would be sprouting anew.

This intricate dance not only determines partners, it also gives a distinctive style to prairie plantings. Most prairie plants are perennials—if planted in traditional perennial garden style, they would be spaced far enough apart to preclude competition. But prairie plants can be (and, for the health of the plants, should be) closely intermingled. So instead of the patchwork bloom that an old-fashioned perennial border provides, prairie plantings bloom all over— again and again.

The trick of prairie planting is more than just matching plant to plant. There is also the matter of matching plant to site. Prairie plants are very sensitive to soil type; that's the reason why Neil has planted his fields in irregular patches rather than the traditional nurseryman's tidy rows. Marsh milkweed (*Asclepias incarnata*), for example, waved its five-foot-tall pinkish crimson umbrellas of bloom over a low patch of muck, while *Penstemon grandiflorus* and its carillons of two-inch lavender bells sat on a dry, sandy blow-out— a high spot where some disturbance had allowed the prairie winds to tear off the topsoil. Generally, nurseries look like farms with some incidental flowers; Neil's had the appearance of a color-coded geological map.

Reading the soil is just one reason Neil prefers to visit a customer's site before he concocts a mix of seed or plants. Exposure— the orientation of the land—also affects his choice of species; and then, of course, there is the matter of who will coexist with whom. But these complex constraints are, for an ecologist, the fascination of prairie design. To some extent, every commission is an adventure. Neil recalled for me the occasion on which he sowed the same seed mixture on two virtually identical soils on the same day. In both cases the result was satisfactory, yet as the landscapes matured, the balance of species in each was entirely different. And, Neil added, he will probably never know why.

Perhaps Neil's most radical departure from horticultural orthodoxy, though, is the method by which he selects seed for his own fields. Like all traditional gardeners, I was trained to watch for outstanding individuals within any planting, with the idea that I would save seeds or cuttings and have *only* outstanding individuals the following season. In contrast, Neil prefers to maintain genetic diversity. As he collected his original seed stock from various prairie remnants, he consciously looked for differing individuals and combined seed from different sites. By enhancing the genetic diversity of his seed, Neil hoped to endow his nursery stock with a greater adaptability.

"Realize, this is not a proven concept. It may or may not be the best way to do this. But theoretically, anyway, it should be."

Over all, Neil interferes as little as possible with his landscapes' evolution. His fear is that too careful management might beget dependence and turn his prairies into something like conventional gardens. Neil describes those as hospitals, "where everybody is on intensive care."

What he aims at is a type of garden that needs no irrigation, and almost no other kind of maintenance either. His plants are not only perennial, but also self-renewing, propagating themselves through runners, suckers, or seed. The areas he cultivates for seed production, Neil figures, will provide him with twenty-five years' worth of harvest before they must be resown, even though the plants are all cut down by combines annually. In addition, Neil's gardens flourish spray-free, too.

Because he doesn't plant in monocultures—large stands of identical plants—Neil's landscapes don't experience the kinds of epidemics that plague conventional gardens. Insecticides are especially taboo at his nursery, because they kill not only pests but also the insect pollinators that give him his seeds. He may use the nonpersistent, "organic" pesticide rotenone in a pinch, but prefers to rely on natural predators. These are abundant—the inspector from the state's department of agriculture who comes every year to check the nursery for sanitation and diseases is consistently amazed at the number of predacious bugs he finds.

The birds that visit his fields also help with insect control, though at a price. The goldfinches, for example, strip Neil's western sunflowers (*Helianthus occidentalis*), rough blazing stars (*Liatris aspera*), and Rocky mountain blazing stars (*Liatris ligulistylus*)—and this despite his offerings of commercial birdseed. What does he intend to do about this? He replies with an easygoing shrug.

There is one maintenance technique on which Neil does absolutely insist. I had learned of it the night before my visit to the nursery, when I had dinner at the Diboll homestead. Before showing me his house Neil insisted on a tour of the patches of prairie he was rescuing from the surrounding scrub woodland; he had begun work on these, he admitted, even before he had the well water tested to see if the house was truly habitable. When we found our way indoors to get a beer, I noticed on the kitchen wall a slate on which someone had chalked a list of chores. These included routine reminders such as:

> Open west prairies
> Remove buckthorn in central ravine
> Spot spray woody weeds

I admit I was intrigued by:

> Clear grotto

Later Neil and I climbed down into this verdant miniature glen of rock, fern, and moss. But of all the reminders on the slate, I was most impressed by the finale:

> BURN EVERYTHING!

The truth is that fire is as native to the prairie as buffalo. It was the means by which the grasslands used to cleanse themselves. When drought had dried the stems above ground to a tinder state, a lightning strike easily set this material ablaze, burning perhaps a hundred square miles or more. The racing flame killed woody growth such as trees, but didn't injure the roots of true prairie perennials. Indeed, here as in the chaparral, fire seems to have been an essential preliminary to the germination of seeds; on the prairie, fire contributes by stripping away the natural mulch of dead leaves and stems so that the earth may be warmed by sunlight.

Neil, like other prairie restorers, uses fire mainly as a weapon against weeds, especially exotic turf grasses. Invaders such as Kentucky bluegrass (*Poa pratensis*), brome grass (*Festuca elatior*), and the greatest villain of all, quackgrass (*Agropyron repens*), are cool-season grasses. Their metabolism dictates that they make their growth and store reserves of food during the cool, moist weather of spring and fall. This makes them more vulnerable to drought than the warm-season prairie grasses, whose period of greatest growth comes with the summer, and which thrive in hot, dry weather. But this difference could give the invaders a potentially lethal head start—except that Neil burns everything (as the slate remarked) just before the prairie grasses awaken.

Vagaries of weather and geography influence the date—and a spring burn doesn't suit all situations, nor all types of prairie. Historically, Neil notes, it seems as if fall burns were more common, or even summer, since that is when lightning strikes are most common in the prairie. But a burn is easier to control when the sap is running in spring (Neil has written a booklet on how to conduct burns safely, and supplies this to customers). Anyway, he has found that on a mesic prairie, the type he cultivates at the nursery, setting the grassland ablaze just as the sugar maple buds are breaking is most effective in defeating the cool-season grasses.

Burning at this time allows a faster warming of the soil (one study found a more than 60°F difference in soil temperature between burned and unburned plots). This extends the growing season of the prairie grasses by a month or so, and forces the cool-season grasses into dormancy that much sooner. In addition, a burn at this time robs cool-season grasses of the fruits of their first flush of growth.

Mowing a prairie once in midspring and raking up to remove the litter has some of the same effect as burning. But fire is better, since it beats the cool-season grasses all the way back to their roots.

What besides pyromania bound this roving ecologist to prairie? At the end of a very, very solid lunch in a country café, Neil admitted that he likes the prairie landscape's dynamism, the chameleon-like way in which it changes every year, bringing one species or another to the fore in response to the weather. Then he confided his feelings about the grasses.

That switchgrass (*Panicum virgatum*), though he grows and plants it—it's real prairie—is an invasive SOB. But little bluestem? Those guys are more cooperative. "See, in about, well, mid to late September, early October, it's in multiple stages of green, blue, and bronze, after the frosts start hitting it. And then it has these white seed heads on top, and the wind comes rushing. It is literally like an ocean. The white seed heads are just like whitecaps. It is excellent, it is excellent. . . ." Persuading a midwesterner to expose the poetry in his soul is a daunting challenge, but prairie plants disarm Neil Diboll.

The time with Neil had whetted my appetite to see how prairie actually worked in a residential setting. For this, I went to see Patricia Armstrong in Naperville, Illinois, a forty-five-minute drive west of Chicago. I had met Patricia at the Twelfth North American Prairie Conference, a five-day event hosted by the University of Northern Iowa. This had featured field trips, learned papers, and a barbecue complete with prairie music and prairie poetry (sincerity was the saving grace of that).

There I'd found nurserymen rubbing shoulders with historians, biologists, ranchers, farmers, environmental activists, even whooping crane specialists and gardeners. Endangered species were the motif for T-shirts. I spotted silk-screened mug shots of grizzly bears, roseate spoonbills, and black-footed ferrets (a predator of the prairie dog that enjoys the unenviable distinction of being the rarest mammal on the continent). As protective coloration I purchased and slipped into a shirt adorned with a tuft of cool-season grass, over which had been stenciled a circle with a slash mark. "No Brome!" read the slogan across my back. In the room devoted to products and services, I met Ms. Armstrong.

She was talking to prospective clients, telling them how she could help them restore their roadsides, pastures, or backyards to prairie. That's her major activity, but only one of many, as I learned when I began picking my way through one of her brochures. She's been busy.

After completing a bachelor of arts degree in biology and English at North Central College in Naperville, she took a masters in biology-ecology at the University of Chicago. She taught for several years at a Naperville junior high school and has worked as an interpreter at various nature centers and arboreta. She conducts natural history workshops and classes at colleges and universities, too, and is a photographer and poet who has published more than sixty articles and four books. Her thesis research on the cliffs and boulder fields of Devil's Lake, Wisconsin, obliged her to master the techniques of technical rock climbing, and since then she has become an expert mountaineer, the first woman to solo climb Mexico's four highest mountains.

The thing she likes about climbing mountains, she told me, is the change in viewpoint. That's why she couldn't agree that mountaineering and writing poetry are an unlikely combination of skills. And the urge to climb mountains has largely to do with a passion for sky and wide horizons—that's what attracted her to prairie, too.

Having grown up in the pinewoods of Michigan, with sandy pinewoods her introduction to wilderness, Pat never saw a real grassland until her sophomore year of college. Even then, the first contact was barely a brush. A field biology course took her to a country roadside, where she was introduced to a relict clump of big bluestem. The tall bluish stems and branched seed heads (the inspiration for the pioneer nickname "turkey foot") opened a door in Pat's imagination.

After finishing her academic work she took a job down the road in Lisle at the Morton Arboretum, where she worked in the education department and, as time permitted, assisted horticulturist Ray Shulenberg in returning a sloping thirty-acre tract of farmland to tall-grass prairie. She stayed with that project for sixteen years, eventually taking over its management when her mentor moved on to other projects.

To Pat, this extraordinary devotion to restoration seems only natural. I believe I got a clue to its source in one of her recollections of mountain-climbing expeditions. Her time in the Andes, she said was disturbing. Why? The sky was backwards there, south of the equator. At night, the constellations were reversed, and so were the shadows, by day.

Pat includes on her résumé the information that she has slept outdoors not only in South America but also in all fifty states, most of Canada and Mexico, as well as parts of Africa and New Zealand. Her relationship to the landscape is close, her reaction automatic. She knows without thinking that what we have done with the prairie is as much a reversal as the southern sky. We've planted trees and tender shrubs where the grasses and forbs should grow. It's a reflex for an enterprising woman like her to set this right.

Increasingly during her last years at the arboretum, Pat found herself fielding calls from people, homeowners, who wanted help with their restoration projects. Finally, in 1986, she went into private practice. She's worked for all sorts of clients, planning and consulting as well as actually planting. Her masterpiece, though, is her own house, Prairie Sun, which she and her husband built in 1983.

Energy conservation was a guiding principle in the Armstrongs' design of their house—it is passively solar heated, so that their fuel bills total less than two hundred dollars per year. Water was what was on Pat's mind when she designed the landscape. Restrictions on landscape watering, or often a total ban, are common now in the Chicago suburbs. They are getting to be as much a feature of the dog days as the cicadas' cry.

As is so often the case, an exploding population is responsible for this: there were seven thousand people in Naperville when Pat first arrived in 1956 and now there are ninety thousand. The escalating withdrawals from the aquifer are causing the water table to drop ten feet a year. The community's response has been to join with its neighbors in planning a huge aqueduct that will run down from Lake Michigan. That will cause water bills to explode, Pat says, and the measure is completely unnecessary. Why not replant to prairie and put a permanent stop to lawn watering instead? Pat has never given her landscape more irrigation than she can deliver with a watering can. Yet it has remained green through summer droughts that turned the neighbors' lawns brown.

Wiping the slate clean is the first step in most prairie restorations, and Pat Armstrong has developed three ways of achieving this. If clients insist, she will use herbicides, but 80 percent of her customers prefer to kill the existing vegetation through nonchemical means. Covering a lawn with giant sheets of black plastic in June and leaving them in place until the next spring will cleanse the earth just as effectively. For instant results on small areas, Pat heaps on a foot or two of fill. She can't use soil from farmland for this, since that is full of the very same tenacious invaders she seeks to eliminate. Instead, she uses muck soils excavated from wetland developments—she welcomes the native weeds that spring up from this. For the more patient, Pat plants right through existing turf, setting in plugs of prairie that grow up to shade out the shorter cool-season grasses. Combined with regular spring burns, this exterminates the original lawn in about five years.

Pat had yet to develop these techniques when she addressed her own yard. There her approach was to hire a local farmer to disk the soil in October. Then she sowed her seed right away.

The following spring brought a lush growth of prairie plants, but also of two aliens: red clover and Queen Anne's lace. Pat hand-weeded a small island of space around all the prairie seedlings she could find and mowed the rest several times that year. Mowing prevented the weeds from setting seed, and by the following season they had disappeared from her land.

In an irregular belt around the house she planted a lawn—but a buffalo grass (*Buchloe dactyloides*) lawn which needs neither mowing nor watering. To help the sod knit faster, and to serve as understudies in case the buffalo grass failed (Naperville is really beyond the eastern edge of that species' natural range), Pat also seeded blue and sideoats gramas (*Bouteloua gracilis* and *B. curtipendula*). All have thrived, making a short, uneven green knap that not only is good for walking, but also serves as a firebreak to protect the house.

Around the lawn she planted a belt of midgrass prairie and beyond that, at the south end of the yard, are the tall grasses. Three types of prairie on a third of an acre isn't plausible ecologically, of course. But for anyone looking outward from the weathered wooden house's big, south-facing windows, the grasses lead the eye out and upward in a swoop over the neighboring suburbia and up to the genuine prairie sky.

Pat's roll call of grasses and sedges underlined the biological poverty of the typical lawn, where the ideal is to restrict growth to a single strain. Pat cultivates twenty-two species: besides the gramas and buffalo grass, she's got both big and little bluestem, June grass, tickle grass, broom sedge, prairie sedge and sand sedge, poverty oat grass, purple love grass, squirrel-tail barley and purple spiderweb grass, porcupine grass—and others.

These plants are as colorful as their names, and change like chameleons with the seasons. The big bluestem, for example, works through from green to tan and bronze, crimson and lead gray; little bluestem caps its rusty red leaves with bluish red seed heads in fall. Purple love grass, when it blooms briefly, gives a purple cast to the yard; sideoats grama picks up this color in the fall with its purplish seed heads, at the same time as prairie drop-seed blades are turning pale pinkish gold. The hues may be more subtle than those of an English perennial border, but they are certainly no less varied.

Pat was enough of a traditionalist that she chose to frame the house with foundation plantings. Her shrubs are not the customary rhododendrons and yews, though, but prairie natives. There is aromatic sumac (*Rhus aromatica*), a three-foot-tall shrub whose red spikes of late-summer fruit and scarlet autumn foliage provide two seasons of color, and gray dogwoods (*Cornus racemosa*), whose creamy June flowers, white summer berries, and purplish autumn foliage provide three. Suckering clumps of wild plums (*Prunus amer-icana*) bear pure white, sugary-sweet-scented flowers that give way to yellow or red little fruits by midsummer, when the lead plants (*Amorpha canescens*), four-foot rounded mounds of gray-green pea-like foliage, are bearing their purple blossoms. I recognized, too, five-petaled ancestors of my garden roses: *Rosa setigera*—the "prairie rose"—with its white-eyed, cerise blossoms; the chaste, pale rose-hued pasture rose, *R. carolina*; and pink *R. blanda*.

Like the prairie that inspired it, this is a landscape of great complexity; Pat included 135 forbs and no less than twenty differ-ent grasses. Between them these plants furnish blooms from mid-April through mid-October. I visited on October 18 and found asters, bonesets (*Eupatorium perfoliatum*), coneflowers, and goldenrods still in flower. Around and among them were the subtler colors of the ripe grasses—golds, coppers, and bronzes—and a collage of textures, like the green fountains of prairie dropseed (*Sporobolus heterolepis*) which would last until spring. There were pleasures for the nose as well. The yellow coneflower (*Ratibida pinnata*) seeds Pat handed to me smelled of citronella, while the blades of the Indian holy grass (*Hierchloe odorata*) had a vanilla perfume. With prairie dropseed, it's the flowers that are fragrant; they smell like buttered popcorn.

This garden is integrated with the house to a unique degree. Besides calculating the views from the windows, Pat has carried the prairie grasses indoors, arranging different ones in the vases of each room, and using the various species as motifs on floor tiles, furni-ture, and rugs. There are prairie grasses carved into the doors, too, prairie roses on wallpapers and towels, and rosewood furniture that

Pat selected because its color is as rich as the dark brown of prairie soil.

The landscape serves Pat in many ways. It is an advertisement of her craft, and while she was showing me around, a couple of prospective clients dropped by to get a taste of what prairiescape could be. It is Pat's laboratory, too. Following Ray Shulenberg's lead, she landscaped a good deal of her yard with nursery-raised plants, but now she has switched to sowing seed in situ. That yields a more natural look, in her opinion, a tissue of plants rather than competing clumps.

Her yard is also a source of flower (forb) seed that she blends into the mixtures she sells to clients. It is a source of herbal teas— she harvests for brewing the minty leaves of the bergamot.

How does she manage the maintenance of her private grassland? Pat burns her yard every spring. She times this to the return of the blackbirds: "That's when spring begins for me." Usually, they arrive sometime in March. She agrees with Neil Diboll that a later burn is more discouraging to the cool-season grasses, but she has found that if she delays the fire much into April it drives away the killdeers who would otherwise nest in her prairie.

Because her prairie sits square in the middle of a heavily developed residential area, Pat must file paperwork before burning. She gets a permit from the fire department, and from the Environmental Protection Agency, too. Burning yard wastes would normally violate air-pollution ordinances, but because prairie grasses burn so hot and clean, Pat gets a special permit.

How has she reconciled the neighbors to the annual fire? She has turned it into a party, inviting everyone to join in this springtime act of renewal. Most do not—attendance is usually limited to other "natural gardeners" and friends—but the invitation disarms potential critics nonetheless.

To the uninitiated, some of Pat's pleasures might seem odd. For example, she took great satisfaction in the appearance recently of grasshoppers in her yard. But these aren't just any grasshoppers, these are *cone-headed* grasshoppers, a species that feeds on prairie seeds. Who can say where they came from? But their return to this land is another small step in its re-integration.

At the end of our walk around Pat's yard, we stood talking by her driveway (which she had edged with alternating purple coneflowers and dropseeds). Looking around her, Pat spoke of the satisfaction her landscape gave her. Absentmindedly stripping fluff from a dried and shattered milkweed pod, she said "We are now—people that are in restoration movements—stewards of the land. We're important. If we weren't here, the land would be worse. You see? So that we've come full circle from being despoilers and exploiters to becoming necessary for [nature's] continuing growth and function. And that's very rewarding."

Taken all together, the result of her work is a truly functional, rooted-in-this-soil landscape. While we said our good-byes, I thought of the photographs she had shown me, views of the neighborhood taken during the 1988 drought. They showed an expanse solid brown except for her stage-managed bit of wild. As I moved toward my car, Pat tossed her handful of milkweed seeds up into the air. Who could tell how far they would drift and where they would take root?

"Where does the rainwater go?"

Lorrie Otto knows. She posed that question as the theme of a program she produced for public access television. Armed with a video camera, she captured the water hitting a roof in her Milwaukee suburb, then followed it as it ran off the shingles, off the lawn and driveway and tennis court, and into the gutter along the street. Right there is where the average homeowner loses interest. As long as the water doesn't back up into the basement, he or she doesn't much care where it goes. Lorrie Otto does, though.

This warm and passionate daughter of a Wisconsin farmer has been working as the truest sort of public defender for more than thirty years. She's the one who speaks up for the environment (an indigent client if there ever was one) no matter how wealthy, influential, and numerous its enemies. She was the one who brought the Environmental Defense Fund to Wisconsin in 1969 and precipitated the hearings which made her state the first in the nation to ban the use of DDT. She recognizes rainwater as the essential resource it is, and she wanted to know: "Where's it all go?"

So she followed it into the gutter, and through an ever-widening series of concrete ditches into what is still called Indian Creek. It isn't until this slips under an expressway and into the village of

River Hills, though, that the creek really becomes a creek. That community has an active garden club, and it wouldn't let the town encase the waterway in concrete.

"So when I asked permission to go through with my camera, to walk this, the first person I got was [a man] in the engineering department: 'Oh, you want to go through that ditch.' And I said, 'Ditch? Indian Creek? That's such a pretty name. What do you mean, ditch?' 'Well,' he said, 'it's filled with, there's junk growing in there.' I said, 'Junk—what do you mean, junk?' He said, 'Well, if you like things *natural*, I suppose you'd like it.'"

Lorrie Otto does like things natural. She likes prairie, too. Unlike most restorationists, she grew up with it. Above all, she hates the abuse of any natural resource. Taken all together, these things have made her one of the most effective agents for change in midwestern gardening.

It was her concern for water conservation that brought me to her garden, but I also wanted to see it because it is an acknowledged masterpiece, authors American and English have hailed it as one of the most beautiful in the United States.

What I found was not tallgrass prairie as you would have found it before the white man's settlement. Lorrie's landscape is a garden much more finished in appearance than Pat Armstrong's. But like the tiny bonsai in which a Japanese gardener concentrates all the rugged, wild spirit of the mountain peaks, Lorrie's "pocket prairie" expresses perfectly the exuberant fertility of early explorers' descriptions.

They wrote about growth so high that a man could become hopelessly lost as he threaded his way along the tracks the animals had made. They wrote of grasses so tall that a rider had to stand up in his stirrups to see above the waving tips. They wrote of the tides of different colors that the various wildflowers made as they came into bloom one after another. Lorrie's sea of grass and forbs covers just half an acre. I felt myself pleasurably afloat nonetheless.

I stepped in a few yards along a path and back thirty years. The green spears and bright flowers towered above me once again, and the flowers I was meeting were ones I remembered from roadsides and hayfields of summer vacations. Black-eyed Susans, milkweeds of course, coneflowers, and ferny-leaved, white-capped yarrow (*Achillea millefolium*) down below; and above, the tall coreopsis (*Cor-*

eopsis tripteris), yellow daisy-like sunflowers, and the purple umbrella-flowers of Joe-Pye-weed (*Eupatorium purpureum*).

I turned one way and looked up at a compass plant (*Silphium laciniatum*), whose deeply cut leaves pointed precisely north and south. Turn around, I was face-to-face with the yellow flower of its relative the cup plant (*Silphium perfoliatum*). I knew that the orientation of the compass plant reduced its foliage's exposure to the hot prairie sun, but why did the leaves of the cup plant join at the base to make reservoirs for rainwater? I haven't been able to discover what advantage that has for the plant, though Pat Armstrong later told me about the cupped leaves' value to people. When lost on the tall-grass prairie, pioneers would draw drinking water from cup plants. That's why Illinois folk were called "suckers."

Had I visited Lorrie earlier in the year I might have encountered a mead of irises, wild roses, and baptisias. Earlier still, and we could have walked over to the woodland area to see Lorrie's spring ephemerals, the bloodroot, violets, trilliums, mayapples, and anemones that bloom in the cool weather, then disappear back underground through the summer heat.

Later, in the fall, I'd have found asters, goldenrods, and fuzzy, white-headed bonesets (*Eupatorium perfoliatum*). In the winter, I might have discovered Lorrie with Japanese rice knife in hand, cutting down the taller stalks—after the birds have eaten the seeds—to stack as a windbreak around her bird-feeding station.

"If we have a wet, heavy snow in November a lot of things are spoiled. They don't make lovely winter bouquets, standing up there stiff and pretty in the snow. So I cut those off." This she does little by little, in the course of casual walks on winter's fine days. How she stacks them varies with her mood and the needs of the birds. This past winter she built a long windrow, since the doves who came to feed need a lengthy runway.

All this towering growth Lorrie has achieved without the use of what she refers to as "drinking water." On the contrary, she purifies natural precipitation, returning it to the environment free of contaminants.

Lorrie Otto doesn't let any—*any*—of the rainwater that falls on her property leave the place. "Because I have a strong feeling that whatever water lands on my property from the air, it's my duty to see that it remains on my property, and not make it be a problem for my village or my city or the Milwaukee river."

She gathers some of the water from the downspouts into two barrels, which she also uses as a decorative element in the garden. The barrels were both decorated by local artists; several years ago Lorrie had commissioned a number of such artworks which she auctioned off to benefit the local Audubon center. Her hope was that this event would also encourage her neighbors to reduce the runoff from their yards, since Lorrie had identified this as a major source of water pollutants. Overall, she maintains, nearly *half* the non—point source pollution comes from lawns.*

"We [suburban gardeners] are worse than any chemically ad-dicted farmer, because we use chemicals more often and in greater quantities than the farmer does."†

Some of the decorated barrels, she complained, ended up inside houses, where the owners display them as artworks, but hers collect water which trickles out through lengths of buried hose to nourish a large white pine. This had been planted in a high, dry spot above the driveway by her house's original owner and would never have reached maturity without the extra moisture.

But most of the rain that falls on her place Lorrie directs into her do-it-yourself wetlands. She excavated these herself, using the spoil to terrace the rest of the yard. She likes the undulating topog-raphy this has produced, and after every major rainstorm and in the spring when the snow melts, a chain of ephemeral pools dots her yard. These last no more than a couple of days, but the mois-ture they leave behind is enough that she has never needed to water, even during the 1988 drought.

In filtering the runoff through her garden soil, Lorrie also clean-ses it of any pollutants it may have picked up in its descent through the atmosphere and across her roof. In a similar fashion, she clean-ses the water from her neighbors' yards uphill. By digging a small channel she tapped the drainage ditch the town has run along the curb. This moisture she has directed into another basin, which she has planted with wetland plants: marsh milkweed and blue flag.

But another key to water retention is hidden in the question with which she closed her videotaped pursuit of runoff. Before we

---

* To be fair, the amount of pollutants generated by lawn care is a point of some contention, with some lawn advocates claiming that lawn care products generate virtually *no* pollutants. The potential threat is clear, however. Collectively we Americans keep some 25 to 30 million acres in lawn, and 40 percent of the home lawns are treated with pesticides.
† Homeowners use three to six times as much pesticide per acre as farmers do.

came here, she asked, what happened to the rainwater? What happened to this resource before we arrived? She knows the answer to that lies in the vegetation the land supported then.

If that happened to be prairie, very little of the rainwater escaped. For prairie is not only able to survive in the absence of rain, it is also adept at retaining it. Her soil Lorrie described as a "cold, greasy clay," and such a medium by itself is almost impenetrable to water. But the prairie plants have perforated it with their deep roots. The channels this has opened, together with the organic matter that decomposing roots contributed, have made Lorrie's soil vastly more absorptive.

Modern lawns, by contrast, are second only to pavement in the amount of runoff they generate. Kentucky bluegrass roots penetrate only six to eight inches into the soil, and often less. What surrounds many American homes is, in effect, hydroponic turf. Every one of the grass's needs is supplied either by the sprinkler system or by a spray from a lawn service truck. Such lawns have no need to send roots downward, since nutrients and moisture all soak in from overhead. There is little interaction between plant and soil in such a situation, and once the inch or so of vegetation at the surface saturates, rain or sprinkler water sheets right off.

As a veteran foe of pesticides, Lorrie detests the chemical lawn services. As the Bronx gardeners who trained me would say, with her it's personal. A couple of springs before my visit, a mist of herbicide—2,4-D—drifted over the fence when a service was spraying the neighbors' lawn and wiped out the front end of her garden. This experience hardened her antipathy.*

Even so, Lorrie managed to turn this misfortune into an opportunity. She demanded that the lawn service relandscape to her specifications. Alternating layers of clean sand with layers of compressed leaves, Lorrie created a raised area where plants would find perfect drainage but also a reliable reservoir of moisture. Here she grows sideoats grama, and prairie dropseed, white and creamy bap-

---

* And rightly so, since Lorrie's experience was frighteningly common. She did not tell me the name of the lawn service that had sprayed her garden, but it's worth noting that Chemlawn, the industry leader among chemical lawn-maintenance companies, had already faced eight thousand complaints of poisoning and/or environmental damage by that point. Although Chemlawn has advertised that its products are "practically nontoxic," it has been sued for false and misleading advertising by the state attorney general of New York and the courts have awarded damages to a number of plaintiffs. Ninety-five percent of what the lawn companies spray are pesticides; of the forty different compounds they use, only one has been completely tested and reviewed by the Environmental Protection Agency for its long-term health effects.

tisia, *Coreopsis palmata* (a three-foot-tall flower with crowfoot leaves and petals like the spokes of a golden wheel), lead plant, and bird's-foot violets. Around them all Lorrie has cinched a border of pink-flowered nodding onions (*Allium cernuum*) and peachy puffs of prairie smoke (*Geum triflorum*).

With Lorrie's story fresh in my mind, I found it unsettling when a tank truck full of poison wheeled by as we walked down the block to see a pocket prairie one of her disciples had installed. What really took me aback, though, was the hostility of the neighbor who came to the fence to demand: "You're the weed expert. What's that?"

When Lorrie explained that the plants he was pointing to were a patch of Canada thistle, her interrogator harrumphed: "I got your friend across the street to thank for that."

Lorrie could have pointed out that for Canada thistles to come from a prairie planting was unlikely, since in fact those plants are not midwestern natives, not even Canadian, but rather immigrants from Europe that probably hitched a ride across the Atlantic in agricultural seed. She contented herself with a courteous good-bye, though, and we moved on.

Obviously Lorrie is adept at handling hostility, and no wonder. She has had to deal with it ever since she put away her lawn mower (a push-type reel model) back in the early 1960s. She had never liked cutting grass. As a child she had particularly admired the strip of more or less intact grassland that ran between the family farm and a railroad right-of-way. She hadn't recognized this as prairie. Prairie was something you read about in school, a place for buffaloes and Indians. Still, this early introduction had formed her vision of what grasses might be.

It was development in her neighborhood that drove her to action—or maybe it would be more accurate to say, a masterly inaction. As the vacant lots around her disappeared under houses, she decided that her children, and the neighbors' too, must have something wild, something natural in which to play. She stopped cutting, and the wildflowers started creeping back—though it was a long time before Lorrie knew how high the grass would grow, since the children kept tramping it down. And then there was the time the town crew came to clear out the "weeds." It did this without warning. A neighbor had called in a complaint, and the village officers decided that a weed ordinance gave them the right to act. In point of fact, nearly every municipality has the legal right to clear out "noxious weeds." But as a farmer's daughter Lorrie knew what those are, and that they are virtually all introduced species. So she invited the village officials out, and took them around through the debris, identifying the remains of her prairie plants and delivering an impromptu lecture on the history and beauties of each. She ended up with an apology, a check for the damages, and a series of requests to serve as an expert witness wherever governments try to force residents to mow wildflower plantings.

Confrontation is not Lorrie's tool of choice, though. In the landscaping seminars she gives, she always advises anyone who contemplates "going natural" to inform their town government first. That helps it deal with complaints in a constructive manner. She has also written a "Natural Landscape Act" that could serve communities as a model for more reasonable alternatives to existing weed ordinances. When enacted, this would still protect a community against plants legally accepted as agricultural pests (all those exotics), but would allow weed commissioners to remove only those unless they could prove that the restoration project posed a clear and present hazard to public health and safety or to agriculture.

To date, however, Lorrie's influence on the local landscape has been felt more through example than through legislation. A lecture she gave at the local Audubon nature center prompted the formation of a natural landscaping club, The Wild Ones, of which she remains program chairman and moving spirit. Membership stood at four hundred when I visited (Pat Armstrong has since opened up an Illinois chapter), but the club's impact is disproportionate to its size since its members are active proselytizers, encouraging neighbors to let their yards go natural, too.

Lorrie Otto argues very convincingly that reducing water consumption in the garden *must* be a part of a healthy environment. Environmental responsibility starts at home. Referring to all the horrifying situations she has been fighting since the DDT hearings twenty some years ago, she posed one more question: Why are we treating the earth this way? "It's because we don't know how to take care of the land right around our houses."

Neil Diboll had ended our lunch by admitting once again that "fighting it out" may not be all the prairie is about. Specifically, he referred me to one of the fathers of prairie ecology, Frederic Clements. "Clements had this completely radical and discounted theory that [in the prairie] there is an organism bigger than the individual, wherein all the individuals are actually linked to one another directly or indirectly. They may very well be working together in some semi-cooperative situation, as well as in a competitive situation. Recent studies on microrhizal fungi [the fungi that flourish in association with the roots of many higher plants] point to the fact that these may connect species to species, that there may be some sort of mutualism. That's a radical concept—a totally radical concept which has deep social implications."

So for Neil, prairie is also a model for healthy coexistence. Pat Armstrong was more succinct:

"I don't think you should pamper plants or people. If it doesn't kill you, it makes you tougher."

And maybe more beautiful too.

Six

Turf Wars

ot so long ago the flawless, velvety green lawn was an American ideal. Like chastity, it was an ideal more often honored than observed, but it was an ideal nonetheless.

Now, though, that same lawn has become an embarassment in horticultural circles. Ecologically minded gardeners (of whom I count myself one) complain that lawns are an insult to the environment. American lawns, such conscience-ridden people point out, consume more nitrogen fertilizer each year than all the farms in India. Lawns are a major generator of non–point source pollution; they fill the waterways with pesticides and nitrates. And what's most relevant to this book, they are terrible water guzzlers, the major consumer of residential water. That's why most xeriscapers shun them.

All these criticisms are true. But they needn't be. The fault lies not in the turf but in ourselves. The way we manage our lawns is what makes them an environmental obscenity.

Fundamentally, lawns are very practical things. That's why we planted so many of them in the first place. To begin with, grass protects your home better than a smoke alarm. If kept short and green and more or less thatch-free, grass makes an excellent fire-break, and can prevent a neighbor's tragedy from becoming yours as well. In addition, like any type of planting, grass helps filter pollutants from the air and cools its surroundings through transpiration of water. It helps replenish the atmosphere with oxygen, too. In short, there is a positive side to the equation.

The fashionable alternative to a lawn is, of course, a wildflower meadow. Through much of the Midwest, that can be a most sensible alternative, especially if what you plant is real prairie rather than that collection of cosmopolitan weeds called meadow-in-a-can. Elsewhere, however, meadow is usually not a climax vegetation,* and human interference is needed to keep it from turning to brush. Interference translates into maintenance, and maintenance of a far more sophisticated kind than a lawn requires. Lawn mowing is easy (if boring) and doesn't have to be more than an occasional chore, if you don't force the grass into unnatural growth with giant doses of fertilizer and water.

I cut my lawn with a push-type reel mower, an antique I bought for fifteen dollars at a yard sale. It doesn't burn petroleum, it exercises my muscles, and the mowing is easier than maintaining a meadow's artificial balance. Mowing not only keeps the grass looking trim, it keeps most weeds in check—my alternatives in a northeastern suburb would almost certainly include either hand-pulling or applications of herbicides. One eco-gardening book I reviewed recently insisted that all I need do was to strip all the topsoil from my yard before sowing wildflower seed—wildflowers and meadow grasses compete better on a poor soil. But how can that be defined as environmentally sound gardening?

I can and do admire the special charm of a meadow, and might include one in my landscape for that reason. I know, though, that such a feature provides excellent cover for mice. In my part of the country, mice host the ticks that carry Lyme disease. So where my son plays, I'll keep the grass cut short.

Obviously, the charge of greatest concern to this book is that lawns are extravagant consumers of water. Once again, that's our fault. We choose our grasses poorly, we plant them poorly and

---

* According to a long held ecological theory, the climax vegetation is the stable, self-perpetuating plant community that eventually develops on any site left undisturbed. Meadow, or a grassland community, is only a step in the succession toward a woodland climax in most regions east of the Mississippi, or in the moister parts of the West.

where they don't belong, and then we demand that they stay green whatever the weather. Correcting these bad habits can dramatically reduce water use. After all, gardeners above the age of sixty remember a time when lawns weren't watered at all.

Before World War II, few American suburbs had municipal water supply systems. Water didn't come from a main then, it came from a well. The well had a definite rate at which it could supply water, and this wasn't generally sufficient to soak a whole half-acre. So we saved our water for the bathtub and flower bed. If the summer brought a month of dry weather, the grass turned brown —but it was only dormant, not dead. Teenagers rejoiced, because dormant grass didn't need cutting, and when autumn brought cooler, wetter weather, the lawn revived.

With the postwar boom, all this changed. America began extending the aqueducts to accommodate more intensive development, and people began moving in large numbers to the arid regions of the West. In the Southwest, if they withdrew enough water from the mains, amateur groundsmen could have green turf all year-round. Homeowners in the North couldn't match that, but they found that with continual watering they could eliminate summer dormancy.*

We have to return to an old-fashioned aesthetic when it comes to lawns. Lawns were not flawless a couple of generations ago. They were full of clover, coarse grasses as well as fine, and they were lush only in spring and fall. If we match this easygoing attitude with some up-to-date know-how, we can have practical lawns —and recognize where lawns *are* unaffordable.

Adapted Turf

The first step to a practical lawn is simple: choose a grass adapted to your area. I like the look of Kentucky bluegrass—that's the turf I grew up with—and I don't particularly care for the coarser look of St. Augustine grass; indeed, I deeply offended a local extension agent in College Station by comparing it to crabgrass. But I would

* For these points about the old lawn versus the new I am indebted to Roger Swain.

have been a fool to grow any other turf in my shaded, central Texas yard.

Choosing a grass adapted to the natural budget of rainfall in your area is easier than it used to be. A generation ago it was difficult to get any guidance on this subject, since the experts were all concentrating on a few of the lushest turfs. Today, though, you'll find your county extension agent full of information, especially if your region has recurrent water shortages. Or contact your town's parks department—it has practical experience of which grasses work well locally. It's even worth calling local landscape maintenance companies, though their customers seem to come mostly from traditional-turf holdouts. But make sure that whatever your sources recommend is a truly adapted grass, not just one that is "drought tolerant."

Tall fescue illustrates the importance of this distinction. Naturally coarse-leaved and springing up in bunches rather than a uniform sod, this grass used to be considered fit for nothing but pastures. Actually, guides to lawn maintenance used to recommend a classic poison-pill defense against this species. Should it appear in your lawn, you were to spray the whole yard with herbicides and start from scratch; tall fescue is so tough it's impossible to eliminate any other way. Then, about a decade ago, someone realized that a turf so tenacious was worth cultivating.

After considerable work, several finer-bladed "turf types" were developed. Because these are remarkably deep-rooted grasses—they reach down as much as five feet into the soil—turf-type tall fescues are extremely effective in searching out soil moisture. This, in turn, means that they flourish with less frequent watering than traditional (more shallow-rooted) turfs such as Kentucky bluegrass. Producers proudly labeled the new fescues "drought-resistant"—which they are, but that doesn't mean they use significantly less water.

Indeed, the ET rate of tall fescues (the rate at which a tall fescue turf loses water into the atmosphere) is very similar to that of Kentucky bluegrass. Tall fescues *can* play a part in water conservation in areas such as the lower Midwest and the upper South, regions with hot summers and irregular but substantial rainfall. Since this turf can weather the dry week or two or three between rains there without help, it eliminates nearly all need for irrigation.

In southern California, however, where tall fescues have also been promoted as a means of water conservation, they are a fraud. In that arid habitat the yearly budget of rainfall is not enough by itself to support tall fescues, and so they must depend on irrigation. Because of the depth of the soil they can tap, tall fescues may need irrigation only half as often as Kentucky bluegrass, but it takes twice as much water to fill their reservoir each time. There really aren't any savings.

Turf Alternatives

As a turf grass consultant in Denver, Colorado, Dorothy Borland has made a name for herself by putting clients on to alternative turfs, ones that demand less water and maintenance than the conventional grasses. Currently serving the City and County as the water conservation officer and analyst, she is still very much involved with lawns, since that is where so much of Denver's water goes.

Fundamental to Dorothy's success is her different attitude toward lawn grasses. Like most gardeners, I tend to lump them together in the single category: turf. I tend to treat them as interchangeable, too. Dorothy emphasizes that gardeners must realize that different grasses are just as distinct in their needs and virtues as different species of trees and shrubs, and that we must use an equal amount of care in where we plant them.

She emphasizes, though, that most homeowners can markedly reduce their lawn's water consumption without replanting. They can achieve this, she has found, simply by giving more attention to irrigation—by making sure that they give the lawn precisely the water it needs, when the grass needs it, and at a rate that the soil can properly absorb the moisture.

How much can they save in this fashion?

Dorothy doesn't have precise figures, but notes that she has seen reductions of as much as 30 percent.*

* Dr. Victor Gibeault at the University of California, Riverside *does* know the figures for southern California. He's found that even accurate watering—irrigation at the recommended rate, at a level equivalent to the daily ET—may be unnecessarily generous. In a three-year test near Santa Ana, he discovered that the irrigation of hybrid Bermuda grass could be reduced to 60 percent of ET without

Switching to a locally adapted alternative turf can produce far greater savings than that, however. If nothing else, Dorothy stresses, the cost of doing this focuses homeowners' attention on their lawn and so encourages them to involve themselves in its care rather than delegating it entirely to a landscape service. Certainly, the alternative grasses sound intriguing.

Selecting the Turf That's Right for You

There are a number of steps to selecting an adapted turf. Before even considering climate, Dorothy emphasized, you should analyze what you need, and just as important, what you want. A turf for a child's play area must be resilient; you may need a more vigorous, high-water-use grass there. At the center of a landscape, in an area of high visibility, you will likely want a fine-textured, dense, richly colored grass; around the periphery you may well be content with something far less lush. There is no one turf for every region—a practical lawn depends on your skill at piecing different grasses together.

A basic decision is how manicured you want the mature lawn to look. Some of the native grasses are extraordinarily tough, and far better adapted to our western climates. Buffalo grass, for instance, flourishes without irrigation in climates where most other turfs require constant sprinkling (it requires only 20 percent as much water as Kentucky bluegrass). My observation, though, has been that the natives do not supply as finished a look.

That's no accident. All the traditional turf grasses are exotic in origin, and the decades of attention turf breeders have given them have produced in the named strains a richness of color, a denseness, and a uniformity that the unschooled natives cannot match. I love the fine, soft look of buffalo grass, and its subtler blue-gray color suits very well the rugged western landscape. But in my opinion, buffalo grass's uneven density and color make it a poor choice for a formal landscape.

---

significantly affecting the turf's appearance. See *Proceedings of the Fifth International Turfgrass Research Conference* (Avignon, France, 1985), pp. 345–54.

That's changing. In 1990, Texas A&M University released a buffalo grass clone named 'Prairie' that is more uniform in height; it doesn't grow taller than six inches, which means that it needs considerably less mowing than traditional turfs, and indeed can be left unmowed in an informal setting. 'Prairie' spreads faster than the wild-type buffalo grass and hence produces a denser turf. Because it is a genetically identical clone, the individual plants don't compete, either, as they do with the wild-type buffalo grass, so 'Prairie' knits into a much more uniform, seamless turf. There's a bonus, too: 'Prairie' is all female, so it produces no pollen—it's a hay fever victim's dream.

This is only a beginning. 'Prairie' buffalo grass's creator, Dr. M. C. Engelke, told me of an introduction from the University of Nebraska, a buffalo grass clone named '609'. According to marketers, this seems to share many of the virtues of 'Prairie', while offering a deeper, blue-green color. Undoubtedly, there will be more buffalo grasses. And crested wheatgrass (*Agropyron cristatum*) bids fair to be the next success. A number of named varieties have already been released by universities and the USDA, though Dorothy Borland said that none of them made a satisfactory turf for her; the individual plants never put on sufficient bulk to merge into a carpet. Still, the next decade will surely bring many natives to the greenskeeper's arsenal. For the present, though, exotics remain the choice for manicured lawns.

Bunchgrasses versus Sod-Formers

The distinction between bunchgrasses and sod-forming grasses I alluded to in the discussion of tall fescues is also an important factor in the selection of a turf. The difference lies in the pattern of growth. Sod-forming grasses such as Kentucky bluegrass send out lateral shoots called rhizomes that knit together into a continuous fabric. Bunchgrasses, such as tall fescues or perennial ryegrass, spring up in bunches, as the name suggests, and don't spread except by seed.

Sod-forming grasses are naturally better suited to high-traffic areas, since they repair themselves much more easily and quickly

—if the turf is healthy and in a period of active growth, rhizomes may knit across a damaged patch in a few weeks. A bunchgrass lawn, by contrast, must wait for another generation of seed to sprout. There is also an aesthetic advantage to the sod-forming grasses: they make a denser turf, one that looks lusher from close up.

Not surprisingly, most of the traditional lawn grasses are of the sod-forming type. But because the bunchgrasses tend to be less "improved" since, as in the case of tall fescue, they are closer to pasture grass ancestors, bunchgrasses often produce extremely hardy, deep-rooted turfs. If viewed from the distance of a few feet, bunchgrasses can give an appearance of density equal to that of sod-formers, and so work well in the outer reaches of the landscape.

You *can* force a greater density on a bunchgrass turf simply by seeding very heavily. This practice may also make these normally coarser grasses produce finer leaves. I've done this with perennial ryegrass, and the result was a very attractive turf. But crowding raises the lawn's water requirement, making it more dependent on irrigation. A better solution would be the compromise Dorothy Borland suggested. If a particular bunchgrass seems especially suited to your needs, yet you want a dense turf, try mixing its seed with that of a compatible sod-former and sowing them together. She, for example, sows blue grama grass (*Bouteloua gracilis*), a dryland bunchgrass, in a 50-50 blend (mixing equal numbers of seeds, that is) with sod-forming buffalo grass.

Cool-Season versus Warm-Season Grasses

The decision that will most directly influence the irrigation requirement of your lawn is your choice of a cool-season or warm-season grass. In the previous chapter I described the different patterns of growth that distinguish the groups; what's of importance here is that warm-season grasses typically lose far less water to transpiration than cool-season grasses. If you look at the accompanying table, you'll note that hybrid Bermuda grass may transpire only half as much water as Kentucky bluegrass on the same warm, sunny day. This gives hybrid Bermuda and all the other warm-season grasses a big advantage in regions where summers are hot and droughts the norm. If a grass loses less water through its leaves, after all, it will need less input from rainfall or irrigation. As a result, warm-season grasses are the standard turfs of the South.

Rooting Depths of Common Turf Grasses *

Shallow-Rooted Turfs—penetration into soil 1–8 inches
    Annual bluegrass
    Creeping bent grass
    Colonial bent grass

Medium-Rooted Turfs—penetration 8–18 inches
    Kentucky bluegrass
    Red fescue
    Annual and perennial ryegrass
    St. Augustine grass

Deep-Rooted Turfs—penetration 18–60 inches
    Zoysia grass
    Bermuda grass
    Tall fescue

* Figures reflect average performance under good growing conditions.

Unfortunately, the warm-season grasses that have been developed as turfs pay for their reduced water needs by being less competitive in cool weather. Few will even survive the cold wet of a northeastern winter. Zoysia, an Asian species, grows well as far north as the New York City suburbs, but with a problem. For many years the gardening supplements of newspapers promoted it as a wonder grass. The advertisements claimed (truthfully) that it makes a dense, almost weed-free turf, and one that requires less fertilization and watering than the traditional favorites. In fact, zoysia's water requirements are similar to those of buffalo grass. Then came the clincher: the ads promised that as a natural dwarf (zoysia grows only two to eight inches high) the wonder grass would rarely need mowing.

What the ads didn't mention was that zoysia turns an unattractive brown at the first hard frost and doesn't green up until fairly late in spring (sometime in May in New York). Buffalo grass, the warm-season turf best adapted to the northern regions of the arid West, follows the same schedule: from October until mid-May in Denver, it's tawny. And as a horticulturist, I've found that most of my clients want green.

Turf breeders are working on that, and the near future should bring warm-season grasses, particularly zoysias, better suited to use in the North. Until that happens, though, warm-season grasses will continue to be best suited to the southern and middle latitudes of the United States, and I will continue to recommend zoysia only for planting around summer cottages north of the Mason-Dixon line. In that situation, gardeners will appreciate the freedom from mowing zoysia provides, and they won't be there to watch it fade.

Planting for low water use

Reducing the water needs of your lawn doesn't end with the choice of grasses. Careful preparation of the soil is also critical— and unfortunately, lawns rarely receive this kind of encouragement. As noted in Chapter Four, the typical pattern is for a developer to strip a site of topsoil before he builds on it. Then, when the carpenters finish their work, he returns a fraction of the topsoil to hide the compacted subsoil, scatters seed on top, and turns on the sprinklers. The wonder is that the grass grows at all. Certainly, it continues to do so only as long as the homeowner force-feeds the feeble roots with fertilizer and irrigation.

Before planting or replanting a lawn, rototill the soil to a depth of six inches, using this opportunity to give it a healthy dose of organic matter such as compost or peat. The size of the dose should be determined by a soil test, though you could try a rule of thumb Dorothy Borland quoted, adding three cubic yards of organic matter per thousand square feet of surface area.

Don't fool yourself that this once-over with a rototiller finishes the job. You've just scratched the surface. Even a modestly rooted grass such as Kentucky bluegrass can reach down eighteen inches into the soil if given some help, and as noted above, the depth of the roots relates directly to a grass's ability to weather drought. The key to deep rooting lies in careful watering.

Sufficient moisture is essential to root growth, of course, but the aeration of the soil is even more important. Overwatering deprives roots of air, especially on dense clay soils, and so discourages their growth. That's why, according to Dorothy, on lawns with sprinkler systems she rarely finds root systems more than four inches deep.

How many Kentucky bluegrass lawns ever get the chance to send their roots down eighteen inches? Those that do certainly don't need weekly sprinkling; they can forage for their own water through the average northeastern summer.

Seed or Sod

There's one last choice to be made before you finally install the lawn. Will you sow seed, or will you lay down sod?

There's instant gratification in a sodded lawn—just roll it out, turn on the sprinkler, and there you are. You pay for sod's convenience in two ways: it's expensive to install and expensive to maintain. To make that smooth carpet, the producer has encouraged the grass to intertwine itself as densely as possible, and this means that a sod lawn's demand for irrigation will remain high even after it sinks its roots into the soil.

Starting the lawn from seed nearly always contributes to water conservation. To begin with, most of the alternative turfs are not available as sod—though Dr. Engelke is currently putting the finishing touches on a zoysia adapted to sod production. (To balance the books, he's also perfecting a zoysia that can be started from seed; one of this grass's disadvantages has been that in the past it could only be planted as sprigs—lengths of rhizomes—and so was relatively expensive as well as slow to establish.)

Besides, if it's a bunchgrass you are planting, sowing the seed yourself allows you to vary turf density. As previously noted, a less dense turf requires less water, so by sowing seeds more sparsely around the outer reaches of your lawn, the parts normally viewed from a distance, you can reduce its irrigation requirements without significantly detracting from its appearance. If you want to make the grass there look thicker, use one of Dorothy Borland's tricks: cut it a little higher.

The beauty of sod, of course, is its uniformity, but that actually is a liability too. The mixture of grasses that can be had in a seeded lawn increases the chance that there will be some strain or species that will flourish in every microclimate of the yard. Also, if herbivorous insects or diseases should discover that seeded lawn, chances are there will be some grass in the mix that the pests will find distasteful, so you won't step out the back door some morning to find a landscape that has been scalped. A sod lawn, though it may include more than one grass, still offers less diversity, and so lacks the seeded lawn's versatile response to pests.

Maintenance for Reduced Water Use

Your style of maintenance will also play a crucial role in setting the water needs of your lawn. If you feed the grass the amount of nitrogen recommended on the turf food sacks at the garden center, it will grow like a weed and use water like a weed, too. You don't have to buy into that cycle. Tests conducted by the Smithsonian Institution in Maryland found that a lawn that was given frequent fertilization, watering, and treatments with the recommended pesticides, and then mowed at the trim height of one inch, didn't look markedly better than a lawn given far less care and mowed at a height of two inches. A third lawn, one that was given no care except regular mowing at a height of three inches, also looked just fine.

There's a double message here. The first is that by keeping your grass relatively tall and allowing it more leaf area, you increase its ability to feed itself. Taller grass also tends to produce deeper, healthier roots and so is better able to find its own water.

Recommended mowing heights vary with the type of turf you grow. Hybrid Bermuda grasses are typically cut at heights ranging from one-half to one inch, while tall fescues are cut at two and a half to four inches. Check the accompanying table (page 213) to determine the height range preferred for your particular turf. Keep the turf on the short side of the recommended range during cool weather to encourage spreading and denser growth, then let the grass gradually increase in height as hot weather settles in. As fall brings back cool, moist weather, gradually reduce the turf's height again. Never remove more than a third of the leaf blade at any one cutting if you can avoid it, since that shocks the grass, leaving it less able to take care of itself. Likewise, keep the mower blade sharp, since a clean cut is less traumatic.

Mowing Heights*

Cutting at the proper height enhances both the health and hardiness of your lawn and so decreases its dependence on irrigation. The proper cut varies with the turf type and the season—refer below for height (in inches) to set your mower's blade.

Cool-Season Grass	Cool Weather and/or Shade	Hot Weather	Last Mow (in late fall)
Creeping bent grass	1/3	1	1/3
Velvet bent grass	1/4	1	1/4
Annual bluegrass	1/2	1	1/2
Canada bluegrass	3	4	3
Kentucky bluegrass	2 1/2	3	2
Rough bluegrass	1	1 1/2	1/2
Smooth bluegrass	3	4	3
Fine fescue	1 1/2	2 1/2	1
Tall fescue	2 1/2	4	2
Annual ryegrass	2	2 1/2	2
Perennial ryegrass	1 1/2	2 1/2	1
Warm-Season Grass			
Bahia grass	2	3	1 1/2
Bermuda grass	1/2	1	1/2
Buffalo grass	1 1/2	2 1/2	1
Carpet grass	1	2	1
Centipede grass	1	2	1
St. Augustine grass	2	3	1 1/2
Zoysia grass	1/2	1	1/2

* Figures taken from Warren Schultz, *The Chemical-Free Lawn* (Emmaus, Pa.: Rodale Press, 1989).

The second message of the Smithsonian experiment is that turf just doesn't need all the help we are accustomed to giving it. Actually, most of the need for fertilizer derives from traditional lawn care, which recommends collecting and removing grass clippings. This drains both organic matter and nutrients from your lawn; if left to decompose in place, clippings can return as much as 1.8

pounds of nitrogen to every 1,000 square feet of lawn every year, enough to supply most of the grass's needs.*

It's important to add that for rapid decomposition, the clippings must not be too long: if you intend to leave them in place, you must either mow frequently or switch to a mulching mower, one that shreds the clippings before dropping them back onto the turf. If you use a reel mower like mine and sometimes (shame!) miss a mowing, you can toss the too-long clippings onto the compost heap, and then return them to the turf as a top-dressing once they have decomposed.

Top-dressing with compost, incidentally, was once a standard practice among greenskeepers, and was abandoned only with the appearance of inexpensive and seductively convenient prepackaged turf foods. Compost still makes the best meal for your lawn, since besides adding nutrients, it also adds humus and so increases the soil's water-holding capacity. For best results, spread the compost in a layer about one-fourth-inch thick, after first giving the lawn a going over with an aerator, one of those machines that punch a pattern of cores out of the soil (they are available at most tool rental businesses). The next rain will wash the compost into the holes, where it will feed the turf's roots while also increasing the soil's aeration and infiltration rate.

A period of active growth is the best time for this treatment, since the lawn will repair the damage most rapidly then. Fall is good for most cool-season grasses, midspring for the warm-season ones. The effect of the compost won't be as dramatic as that of the bagged turf foods. Gradually, however, over a series of topdress-ings the lawn will become not only thicker and greener, but also more drought resistant.

The drawback to this practice is that it requires large quantities of compost—almost a full cubic yard for my small, twelve-hundred-square-foot urban lawn. Owners of large lawns will prob-ably find a compost feeding too much work.† But they can obtain some of the same benefits by using a mulching mower to shred

* This figure comes from a study performed by the Connecticut Agricultural Experiment Station; a summary can be found in Warren Shultz, *The Chemical-Free Lawn* (Emmaus, Pa.: Rodale Press, 1989) p. 69.
† It's worth noting, however, that in 1991 Walt Disney World began a study to determine the feasibility of switching its two thousand acres of grounds to a compost maintenance program. The goal is partly to dispose of the resort's millions of tons of organic wastes (it generates about as much of these as a city of half a million), but also to free itself from dependence on chemical fertilizers. So maybe your half-acre isn't too big.

autumn's leaves into the turf rather than raking them up and removing them. Composting in situ is what that is.

If you are determined to fertilize, by all means fertilize naturally. Sow your lawn with clover, either by mixing clover seed into the original seed mix or by scarifying an established lawn's surface with a heavy rake and then sprinkling it with the clover seed. Because it is a legume, clover absorbs nitrogen from the atmosphere and converts it into a form available to plants; in effect, it feeds itself and the surrounding lawn, slowly but continuously.

The benefit is considerable. Obviously, you aren't going to plant a pure stand of clover, but if you did, it would add as much as 160 pounds of nitrogen to the soil per acre per year. That works out to almost four pounds per thousand square feet, which is at least twice as much nitrogen as your low-maintenance, reduced-irrigation lawn requires. Turning over a fraction of the lawn to clover should, along with top-dressing, eliminate all need for bagged fertilizers. Besides, clover provides a bonus: its leaves stay green long after summer heat forces turf grasses into dormancy. Because it spreads by rhizomes (like a sod-forming grass), it is also useful for binding bunchgrasses together into sod.

If you still feel the need to get out the fertilizer spreader every spring (old habits die hard), use it to lime your lawn. Test the soil's relative acidity first, of course, with an ordinary pH test kit. Your soil may already be in the 6.0 to 7.4 (slightly acid to neutral) range that turf prefers, but in the eastern half of the United States, a combination of natural conditions and acid rain makes it likely that the pH is too low (too acidic).

Since pH affects a plant's ability to absorb nutrients, excessive acidity will starve your turf. A weakened turf will make only feeble roots, and that means it will require more irrigation. So if your soil's pH tests lower than 6.0, "sweeten" it with ground limestone. On average, a topdressing of five pounds of lime per hundred square feet is sufficient to raise the soil's pH by one full point.

Ultimately, the most important step you can take to reduce your turf's water consumption is to recognize the places where turf should never be planted. Turf is an extremely unnatural kind of vegetation in the desert, and should be treated there as a special feature, something to be savored, like a spice, in very small quantities. Even in well-watered areas, banks and berms are also inappropriate spots for a carpet of clipped turf. Water, whether from rainfall or a sprinkler, will mostly run off before it can be absorbed, and the turf will suffer from drought even during a moist season. Explore other ground covers for use on such spots.

Don't plant turf in that strip of earth that runs down the center of the driveway. It's too hot and dry there for the grass ever to flourish, so dress that area with a mulch instead. Take a hint from the xeriscapers and eliminate the hard-to-water, hard-to-cut corners and peninsulas from your lawn. Turf makes a wonderfully practical ground cover; no other plant will stand so much traffic or recover so quickly from injury. But you can have too much of a good thing.

As Owen Dell pointed out (see page 35), we have tended to use turf as the default planting—if nothing else comes to mind, we reflexively sow grass. In consequence, we have already turfed over an area of the United States greater than the whole state of Virginia. Do we need more? Probably not. Should we convert all this to wildflower meadows? Don't be ridiculous. Just learn to cultivate a sensible lawn.

That may not free you completely from a dependence on sprinklers. Even with her use of alternative grasses and more skillful cultivation, Dorothy Borland still recommends irrigating a Denver lawn (if it's buffalo grass) once a month (giving it an inch to an inch and a half of water at a time) during the growing season. That treatment isn't necessary for the survival of the lawn, but it keeps the grasses from going dormant and brown. It's a luxury, but still a great savings when compared to her neighbors' thrice-weekly soakings of their bluegrass.

What really sells her dryland lawns, Dorothy says, isn't the water savings, nor their distinctive beauty. It's the reduced need for mowing that her clients like best. And I must admit, that sounds very good to me.

Denver, Colorado

"Clean and green" has long been the the creed of Denver's landscapers, and the city is as green now as any in the United States.
It's utterly familiar. Once again, it's the bluegrass lawns, the foundation plantings, the "specimen" trees in front, and in the back, the
sprinkler for a child to run through. With the endless blocks of
modest bungalows, you could be anywhere—until you look up.
Then the wall of grand and rough-hewn peaks—the Front Range
—reminds you that you stand, literally, at the edge of a watershed:
the Continental Divide.

It's Denver's luck to sit on the dry side of that, in the rain
shadow on the mountains' eastern side. Weather moves from west
to east here, and by the time the winds have crested the mountains,
the high altitude cold has wrung all the water out of them. Consequently, Denver's annual precipitation averages only fifteen inches.
That's less than Santa Barbara. The truth is that Denver's lush
landscape is an illusion.

It's an illusion maintained with increasing difficulty. This, after
all, is the community that invented xeriscaping. The "xeriscapes" I
saw in Denver, however, couldn't rival those of Austin, Texas,
either in number or flair. But there is pioneering work being done
in Denver nonetheless. There's a circle of gardeners—they all
know each other and have at various times worked together—who
are creating some of the most innovative gardens in the country,
and saving rivers of water in the process. There's no clearly defined
membership for this group, but there is a clear leader. He's Panayoti Kelaidis.

Panayoti's singular approach to gardening derives, I suspect,
from his most unconventional education. Growing up in Boulder,
he learned his horticulture in the rock garden that an older brother-
in-law planted in front of the family home. Growing alpines may
seem an obvious response to living in the Rocky Mountains, but in
fact it was an unusual, almost eccentric, decision for a Coloradan a
generation ago. But that is why Panayoti took for granted that the
plants you grow in a garden will be adapted to local conditions.

He learned differently when, fresh from college, he moved to
Denver. There he noticed that the landscape plants were mostly
doing poorly. Their foliage was yellowed and sparse, the tips of

branches were dying back. No wonder; these plants were all flat-landers, trucked in like the migrant workers. But there were some nice displays—lush foliage, vivid flowers. These were found among the weeds in vacant lots. So why not grow something more like weeds?

This is the type of obvious departure that would not occur to a professional such as myself. But Pananyoti was an amateur; and despite the senior position he now occupies at the Denver Botanic Garden, he continues to identify with home gardeners. To me, he described himself as "one of these typical damn horticulturists who came in the back door."

What he means is that he never took a single class in gardening. Indeed, his education is in classical Chinese. He's also fluent in a variety of other languages: I watched him offhandedly translate a passage from modern Russian for a friend, and when he learned that my university major was Latin and Greek, he happily launched into a chant that I, mercifully, managed to recall as the opening lines of Homer's *Iliad*. Panayoti delivered the lines in the original language, of course, for Greek is his ancestral tongue.

As Panayoti pursued his interest in high-mountain plants at home, his reputation spread, largely due to the articles he was contributing to gardening magazines. So when the Denver Botanic Garden began laying plans to install an alpine rock garden in 1980, it turned to him. What else could the Garden do? All the professionals had been too busy watering lawns and junipers to learn how to grow more appropriate vegetation.

Panayoti, who had already been associated with the Botanic Garden as a member and volunteer, responded to its invitation by submitting a sixty-page outline of what he considered a "dream garden." This document listed all the plants he'd like to try in Denver. To Panayoti's astonishment the Garden hired him as a consultant, first on the design and then on the construction of the alpine garden. As the soil settled around the rocks, Panayoti was asked to stay on as curator—there was no one else on staff who could manage the kind of garden he had envisioned.

In his whirlwind first year, Panayoti tested fifteen hundred species and varieties. That process has gone on, though at a slightly less killing pace, and what Panayoti has learned is that infinitely more species will grow in Denver than even he had imagined. At any given time, he maintains a collection of roughly twenty-five hundred different plants, and it gives some idea of the originality of his planting to note that only 2 percent come from commercial sources. The rest he has either collected from the wild himself (usually as seed), or obtained from other enthusiasts and botanical gardens. The story of the Alpine Rock Garden, Panayoti says, "has been the constant expansion of our horticultural palette and ambitions."

Ambitions that to my eye approached hubris as this Homer-spouting autodidact took me round his one-acre domain. Along a network of paths we strolled down into deep canyons, along the tumbled foot of screes and moraines, past a waterfall and a bog, and then up, rising easily as Olympians, to the peaks and high mountain meadow. This illusion was near perfect—the geology was inspired, mimicking in vastly reduced scale the mountains that block the western horizon. Only the vegetation gave the business away: it was impossibly rich.

There were the daphnes, for example, neat mounds of azalea-like foliage which in spring would swarm with tiny, four-pointed fragrant pink flowers. Native to northern China and Korea and to the mountains of Europe, daphnes are a favorite of English gardeners but had been unknown in Denver before Panayoti tried them. The success of one type, the Burkwood daphne 'Somerset', has been such that its introducer refers to it as "the Daphne that ate Denver." Then take the ice plants—"Oh my God," I heard my host moan, "is she cutting my acanthus?" Panayoti hustled off to check the work of a volunteer gardener.

He returned much relieved a few minutes later from what had proved to be a false alarm (the exceptionally dedicated band of volunteers are essential to the maintenance of this small but intensively planted garden). Then Panayoti related to me that story of his ice plant promotion.

This South African genus of succulents (*Delospermum*) had won a secure place in the gardens of the southwestern United States with its extravagant blooms of daisy-like flowers and extraordinary tolerance for drought. Their name might suggest that these are plants of the frozen north, but actually it derives from wishful thinking on the part of a parched European botanist: the sunscreen of tiny reflective hairs that covers these plants' leaves gives them a deceptively icy glisten. In truth, ice plants had been thought too tender for northern climates, until Panayoti began experimenting with two species: a purple and a yellow-flowered type (*D. cooperi* and *D. nubigenum*).

These plants had been available from a few rare-plant nurseries, but Panayoti believed that they deserved wider exposure. In the garden they had proved practically unkillable, eventually spreading to cover an area up to a yard across. Both species bloom heavily in the spring, and occasionally in the summer, and the foliage of the yellow-flowered type, which turned red with the onset of cold weather, offered a note of winter color as well.

Panayoti had made a practice of taking promising plants around to the nurserymen, but he found that only made them suspect the quality of the offerings.* So in the case of the yellow-flowered ice plant, he propagated two or three hundred potfuls himself. These he sold at the botanic garden's plant sale, thereby creating a popular demand that the nurserymen couldn't very well resist. Within a couple of years, this plant was selling by the tens of thousands all over the metropolitan area. But his real triumph was the purple-flowered ice plant—he grew that from seed he had obtained from the Munich Botanic Garden and introduced it in the same way. One year later he saw it on display in the shelves of a local K-Mart.

Local gardeners with whom I conferred agreed that Panayoti had transformed the local nurseries. When I asked Panayoti about this, he claimed to have managed it entirely by a strategy of staying put and chatting up his selections with the botanic garden's visitors. He admitted, though, that he had taken pains to identify plants that would be good for nurserymen as well as gardeners. Panayoti's selections are easy for the nurserymen to propagate—generally by cuttings—and easy for home gardeners to grow.

"I don't want something that's hard to grow," he explains, identifying with his constituency. "Because if it's hard to grow, I have to work hard. I don't want a garden full of invalids." And if a plant is to flourish in Denver, it must be reasonably drought tolerant.

Water use is the "subtext" of all Panayoti's planting. His alpine garden is served by an elaborate irrigation system with twenty-seven distinct zones. But this lifeline breaks down with some frequency, generally (Panayoti claims) when he is away. In 1989, for instance, the line to the central bed gave out right before the

---

* "Timeo Danaos et dona ferentis," warned the priest in Virgil's *Aeneid* when a wooden horse turned up at the Trojans' gate: beware of Greeks, even when bearing gifts.

hottest five days in Denver's history, a stretch when the temperature rose above 105°F every day. Panayoti returned from a vacation to find what he described as "a worst-case scenario." He had lost about half the plants in the affected area. What did he do? He replaced the dead plants, of course—but with something tougher.

As we sat and talked in his potting room, Panayoti expanded on this theme. "Whenever there is a choice between a water-thirsty plant and one that will take a potential drought"—*bang*, his fist hit the table—"I go for that. That's why," he added, "my garden is so silver and white."

Those are colors I had come to recognize in Texas as typical of xerophytes. Now I learned that they are also the reflective colors of plants that can survive the intense high-altitude sunlight. Like cacti, alpines also contend with dehydration. The wind on the peaks, though not hot, is strong and soil moisture, while often abundant, is typically unavailable, locked up as ice. Not surprisingly, many alpines make fine water-conserving plants.

Like lowland xerophytes, alpines commonly shield themselves with coats of fine hairs, but they employ another strategy, too: they extract lime from their rocky soil to encrust leaves with whitish crystals of calcium oxalate. In addition, these plants have learned to shelter themselves in hollows and crevices. That's why alpines typically grow in an architecturally compact fashion—in regular rosettes or pincushions of foliage that reduce surface area to a minimum.

Not all of Panayoti's plants ("my little godchildren," he calls them) are alpines, however. He is fascinated by the field of geobotany, the science of relating flora to geography, and he long ago identified Colorado's high plains as steppe or grassland. So he has looked to that type of habitat for a source of plants that would flourish through Denver's hot, dry summers and cold winters. His explanation of the science involved quickly passed into terminology that I could not follow (yet another of the day's linguistic humiliations), but the upshot is that Panayoti has found that plants of the central Asian steppe perform well in Denver.

So do plants from South Africa's karoo and the Patagonian pampas, plants from the Mediterranean maquis and phrygana, even those from other European mountains. Actually, almost any herbaceous perennial thrives in Denver (and Panayoti can identify some four thousand at a glance). Most come, he explained, at least originally from montane areas, or middle- and lower-elevation grasslands—all habitats easy to simulate in Denver. "The Rocky Mountain climate," Panayoti maintained, "is one of the most ideal for planting a garden."

Surely it's dry?

Not if you manage your garden right, Panayoti insisted. Yes, there are only fifteen inches of rain a year, but it all comes at the right time, and in the most effective manner. Denver receives precipitation of some sort in every month of the year, the bulk of it during the peak growing months of May, June, and July.

"So in many ways, when it comes to several of the largest families of ornamental plants [herbaceous perennials], Iridaceae [iris], Lamiaceae [mint], Scophulariaceae [snapdragon]—you know, the very largest genera of plants available to our gardens, penstemon, salvia, on and on and on—we can probably grow a larger spectrum of species than can any other climate. And that includes southern California. Because it doesn't have winter, and a lot of steppe-climate plants need that. Southern California can't grow tulips. In Denver, most are highly perennnial. Virtually all of them, even many of the fat little Dutch hybrids, are long-lived plants here. They go twenty, thirty, forty years."

Panayoti is trying to promote what he calls "a steppe-climate awareness." He notes that "there has been a great deal of feeling inferior to the Midwest, the Northeast, and definitely England, a feeling that somehow or other wet, maritime climates are optimal for cultivation of herbaceous plants. But my thesis has been that they are optimal for the growing of rhododendrons, and mosses, and certain kinds of woodland plants. But when it comes to the standard perennial, a perennial border is just a kind of glorified meadow from a steppe climate."

Other gardeners told me that Panayoti's efforts have been central to Denver's development as a center of the perennial nursery trade. They've also helped to give the city many more months of bloom. Panayoti despises what he calls "fair-weather gardening," and "the vegetable mentality." Though we think of Denver as a northern city, in fact it's on the same parallel as Rome, and, because of its altitude (Denver, "the mile-high city" stands at 5,280 feet above sea level, Rome at 377), the Coloradan capital actually receives more intense solar radiation. The earth's atmosphere works as a filter, scattering, absorbing and reflecting sunlight; Denver, with a filter five thousand feet thinner than that of Rome, receives (all other factors being equal) a sunlight anywhere from 11 to 18 percent more intense, depending on the season.* The result, according to Panayoti, is that his garden gets as much sunlight as it would in Cairo, and there is no reason to stop gardening when summer ends.

"June, July, and August are actually our worst months. It's really much more comfortable in September, October, and November here, because it's never hot. It's not all that cold and it's never hot. So you can garden beautifully really up until Christmastime. . . . We get bloom every month of the year."

He's been pursuing autumn-blooming plants, species from areas with dry springs where flowering is put off until fall. So come September now, phloxes from the uplands of northern Mexico drift across the alpine garden in shades of rose to white, while helichrysums and zauschnerias of the South African Drakensberg bear their counterfeits of fuchsia blossoms.

Through the cold-weather months, Panayoti relies on foliage for landscape color. Indeed, when Panayoti is choosing material for the garden, it is the state of a plant's leaves from November through February that he checks first.

"Evergreen, ever-silver, ever-purple, or whatever color it is, is it there? Because I can't afford to grow a lot of plants that are gone for six months, ten months. December is *the* month to garden for. If you create a garden that looks good in December, I can guarantee it will look good in May."

Anyway, as he points out, dormant plants, ones that have disappeared underground, leave windows of opportunity for weeds.

All of these beliefs Panayoti is spreading now through his classes. Though he never studied horticulture formally himself, for a decade he has been teaching a natural gardening and rock gardening class at a local community college. The clientele he aims at is landscape contractors and nurserymen, and he finds them receptive, especially with regard to new plant materials. One of the advantages of Denver's geographical isolation, Panayoti believes, is

* Figure taken from Clarence Frederick Becker, *Solar Radiation Availability on Surfaces in the United States as Affected by Season, Orientation, Latitude, Altitude and Cloudiness* (New York: Arno Press, 1979), pp. 50–56.

that the distances keep outside influence weak, making it easier to develop a regional gardening style. But the issue of water conservation he finds difficult to sell.

"Watering is synonymous with gardening in Denver. To try and change that is tough." With water bills unrelated to consumption (Denver shares with New York the distinction of being one of the last cities in the country where water metering is not obligatory), the rewards are mostly spiritual. Panayoti told me that he knew of only three truly unwatered landscapes in Denver. One of these was at his house. He was quick to make clear, though, that this wasn't his garden; it belongs to his wife, Gwen.

The distinction is important, because Gwen is as dedicated a gardener as Panayoti, with just as many interests and projects. She was, at the time of my visit, editing the bulletins of the American Rock Garden Society and of the American Penstemon Society, as well as operating a mail-order business in uncommon Rocky Mountain wildflower seeds with twelve hundred subscribers, half of them abroad. She grows plants for sale to other rock gardeners and to local nurserymen—she showed me that year's crop, 125 flats of twenty-four plants each, enough to cover the entire driveway.

So Gwen needs her space just as Pananyoti needs his, and their nuptial agreement is that *his* plants stay in *his* garden at the botanical garden. He may bring one or two home, he admitted; Gwen grinned as she reminded him of the previous spring when he'd arrived with some three hundred, airily suggesting that she work them into her design. But basically, the garden around their comfortably solid Denver bungalow belongs to Gwen. It included fifteen hundred distinct types of plants when I saw it. She was sure of that number, because she'd spent much of the preceding spring creating a computerized record-keeping system.

When Panayoti and Gwen had moved to this house four and a half years before, the yard—just fifty-two by a hundred feet—was a typical city lot. But not for long. The first spring, she went to work with a power sod-stripper. She had planned to remove a strip of useless turf from the front parking area. But when Panayoti called home, she told him that oh, by the way, she had gotten rid of the whole front lawn. "He was ecstatic."

What replaced the turf was a Continental Divide in miniature, a range of rocky mounds that she mulched with a granite gravel from the back side of Pike's Peak. Building this was no easy task, since Gwen was seven months pregnant at the time. She let someone else place the rocks, a sensible decision whose results she immediately regretted. Two months after delivery, she redid the job to her own satisfaction.

The mounds suit the high-mountain plants that Gwen, too, loves—these plants with their deeply penetrating roots need perfect drainage. Her object was also to give the flat site some topography and to screen the house from the street. To appease the neighbors, she has planted the outer face of the range with ground-cover plants that will give the slopes there a "clean and green" (if genuinely western) look.

There we found Panayoti's yellow ice plant; partridge feather (*Tanacetum densum amani*), a relative of the common tansy that makes an elegant tuft of plume-like, whitish leaves; and *Penstemon crandallii*, a native of Colorado's brushy slopes whose sprawling stems bear thimbles of purplish blue. Yet another mat of ground-hugging foliage proved to be *Veronica liwanensis*, which celebrates late spring with clusters of blue flowers, at about the same time that *Arctostaphylus nevadensis*, a glossy, evergreen look-alike of the eastern bearberry, is ending its season-long display of pink, bell-shaped blossoms.

Panayoti has described Gwen's style of garden making as "design by trowel and spade," and there's a good deal of truth to that. She's a collector who cannot resist a beautiful plant, and though her tastes run mostly to the high-mountain species, she seemed unable to resist any wildflower, as long as it remained compact and mannerly and could adapt to her dry, sunny beds. They come home with her from visits to nurseries or plant sales, and then she hunts around for an opening.

What unifies all these different elements is the blanket of tawny gravel. This also serves the purely practical purpose of protecting the soil from Denver's dessicating atmosphere (after just a few days the skin was flaking off my face), and keeping the soil surface loose enough to absorb whatever rain strikes it. The gravel makes good footing, too, for the mailman; Gwen left a pass through the mountains for him, so that he can cut across to the mailbox without rock climbing or stepping on plants. Persuading paper boys that this is a garden has so far, according to Gwen, proved beyond her abilities.

In the details of the design—what goes where—Gwen often lets her plants take the initiative. Much of her garden's color comes from annuals like the rocket larkspur (*Consolida ambigua*), which bears delphinium-like spikes of blue, white, and pink in early spring, or the white cosmos I spotted blooming in a distant corner. Rather than dead-heading these as the flowers fade, she lets them set seed so that a spontaneous crop will arise the following season. She even treats some of the perennials this way. *Penstemon palmeri*, a robust southwesterner that turns into something like a rose-and-gold snapdragon in May or June, would return year after year. But it's unattractive after the bloom ends, so after it has scattered seed, out it comes.

Letting flowers self-sow eliminates the need to be constantly buying new seed, but it offers other benefits far more substantial. Many, perhaps most, of the self-sown seeds never germinate, of course; only the seeds which find the right niche take root. But those that sprout do well, since plants know best what they need. Besides, Gwen's policy of non-interference saves seedlings from trauma. Western natives as a rule do not transplant easily. One of their adaptations to recurrent drought is their long, tenacious roots; these are useful for tapping hidden reserves of water, but impossible to dig up without damage. Even if the plants survive, they are far less able to scavenge their own water.

The healthy roots of Gwen's plants make for a remarkably unthirsty garden: Gwen sprinkles the front garden only a few times a summer. "When it's been 102° five times in a week then I usually give it [the front garden] a squirt. But I only water the new stuff." She doesn't like drip irrigation—it's too static to suit a planting as unstudied as hers. And she thoroughly disapproves of the automatic sprinkler system that has been installed in the xeriscape demonstration area at the botanic garden—"unconscionable" was her word for it.

More and more, Gwen says, she is coming to value really aggressive plants, the ones most gardeners label "invasive" and shun. Friends laughed when they caught her planting butterfly weed (*Asclepias tuberosa*), an orange-flowered type of milkweed. Yet in July, its flowers make a vibrant contrast with the pale blue mist of the

Russian sage (*Perovskia*) flowers. Perovskia is another plant that Coloradans tend to hold in disfavor, because in western soils it rapidly colonizes by means of underground runners (I have grown it on the East Coast and have not found this to be a problem, perhaps because of the difference in soil moisture). But like the butterfly weed, the Russian sage has proved nearly invulnerable to drought. That's important, because Gwen doesn't water these plants at all. Indeed, when I saw them it had been two years since she had irrigated the "herb strip" in which they grow.

Stretched between the south side of the house and the driveway/nursery, the herb strip occupies an especially hot, dry spot, so its self-reliance is particularly remarkable. Among the other plants that adorn this spot are the culinary sage (*Salvia officinalis*), the lavender (*Lavandula officinalis*), the various thymes, bluish-leaved rues (*Ruta graveolens*) with their lemon yellow flowers, and gray-foliaged lavender cottons (*Santolina chamaecyparissus*), whose flowers are an even more startling shade of gold. What care does Gwen give these? She shears them like sheep in the autumn to keep them more or less compact, and to open the way for the early spring show.

This consists of "botanical" tulips—the wild species of Panayoti's beloved steppes. These bloom not with the familiar (and to my eye, lurid) goblets of the Dutch hybrids, but in a galaxy of exquisite stars. There are yellows tipped with cream (*Tulipa tarda*), crimson flowers with black hearts (*T. linifolia*), and others of shining vermillion (*T. wilsoniana*). Spring bloomers, these plants retreat underground as the dry weather of summer sets in, and as Panayoti had claimed, they perform as true perennials. In fact, they are something of a pest—the tulips set so much seed that they too have become a weed.

Not all of Gwen's garden is water efficient. Such a passionate collector doesn't reject fine plants simply because they aren't drought proof, and she has beds in the backyard that she waters twice a week during the dry part of summer. Nevertheless, when she and Panayoti requested that a meter be installed on their water line (Denver encourages such voluntary conversions), their bill, now based on actual rather than typical usage, dropped by half.

Eventually, my single-minded attention to water conservation began to irritate Gwen. Her alpines have so many other virtues. She likes the textures of the foliages: the jets of the bear grass's

(*Nolina texana*) spear-like leaves; the furry, silver tongues of the woolly mullein (*Verbascum bombyciferum*); and the pinked leaves of the Himalayan catnip (*Dracocephalum calophyllum*). Did I know that alpines are hail resistant, too?

I did know that hail is a problem in Denver. I had already weathered one such storm since arriving in the city two days before, and one of Panayoti's students had pulled hailstones the size of golf balls from her freezer. Those were relics of a storm of the previous month, and had been as big as tennis balls originally; they had struck with sufficient force to shatter Plexiglas plant labels. Gwen took me to the far end of the backyard to show me the lacerated leaves of a squash, then told me to compare that with the perfect foliage in her rock garden. No question; she was right.

One virtue of the alpines that Gwen forgot to mention was their usefulness to steam locomotive enthusiasts. But she didn't have to; that assignment was ably handled by two of her friends, Barbara and Marc Horovitz.

Marc has a fleet of locomotives that would do credit to a Harriman or Vanderbilt—"about six dozen" working steam engines was his estimate. In addition, there is the electric railbus, the boxcars and flatcars, even a plow so that their Ogden Botanical Railway can run right through the snow. It's only right, then, that to house these he and Barbara should maintain such an ambitious estate. They have three rock gardens, a garden devoted to fragrant herbs, a rose arbor, and a classical folly, as well as a loop of railroad track and a private station. And they've managed all of this on a back yard thirty-six feet deep and fifty feet wide. Everything they've built or grow is to the same half-inch scale; that is, one-half inch of track or tree trunk in their yard is equivalent to a foot outside. They didn't do this to conserve water, but that's certainly the effect. Their plants use just one-twenty-fourth the normal budget of water, too.

The Horovitzes are healthy, normal and practical people—I must admit that surprised me a little. Their garden and their railway just happened to result from passions that synergized. Marc is an architect by training and a self-confessed "technology junkie." Going down with his father to the Dallas station every Sunday morning to watch the Texas Zephyr pull out on its run to Denver is one of his strongest childhood memories. As far back as he can remember, Marc says, there were always trains, and he had collected all sorts of rolling stock, from wooden toys to Lionel electrics. Barbara is an artist who has loved miniatures ever since she got her first dollhouse, so her attraction to alpines was immediate.

Curiously, it was in England, not Denver, that she first encountered these plants. That was in 1979, when the Horovitzes were taking a vacation from their architectural graphic design business. They'd gone to England, and while there they visited an outdoor model railway, a "garden railway," of which Marc had read. "That just pushed us over the edge."

Marc knew immediately he had to build something similar for himself; Barbara laughs now to remember how she wondered if she was going to be able to grow the same plants (nearly all alpines) in her high-altitude home in Denver. A simple garden railway took form in the front yard of their duplex (which overlooked Ogden Street—that was the source of the line's name). Soon Barbara was ordering plants through the mail, shopping the local garden centers (which were quite remarkable, thanks in part to Panayoti), swapping plants with other gardeners, and begging "pinches and starts."

They joined the local chapter of the Rock Garden Society, where they met Gwen and Panayoti; "of course, that blew everything wide open." Meanwhile, the steam locomotives they had begun importing from Germany for resale turned into a line of train-related products, and they started to publish a bimonthly newsletter to keep their customers apprised of new products. In the end, that turned into a full-fledged magazine, *Garden Railways*, which pushed everything else out of their professional lives, including the graphics business. Today it has a circulation of over eleven thousand, with subscribers in all fifty states and twenty-four foreign countries (including Egypt and Malaysia).

It was when they bought their own house (yet another of the ubiquitous Denver bungalows) at the end of 1985 that they at last had the opportunity to plan a really ambitious garden railway. Plan was all they did, too, for more than two years. Marc is meticulous in that respect. He began by calling a friend at an architectural firm who could borrow surveying equipment. With the information it provided, Marc drafted a topographical map. That may seem excessive, but Marc insists that it was not; to run his steam locomotives without constant refueling, Marc needs a level track. It was only after determining where he would site the station and lay the track, and therefore where he would have to raise the grade with soil-filled timber cribs (still in half-inch scale), that Mark could set shovel to ground.

Barbara's style of designing is much more offhand, Marc told me, remarking that he's depended on this strength of hers ever since they started working on projects together as undergraduates at the University of Texas. So he left the landscaping entirely to her—she's the plants person.

By the time I saw it, the effect of her work was both charming and disconcerting. As I stepped out the back door of the Horovitzes' house, I felt as if I were blowing up like a balloon in Macy's Thanksgiving Day Parade, and it wasn't until I dropped to my hands and knees that I could properly appreciate the landscape. Make no mistake, it was impressive at firsthand. Yet I've concluded since that the camera's eye saw truer than mine. My perspective was still too lofty, and I was too distracted by the artifacts.

For quite a while, I couldn't see past the astonishing architectural details: the brass rails pinned with tiny steel spikes to the hand-cut redwood sleepers; the trestles Marc had run over rocky gullies; the black, paved station yard abandoned except for a stray pig. A sense of the landscape came only as Marc set out a locomotive, an Aster Baldwin -4–2T, and I imagined stoking the firebox, building up a head of steam, and chugging round the Ogden Botanical's line myself.

I wait for the train enveloped in the clean, old-fashioned fragrance of lavender—a hedge of 'Munstead' dwarf English lavender, a magnificent stretch of needled foliage 480 feet long (in half-inch scale) that runs across the back of the station and train yard. As I board, I can't help noticing the rocky knoll that rises up across the track. Its flank is a tufted cascade of aromatic foliages and flowers: *Alyssum montanum* 'Mat of Gold', Lebanese oregano (*Origanum libanoticum*), silver saxifrage (*Saxifraga paniculata*), caraway thyme (*Thymus herba-barona*), silver-variegated thyme (*Thymus vulgaris* 'Argenteus'), to name a few. Here and there rises a hardwood—a littleleaf mountain mahogany (*Cercocarpus intricatus*) and a miniature Chinese elm (*Ulmus parvifolia* 'Seiju')—that contrasts with the coarser, somber spill of a dwarf Norway spruce (*Picea abies* 'Pumila').

With a hiss the train eases into motion, and we round a curve with a stand of herbs off to the right: variegated sage, a big silvery horehound, oregano in bloom, bee balm, lemon balm, all the old-fashioned fragrances that Barbara loves. As the train glides over a redwood trestle I poke my head out the window to catch a quick glimpse of white foliage carpeting the tumbled slope below: woolly veronicas (*Veronica pectinata*) of both the blue and rose-flowered forms, and the crimson-jeweled cushions of cheddar pinks—*Dianthus gratianopolis* 'Tiny Rubies'. There's just time for a glance at the green-needled mound of a dwarf Swiss mountain pine (*Pinus mugo* 'Valley Cushion') before we slip into the shade of a sequoia-tall white lilac.

To the left there's a cluster of flowering mimics. I spot the red and yellow blossoms of Canadian columbine (*Aquilegia canadensis*), that to our ancestors recalled a quartet of doves sipping at a fountain (*columbina* is Latin for dove), and the monkey-faced flowers of viola 'Freckles'; there's a belfry's-worth of white Carpathian harebells (*Campanula* 'White Clips') amid the glossy, broad evergreen leaves of periwinkle (*Vinca minor*) and the even broader silver-spotted foliage of dead nettle (*Lamium* 'Beacon Silver').

There's the folly—"Our Lady of the Railway," Marc and Barbara call it—a classical temple fashioned from a garage-sale light fixture, a mock-granite plinth (a scrap of countertop saved from a friend's kitchen renovation and turned on a lathe), and a female figure cast in pewter.

Another bridge—this one cleverly designed to lift out whole so that a Brobdingnagian lawn mower can be brought in to trim the patch of grass that remains at the garden's center. We pass over the trestle and past a Colorado blue spruce (a miniature clone, *Picea pungens* 'Montgomery', that grows at a rate of a quarter inch a year —a modest half-foot even by the railway's reduced scale). Around a meadow sprinkled with white catalpa-tree blossoms and past a shady savannah of trees, grasses, and ferns—I recognize among them a miniature false cypress (*Chamaecyparis obtusa* 'Nana'—a cumulus cloud of emerald green), elegant tufts of black mondo grass (*Ophiopogon planiscapus* 'Nigrescens'), and the burgundy carpet of a variegated bugle (*Ajuga reptans* 'Burgundy Glow').

A straight fast run, and then to the left again around a mountain landscape of *Acantholimon venustum* (silver prickly thrift—it lives up to its name, the cushion of sharp hard foliage stabs my hand when I try to stroke it), alpine pinks (*Dianthus alpinus*), and a variety of conifers: another dwarf Colorado blue spruce (this one named

'Thume'), the hunched cone of a dwarf Alberta spruce (appropriately named *Picea glauca* 'Gnome'). Finally it is under the arbor of
miniature roses, one of which—'Si'—makes buds hardly larger than
a grain of wheat. Past a hedge of tooth-leaved germander (*Teucrium
chamaedrys*) and back into the station.

Stop.

Barbara—who has studied with Panayoti—emphasizes foliage
in her garden, but with her artist's sensitivity for color and texture
comes something more: a special enthusiasm for fragrances. She
described her garden as a potpourri, and the wealth of herbs did
ensure that it appealed to nose as well as sight and touch. I found
it a garden of contrasts. There was the contrast between the sharp-
smelling artemisia 'Silver Mound', and the savory aroma of a creeping thyme turf around the station yard. A carpet of Scotch moss
(*Sagina subulata* 'Aurea') was seductively soft to the touch—yet I was
still nursing my fingertip after the encounter with prickly thrift.

The garden had its harmonies, too. A purple barberry (*Berberis
thunbergii* 'Crimson Pygmy'), for example, called across to purple-
leaf wintercreeper (*Euonymus fortunei* 'Coloratus'). Barbara told me
that she had selected roses for the garden in the fall, when she
could form no idea of the flowers. "I frankly didn't care because the
flowers were secondary. The color of the leaf, the color of the
stems, the contrast of the new stems and the old canes, the hips.
. . . Flowers are fun, they're bright and cheerful, I do love them,
but they're not everything."

Barbara made a point of showing me her collection of more
than fifty miniature flowerpots, many of them planted and set out
around the railway buildings. She takes a pinch of a succulent, a
sempervivum or sedum perhaps, potting up a tiny sprig of the most
delicate new growth with the help of a toothpick. One of her
favorite subjects for this is the poplar-leaved sedum (*S. populifolium*),
a Siberian species with toothed, tiny, poplar-like leaves that Gwen
Kelaidis gave her. Its stems are stiff enough that she can train it as
a standard, like a little tree; grown in a pot an inch tall, "that scales
out to two feet tall. It's quite a statement pot, with a tree in it.
Those are my big plants."

I asked and Barbara told me, no, there's no sprinkler or drip
irrigation system here. She admits rather ruefully that she planted
by eye and by touch, composing in textures and colors rather than
grouping plants by water needs as a xeriscaper would. Because she's

continually changing the garden, there are always new plants that need extra irrigation, too, until they root in. Only hand watering permits the individual attention the Horovitzes' plants need—it's so easy to overwater when a pot measures just an inch deep.

Barbara wasn't irrigating at all when I stopped by. Denver was receiving a bit more than the average rainfall, and Barbara claimed that her plants were yellowing as a result. She said that she missed watering, that it's a kind of therapy for her. But she doesn't approve of waste and she hates fuss—so she won't tolerate a shallow-rooted irrigation-dependent landscape.

Clearly, Barbara Horovitz is not a xeriscaper in the strict sense of the word. Still, she and Marc are hunting for another, more spacious, house, and she plans to group plants more according to need in her new garden. She says she finds herself increasingly offended by the people she sees squandering resources, people who think that conservation is everybody else's responsibility. She has episodes of discouragement.

She and Marc, though, could take pride in having changed some people's thinking—if they were the missionary type. Their magazine is about fun, pure and simple, and they never suggested to me that it had any other mission. Yet it is promoting a more sophisticated understanding of gardening among their readers. Barbara and Marc do not recommend specific plants, since no one plant could suit all the widely varied circumstances of their international readership. Instead, they stress exploring local resources. Every article about an actual railway must include a list of the plants that gardener used—readers can draw their own conclusions.

Barbara has been particularly excited to watch the horticultural awakening that's occurring in the Denver model railway club. Some members who previously regarded plants as nothing more than backdrops have developed a genuine interest in alpines. Several have joined the local chapter of the Rock Garden Society, and others, though they don't know plant names, have become first-rate growers.

When I met them the Horovitzes were about to disassemble their garden in preparation for their move. They didn't know exactly where they would end up, but they were sure that wherever it was, Marc would soon be laying track. Barbara would surely bring her collection of catalogues and a host of "pinches and starts." They were making big plans—on a modest scale.

Steve Olsen

When Steve Olsen got married Panayoti Kelaidis was his best man, and the gift he gave the groom was a flat of plants. There's nothing Steve would have valued more. He told me that plants are like children to him. He said this several times in the course of our afternoon together, and never once did it strike me as sentimentality.

Steve saw a lot of plants while he was getting his graduate degree in ecology, and afterward when he went to work as a Co-operative Extension agent. He's seen countless more since he went into business as a landscaper. Yet somehow he's never grown blasé. He still responds with the genuine wonder that most of us lose along the way.

What's more, he's has something exceedingly appropriate for a water-wise gardener: a dry sense of humor. I noticed it as he told me about moving into his present home in one of Denver's quiet residential neighborhoods.

His yard had looked like every other yard up and down the street—"just crummy grass." So the first thing Steve did was to spray it with a contact herbicide. Naturally, the neighbors wanted to know why his lawn suddenly turned brown. All brown. "And I kind of grinned a little bit, and I told 'em—I killed it."

"They were real interested." They were even more interested when Steve rototilled the dead grass into the soil and mulched the whole with three inches of crushed granite. What was he planting, they wanted to know—a desert?

Hardly. On a street of might-as-well-plant-lawns, his yard is a colorful oasis. With his children all grown up now, the garden has a quirky exuberance that is irresistible.

Categorizing this garden is a problem. The mulch gives it the flavor of a rock garden, and Steve maintains a fair collection of Rocky Mountain foothills flora. But he's no nativist. You find dwarf conifers here cheek by jowl with giant sunflowers. The plant material is different, but in spirit what Steve's garden is closest to is an old-fashioned cottage garden. It's got the same ad hoc appeal.

Steve enjoys the unexpected. The seedling oak in what had been the green strip between sidewalk and street is a hybrid with some bur oak (*Quercus macrocarpa*), a prairie native, in it. Steve is pretty sure of that, and believes that's why the tree flourishes un-watered. Where did he buy it? I wanted to know. Steve grinned again, and confessed that it had been planted by a squirrel.

That was why self-seeded plants played so large a role here. Steve values their adaptation to a dry landscape; he waters *maybe* once a month. He likes the fact that such "volunteers" are adept at finding moister spots where they can survive unaided. The dianthus on his street-side slope, for instance: Steve had planted it at the top, but it had migrated to the bottom where (presumably) the moisture collected. That kind of self-reliance is fine. But what really excites Steve is the genetic variability that manifests itself in chance-pollinated offspring of nursery-grown parents.

His simple marigolds would be boring—except that after a couple of years of planting themselves, no two are exactly alike. His snapdragons have also increased, and though annuals in my garden in Connecticut, they have proved perennial in Denver. That's why Steve was able to show me how a single set of parents had spread yellow, pink, and white offspring all around the yard. Why they didn't clash with the sulphur flowers (*Eriogonum umbella-tum*), tufts of wild and (literally) woolly, yellow-crowned flowers from the nearby foothills, I don't know. I wouldn't have tried that combination. But then, I wouldn't have combined domesticated sunflowers and the almost equally tall purple spikes of gay feather (*Liatris punctata*) in the same landscape. Nor would I have coupled for my "statements" (Steve's expression) so unlike a pair as a choke-cherry (*Prunus virginiana*), an almost ethereal tree of woodland edges and hedgerows, and a golden arborvitae—a bright dwarf evergreen that is the epitome of suburban respectability. But the effect wasn't, as you might expect, a hideous discord. It was cheerful.

That was something very pleasant in the affectionate way Steve addressed every plant we encountered. So, in the backyard, when we came upon a tiny bouquet of foliage and flowers: "Isn't that neat?" Then in hushed tones: "It blooms late, doesn't it? And it's a yellow-flowering one, and it is dianthus."

And moving farther back: "There's a nice gentian . . . and I love the morning glories here in the alley. In the morning I can say 'Good morning, morning glories'—you know they're all blooming, they're all nice and everything."

If Steve's reactions were artless, his gardening certainly was not. He was as clever at exploiting microclimates as anyone I've met.

Cold spots, hot spots, wet spots or dry—these pockets of aberration can be an enormous resource for the gardener or a terrible frustration, depending on sensitivity and skill. Steve pays attention to his plants—he's a good parent in that respect—and it pays off. After watching his dianthus's migration, for example, Steve applied the same principle to his planting in the backyard. His cactus went in at the top of a bank, where it is sunny and dry, while his wife's collection of gentians went in at the moister base—two plants with totally dissimilar needs, but both contented and growing within five feet of each other.

Steve has also created his own microclimates with the twists of gray juniper wood he collects on trips to the high country. In the front yard, one such tortured-looking log cradles a delicate primrose. Sitting in the lee of the wood, the plant is sheltered from the drying wind, and since it lies to the north, on a slight north-facing slope, the primrose receives relief from the high-altitude sunshine as well. To the south of the wood lay another of Steve's cacti—that specimen appreciates the extra heat this side of the log collects.

Really, Steve has no "yard" left, for he's filled every scrap of it, even the green strip between sidewalk and street, with his plants. There came a point where I had met as many of these as I could stand, and I was beginning to feel like I was back on one of those class trips to the endless art museum. But Steve insisted that he had one more experiment to share with me. He sat me down behind the house in an English teak chair at the English teak table (he was very proud of the furniture and made sure I appreciated its origin). Then, a few minutes later, he brought out a pitcher of margaritas; he wanted my opinion on a new formula he was developing. It was fine—but I suspect that the drink's relish derived partly from the aridity of our conversation—we were talking dry times in the garden.

It's a given of xeriscaping that eliminating the lawn cuts water use drastically. But never before had I heard this case made more effectively. Drawing on his professional experience, Steve calculated that it costs one of his clients (if their water is metered) a hundred dollars' worth of water every month to support a five-thousand-square-foot expanse of bluegrass. Many of them have up to twice that much turf. So Steve invites all customers to his water-conserving landscape for a twice-annual open house. Always these visits bring demands for relandscaping; that constitutes a third of his business now.

I admired Steve's mulch for the stark backdrop it provided: a snapdragon or primrose has a startling delicacy when set in granite. When I raised this point with him, though, he at once moved on to the gravel's practical benefits. It keeps the soil moist. Some gardeners go even further, stretching a sheet of polyethylene over the ground before spreading the mulch. That not only reduces water loss even more, it also excludes weeds. Steve doesn't hold with the practice, though. Gardens are dynamic, he believes, and sealing the soil prevents the self-seeding evolution Steve treasures. Besides, he finds such extreme measures unnecessary. Instead he avoids cultivation. Turning the soil creates opportunities for invading weeds and also exposes buried weed seeds, encouraging their germination. Steve doesn't cultivate except to plant, and he is certain that's why he hasn't had to weed for several years.

When I asked Steve how he had developed his interest in xeriscaping, he stopped me, gently but firmly. "I'm just interested in plants," he explained. "Because of your background in ecology?" I asked. "Well, just like friends. I never had children, I want to have a lot of different kinds of plants. You have to have a home for them."

A *healthy* home. Panayoti made a stong case that this is what Denver offers, naturally. But nature can change.

A scientist at the University of Colorado told me that he had charted alongside each other on the same graph a history of the totals of cloudy days Denver has experienced every year since the turn of the century, and a history of the region's irrigated acreage over the same period. The two curves rise in nearly perfect parallel. Could this be coincidence? Maybe. But it suggests that there is a relationship between the number of sprinklers and deterioration of the local climate.

For Denver, water-wise gardening can be more than a money-saver and a way to preserve the flow of trout streams. It has been the way to gardens as remarkable as any. It can be the means of preserving the special climate that supports them.

Seven

Recycling

ow much water do you waste? You've planted your garden with adapted species, and installed a drip irrigation system in the vegetable garden. You've removed the automatic controller from the sprinkler system, and you've swathed all your plantings in mulch. So you say: not much. And you are wrong.

If you take an average eight-minute shower every day, you wash as much as forty gallons of slightly soiled water down the drain. Even if you've installed a low-flow showerhead and limit yourself to a brisk five minutes, you still send ten gallons to the septic tank or sewage treatment plant. An average bath sends thirty-six gallons down the drain; washing a load of dishes with the tap running uses twenty-five gallons; washing a load of clothes uses forty, and just washing your hands uses two or three. In each case, the water used is only slightly soiled. You wouldn't want to drink it, but it's fine for irrigation. In fact, it's probably purer than some of the water farmers draw from the rivers out West. Yet you flush it down the drain.

All in all, you and your family may easily waste in this fashion a hundred gallons of water every day. That's enough water to keep a twenty-by-forty-foot panel of turf emerald green in the average American climate. It's enough water to see an orchard of fifteen fruit trees through the summer in southern California, or to irrigate a five-hundred-square-foot vegetable garden. Chances are you already recycle paper, cans, and glass—so why not recycle water?

Of course, if you do, it will make you a criminal in much of the United States. Currently, California is the only state which permits homeowners to recycle this so-called gray water, and even there, this marks a recent change in the plumbing codes. Santa Barbara County was the first county to rewrite its plumbing codes to allow for the distribution of gray water to the landscape—it did this in 1989. Several counties followed suit the following year, but it wasn't until 1991 that the state itself legalized gray water use.

As of this writing, the International Association of Plumbing and Mechanical Officials, the body which establishes plumbing codes for twenty-two western states, had recommended the legalization of gray water. If approved by a vote of the full membership, this would make gray water irrigation legal in every state west of the Mississippi. But gray water use would continue to be tightly controlled.

There's good reason for this. Gray water may contain various potentially harmful microorganisms, especially if a resident of your house is sick. Careless storage and distribution of gray water could conceivably spread typhoid fever, dysentery, and infectious hepatitis. But then, many of your cleaners and polishes are deadly poisons, and the can of gasoline you keep for the lawn mower could blow up the garage. Safety in each case depends upon taking sensible precautions. If you make a commitment to be careful, gray water can be a useful and healthy resource.

For guidance on this subject I went to consult Robert Kourik, the horticulturist who helped Santa Barbara write its gray water code. He lives well to the north, in a mixed redwood/Douglas fir forest above San Francisco in Santa Rosa County; it's a lush place, but that's largely because the forest waters itself. Robert had noticed that trees around his house seemed to harvest water from the fogs that roll in to his area, and by setting a rain gauge under the branch tips of one Douglas fir, he found that this tree might harvest an inch or two of water a week.

That's important, because Robert's well draws from a perched aquifer, a small underground pool that sits above the water table and so is only replenished by seasonal rains. The yield is enough to satisfy his personal needs, but any substantial irrigation system would soon suck the pool dry. Then he'd be dry too, maybe for months, until the next round of storms. Robert can't spare any drinking water for irrigation. Nor can many of his clients, since high-yield wells are uncommon in his half of Santa Rosa County. As a result, Robert's livelihood depends in a very real way on gray water. If he wants to sell a garden to his customers, it's important that he can sell them an alternative water source, too.

Robert has written the definitive do-it-yourself manual for gray water use,* and he provided me with a copy of this, then amplified with personal observation. What I learned was this:

There Are Many Shades of Gray

Obviously, you shouldn't be irrigating with the raw sewage that drains out of the toilet—Robert calls that "black water." If you are pinning your baby into cloth diapers, and you wash them yourself, you shouldn't apply the water from that load to the garden either. Water from dishes can be problematic too, unless you scrape the plates carefully before washing; grease and food bits aren't good for the soil and may attract vermin.

Water from the bath, shower, and bathroom sink is usually the best for irrigation, although recycling them requires tapping into the drain lines. For guidance on how to do that safely, check Robert's book, and contact the E.P.A. National Small Flows Clearinghouse,† a federally funded agency that can furnish you with the pertinent parts of approved plumbing codes. Those who aren't handy with tools will find the washing machine the most convenient source of gray water, since it has its own pump. It's a simple matter to redirect the wash water from its drain into a barrel, and from there siphon or pump it out into the soil.

---

* *Gray Water Use in the Landscape* (Santa Rosa, Calif.: Metamorphic Press, 1988). Available for $6.00 from Edible Publications, P.O. Box 1841, Santa Rosa, CA 95402, this is an essential guide for the would-be water recycler.
† Its address is: West Virginia University, P.O. Box 6064, Morgantown, WV 26506-6064.

Garbage in/Garbage out

What you put into the water—the kinds of cleaning products you use—will determine the quality of the gray water that flows out onto your plants. Chlorine bleaches are highly toxic to plants, so when you are whitening your whites, send that water down the drain. Borax or any other cleaners that contain boron are toxic, too. Ammonia, is not; in fact, it is an excellent source of nitrogen and is often used in its anhydrous form as a fertilizer.

The most common problem with gray water is a high sodium content. Water softeners and detergents are the main contributors of this pollutant; you can reduce its level in your gray water by switching to old-fashioned soap flakes such as Ivory, and by staying away from products that advertise a "softening" or "enzymatic" action. However careful you may be, though, you will almost certainly boost the sodium levels in your soil if you irrigate with gray water.

If sodium builds up to a sufficient level, it can destroy the structure of a clay soil, and thus may cause problems with drainage. In addition, it is alkaline, so that its effect is to gradually raise the soil's pH. This makes gray water a poor source of moisture for acid-loving plants such as ferns, rhododendrons, or citrus trees. But sodium's effect on the pH, as Robert Kourik pointed out, also makes it easy to monitor its concentration in your soil.

Use an inexpensive soil test kit (available at most garden centers) to check the soil's pH after the first season of gray water irrigation. If the pH has risen above 7.5, the sodium level is probably excessive, and you should neutralize it by spreading gypsum over the soil at a rate of two pounds per hundred square feet every month until the pH drops below 7.0. Robert also suggested forestalling sodium buildup by routinely dosing the soil with gypsum at a rate of one pound to every hundred square feet per month for every twenty gallons of gray water discharge. That may be unnecessary, though, if you live in a region of heavy precipitation, since a heavy rain will wash much of the sodium out of the soil. On the whole, it's better to make periodic soil tests a part of your gardening routine if you recycle water—and base your treatments of the soil on those results.

Finally, there's one more kind of pollutant that can afflict a gray-water irrigation system: suspended solids—all the lint, dirt, hair, etc., that washes down the drain. This problem may be severe if you use a washing machine as your source of irrigation water. The solids won't trouble the plants, but they may plug the irrigation system. That's why you should install a filter at the intake.

Robert Kourik has developed a particularly elegant solution. In the system he installs for customers, gray water collects in a barrel before a sump pump sends it on to the plants; the water cascades into the barrel through a basket of quarter-inch hardware cloth which he lines with straw. The straw filters out the suspended solids, and when the organic filter begins to clog, Robert dumps the mess on the compost heap. Then he scrapes the hardware cloth clean, relines the basket with fresh straw, and sets it back in the barrel.

Potential Hazards

Gray water is not something you should save for a rainy day—or any other kind of day, either. Letting gray water sit in a barrel allows any pathogens it may contain to multiply, so always send it on immediately to the garden, and into the soil where the soil flora and fauna will cleanse it.

Health authorities insist that gardeners must avoid as far as possible any contact with the gray water—although as Robert pointed out, any pathogens in the wash water presumably came from the gardeners and so don't pose any risks to which the gardeners haven't already been exposed. Still, he agrees, it can't hurt to be cautious. So before cleaning the filter or working on the system, put on a pair of rubber gloves. Wash up afterward, too.

It really is dangerous to apply gray water via sprinklers, since that fills the air with a polluted mist. Instead, irrigate with a subsurface system of perforated pipe—the kind sold by plumbing supply stores for use in leach fields works well. In fact, the best way to distribute gray water (and the only way approved by the state of California) is through a shallow leach field of pipes set in trenches filled with pea gravel. An arrangement of that kind is ideal for irrigating deep-rooted plantings such as hedges, orchards, shade trees, even masses of shrubbery. It's not well adapted to the needs of ground covers that spread their roots closer to the surface of the soil, or to flower gardens where the bands of exposed gravel would be unsightly.

In addition:

- Don't apply more gray water than your soil can absorb. If the gray water comes out of the subsurface pipes in such quantities that it puddles on the soil surface, it could create a health hazard, and will certainly furnish a breeding ground for mosquitoes. The amount of gray water you can apply at once will depend on the infiltration rate of your soil (see table on page 121). Robert Kourik recommends as a rule of thumb figuring that a rich loam can absorb without damage about one quart of gray water per square foot of bed each week. Sandy soils can absorb more, clay soils less. So before installing your gray water system, figure out the gallons it will supply each day, and design the leach fields to accommodate this input.
- Don't apply gray water directly to the edible portions of fruits or vegetables that you will eat unpeeled and uncooked. To be 100 percent safe, save it for use on ornamental plants, or fruit trees, bushes, and vines.
- For the sake of peace in the neighborhood, don't irrigate with gray water right next to your fence line. Your gray water may be good for the plants next door, but it may worry their owners.
- Above all, don't irrigate with gray water right next to your well. Check with the county health authorities to find out the distance you must preserve between the well and a septic leach field, and take that as your minimum.

To put all of these hazards in perspective, remember that the water we routinely filter through septic fields is far more polluted than gray water, and that we rely on the same natural processes to cleanse both. Gray water won't pose a significant threat to your health or the health of your plants if you handle it intelligently.

That's why it's essential that you know what you are doing before you alter your plumbing in any way. Before cutting any pipes or installing any leach fields, get a copy of the pertinent section of the State of California's uniform plumbing code. Or consult Robert Kourik's handbook.

As Always, Too Much of a Good Thing . . .

The real secret of the successful use of gray water is to make it just one element of your irrigation system. A system that collects twenty gallons of gray water each day can furnish all the moisture needs of eighty square feet of bed, but it's wiser to distribute its water through two hundred, three hundred, or even four hundred square feet. In that way, you can alternate doses of gray water with doses of fresh water to protect the soil from sodium buildup. What's more, you have built a system that can handle an influx of house-guests.

There is an insoluble problem with recycling water in this fashion: your needs don't always coincide with those of your plants. You won't want to wait for a dry spell to wash your clothes, nor will you want to stop bathing simply because it is raining outside. To deal with eventualities of that kind, you must install valves in your plumbing that allow you to choose whether you wish to route water to the irrigation system or down the drain. You probably won't need to irrigate at all during the winter, for example, so you must have some way to shut your gray water system down easily and safely.

Robert took me on a tour of the Santa Rosa area, and everywhere we stopped he disappeared under the porch like a rabbit diving down its hole. I'd join him, and he would show me the drains. After cleaning a filter at one house, we'd emerge to meet the startled house sitters, who had wondered *who* was in the crawl space. Pretty soon, though, they were under the porch too, absorbed in Robert's explanation of the gray water system. Eventually, I come to believe that the blue plastic barrels sprouting hoses and electric cords are his spoor—they are the sign that a garden is his creation.

I had arrived in Santa Rosa thinking of gray water as an expedient useful for periods of drought, but Robert soon set me straight. He and his clients have found that if the gray water system is properly designed and managed, plants actually grow better on its flow than on city water. What we call pollutants, plants may regard as nutrients. In the future, Robert believes, gray water irrigation will become a standard horticultural practice for that very reason.

He realizes that gray water recycling isn't for everyone. He calculates though, that if 1 percent of all Californians installed gray-water collection systems in their homes, the annual yield would be 9 billion gallons. That's 9 billion more gallons available to the landscape, and 9 billion less that we must purify in septic tanks and sewage treatment plants.

For me, the most interesting part of my visit with Robert Kourik was what I found at his house. And that was almost nothing at all.

There were the mounds of herbs and adapted plants, the fifteen types of rosemary, and the euphorbia that had been making the same huge yellow balls of blossoms for four months. One lavender —the *Lavandula dentata*—blooms every day of the year, and the *Lavandula stoechas* had been blooming continuously for two to three months when Robert showed it to me. But none of this is due to gray water. Over the course of the five-year drought he has cut back on his personal water use—he boasts of taking the fastest showers in the West—until he generates only five to ten gallons of usable waste a day. That's barely enough to satisfy the fourteen fruit trees he has planted in his own miniature orchard.

That's all right. Because Robert believes that a garden, ideally, shouldn't need irrigation. Xeriscaping, he says, doesn't go nearly far enough. Xeriscapers boast of reducing irrigation by 75 percent. Well, what about the other 25? Robert demands. We ought to turn off the tap altogether.

That's a point of view he doesn't try to impose on clients, who want to surround their homes with more conventional landscaping. For them he'll continue to recycle. But at home, when a plant wants extra water he sets it at the base of one of his fog-harvesting Douglas firs. That's the original drip irrigation system, he insists. I have to agree: you can't recycle what you don't throw away.

Brooklyn, New York

Wildflowers have no street value, Patti Hagan explained. That's why she started growing them. The annuals she planted in front of her Prospect Heights brownstone kept walking away; persons unknown helped themselves, taking the plants, roots and all. But wildflowers are weeds, and the perpetrators didn't care for them. At any rate, no one disturbed the micromeadow she planted right there on St. Mark's Avenue in 1984.

But there's a second reason why Patti planted wildflowers. Once established, they don't require watering. Patti's house has no outdoor faucets in front and she was tired of the endless trips with the watering can. Of course, the backyard had been the real problem. When Patti began replanting that in 1980 (the year after she moved in), she had no direct access except through the basement, and that was a tenant's apartment. So until she had the deck and stairs built, she entered the garden by a ladder propped up against a window. Negotiating that with a watering can was a job for a Sherpa.

Patti Hagan is a gardener's gardener. She's the kind who always has room for a new plant, even when her narrow slice of cityscape clearly can take no more. Yet she's equally devoted to the craft of writing—her taut, deft prose always has an unexpected point of view, since she's a relentless reporter as well. Patti has managed to synthesize her interests in the column she contributes to *The Wall Street Journal* and her articles for *HG*; there you might find an exposé of the international trade in illicit bulbs, or perhaps the secret of bringing gardenias into bloom (a coffee-grounds mulch).

But if Patti is a bit difficult to classify, her garden isn't. Of all the gardens I know, it comes closest to the absolute prototype, the one I learned about in Sunday school. There is no serpent or apple here, but there is a feeling of peaceful remove in this gentle, flowery jungle. And it's as Brooklyn as a Dodgers' doubleheader.

This place the Dutch named "Broken Valley" (*Breuckelen*) was always a good place to garden. It has, according to a seventeenth-century advertisement of the Dutch East India Company, "the best clymate in the whole world [such that] seed may be thrown into the ground, except six weekes, the yere long." So maybe that's optimistic, but just a few miles from where Patti lives is the site of

Prince's Linnaean Botanic Garden, America's first commercial nursery and a supplier of trees and shrubs to George Washington. Patti can walk to Prospect Park—the masterwork of Frederick Law Olmsted, America's first landscape architect and arguably still the greatest. A tree grows in Brooklyn? Millions of trees grow in Brooklyn, for it's a place with a great horticultural past, and perhaps an even greater future.

As a borough of New York City, Brooklyn also draws on the world's finest municipal water supply system. Eighteen reservoirs and six thousand miles of tunnels (many so large you could drive a truck through them) feed New York 1.5 billion gallons of water every day. Like everything in that city, the water system faces enormous problems, most of which are outside the scope of this book. What they add up to, though, is a growing discrepancy between supply and demand. The city's population is shrinking—it has lost half a million residents in the last twenty years—yet water consumption continues to increase at a rate of about 1 percent annually. No one knows exactly where the extra water is going, but the general answer is clearly—waste.

Waste is partly the result of an aging system with leaking mains. But waste is also an attitude. Waste is charging water customers a flat rate for service (as the city does) so that it's cheaper to let leaking faucets run than to call the plumber. Waste is letting water run for years in abandoned buildings from which scavengers have stolen the plumbing fixtures. To a lesser extent, waste is also a style of gardening.

Landscape use occurs on the grand scale in Brooklyn. The greatest ornament of Prospect Park is its waterworks—the waterfall that feeds a stream that runs through the woods as a babbling brook to become a river and then a sixty-acre lake. Natural as this complex may look, it is in fact entirely artificial. It was brought into existence by Frederick Law Olmsted and it comes from a pipe. How many hundreds of acre-feet are consumed this way every year, not even the park management knows.*

Because these waterways serve to cool and please some 5 mil-

---

* To be fair, I should add that the park administration maintains a well which can be pressed into use in time of drought. As long as the city continues to provide water for free, though, the park managers cannot justify the expense of pumping the water up from the aquifer; park budgets are tight these days. I should also note that the Prospect Park staff is also beginning a restoration of the waterways, working to reseal the beds and banks so that water use will be reduced.

lion visitors every year, one could reasonably argue that this consumption isn't extravagant at all. There's no doubt, though, in Patti Hagan's mind about what went on in her yard prior to the summer of 1988.

By that time Patti had solved her water "problem." She had cleared all the brush and rubbish out of her backyard and was planting in earnest, and so naturally she had a faucet installed. After that, she watered constantly. All her neighbors did it (the ones that had gardens), so Patti thought that's what you had to do. That's what she thought until the dry summer of 1988, when the city government temporarily prohibited the use of garden hoses and she had to put her oscillating sprinkler away.

The immediate effect of this was . . . negligible. It provided Patti with material for a column about xeriscaping. In it, she promised to replant with silver-leaved xeriphytes. She looked forward, she said, to growing gray with her garden. But nothing of the sort has happened. Rather, the garden has grown yet more lush.

Patti found that the front garden, the eight-by-ten-foot rectangle tucked in between house and sidewalk, didn't need any help in surviving the drought. The wildflowers were all true Brooklyn natives—Patti hadn't bought a single one. Instead, she collected the seed from the vacant lots along Atlantic Avenue.

There she found a giant bouquet of overlooked blossoms. There was Queen Anne's lace, moth mulleins, chicory, fleabane, butter-and-eggs, cinquefoil, spotted knapweed, clover, black-eyed Susans, bladder campions, St. Johnswort, evening primrose, wild petunia, and even Deptford pinks.* All flourish beside her stoop, but beautiful as the tangle of flowers was, I wondered if for Patti the appeal wasn't largely to the ear: the roll call sounded so rich as it rolled off her tongue. It certainly made good copy for the article she supplied to *The New York Times.*

Arriving four years after that drought, I might have missed Patti's house altogether if it hadn't been for the meadow; a mask of vines, hardy kiwifruit (*Actinidia arguta*), hid its features almost altogether. After I admired that, she took me through the house to the hidden pleasures behind.

Fragrance had been one of Patti's absolute requirements. She's

* Botanical names, in their respective order: *Daucus carota, Verbascum blattaria, Cichorium intybus, Erigeron philadelphicus, Linaria vulgaris, Potentilla sp., Centaurea maculosa, Trifolium sp., Rudbeckia hirta, Silene cucubalus, Hypericum perforatum, Oenothera biennis, Petunia sp., Dianthus armeria.*

fortunate in that she works at home much of the time, so she can enjoy the garden at all stages of the day. For a commuter, though, and for Patti too when work keeps her away from the house until dark, perfumes are a garden's chief reward. She keeps a heady blend outside the back windows on her deck: pots of gardenias (her coffee grounds do awaken these reluctant bloomers), a Valencia orange, two kinds of jasmine, and two frangipanis. Down below, she's planted winter honeysuckle (*Lonicera fragrantissima*), a shrub which whispers its intense sweetness halfway down the block when January brings it to bloom.

We descended past curtains of Asiatic bittersweet and four kinds of grapes to the base of the deck's substructure and an old one-holer that Patti has converted into a toolshed—not all odors are desirable. There's a square of flagstones Patti discovered when she stripped the brush from this lot; the flagstones that meander off as paths into the plantings she had to carry home on her back from demolition sites. I stooped to admire a pot with ivy-form leaves and blue, pansy-like flowers—an Australian violet (*Viola hederacea*), then stepped over to the bog.

There, a turkey roasting pan sunk flush with the ground provides a home for a sheet of sphagnum moss and spikes of pale pink turtleheads (*Chelone glabra*) and Lobelia x Gerardii, whose purplish flowers will appear in late summer—the sunken iron pot overflows in springtime with the gold of marsh marigolds (*Caltha palustris*). Looking up, I spotted an old friend in the expansive green knot ahead: 'Jacques Cartier'.

Or maybe it's 'Marquise Bocella'; nobody is quite sure about the right name for this hybrid perpetual rose of the year 1842. I'd missed the first flush of pink, powder-puff flowers—spring comes early in Brooklyn—but the bush would continue to produce the odd flower throughout the summer and fall.

This old French aristocrat was blooming in seclusion; one of Patti's first projects was to line the surrounding chain-link fence. For this she used swags of *Akebia quinata*, a fast-climbing vine with dainty, five-fingered leaves, and the rambling canes of 'Dorothy Perkins' (another old-timer, an American rose of 1901 that in springtime explodes in pompoms of pale pink). Then she laced in hedges of *Macleaya cordata*, a monstrous eight-foot-tall poppy relative that bears feathery white plumes of flowers above the doily-sized blue-green leaves.

But if Jacques (the Marquise) finds himself hidden away from the neighborhood, he has plenty of company nonetheless. Patti likes clematis—a lot. She's planted a hundred or so of these flowering vines in a yard that measures one hundred by twenty-one feet. Some are duplicates—she has several specimens of 'Betty Corning', for example, a *Clematis viticella* hybrid that bears bell-shaped blossoms of smoky blue throughout the summer. Even so, there are about eighty different cultivars and species back there, tumbling across the ground and embracing shrubs, climbing from branch to branch toward the sun.

Though relatives all, these vines furnish a whole repertoire of different floral effects. Compare, for example, the serene blue saucers of 'Ramona' with 'Duchess of Albany's' vivid blooms—despite its high-flown name, the latter flaunts curved petals as long, pointed, and hot pink as any neighborhood bimbo's nails. Differences among the foliages—finely cut, tooth-edged, or elliptical; expansive or petite—are more subtle but no less important to Patti. She explained that when she started this garden, the first she had had since childhood, around 1980 she was crazy for color—"Lots of color; color, color! The more colorful the better!" She didn't even distinguish much between annuals and perennials; all she cared about was that there should always be lots of flowers. "*Now* I'm much more interested in green." In the writing assignments that take her to other gardens, she savors the subtle interplay of light and weather with the different shades of green; a misty vista of woods, the view of a field in the rain. "Too much color disturbs me. Does this happen to everyone—you get beyond all the color?"

Reflecting on my own past, with incidents of carpet bedding and marigolds planted in pinwheels, I shuddered and concentrated on Patti's clematises. The books insist on rich, moist, and cool soil for these, and that's what Patti's got. She doesn't mulch, except to drop weeds back onto the ground as she pulls them, but the dense canopy of foliage that covers every square inch of her land provides much the same benefits. When these leaves fall, she lets them lie, too; she rakes only the paths and terrace. *And* she composts—not only the organic part of her own garbage but also that of her downstairs tenants.

The result is a soil to kill for—an earthworm's paradise that never needs irrigation. That's fortunate, because although the faucet is still there, Patti gave the sprinkler and even the hose away four years ago. She's still got the plastic two-quart watering can, but two trips with this now suffice; only new plantings get any more water than the natural budget.

"In my Father's house are many mansions. . . ." It must have been the cloistered peace of this inner-city garden that put me in mind of this tag from the Gospels—that and the ingenuity Patti has shown in fitting many distinct experiences into what could have been a constricted plot. There is, for instance, the scrap of prairie she put in for her tenants (who come from Wisconsin). Neil Diboll sent her Queen of the Prairie (*Filipendula rubra*), marsh milkweed (*Asclepias incarnata*), and nodding pink onion (*Allium cernnum*) for that. Turn a corner in the path and you make eye contact with a crumbled female head—it fell off a building on Atlantic Avenue and Patti brought it home to wedge into the crotch of a crabapple. Under the mulberry there's a spring garden of jack-in-the-pulpits (*Arisaema sp.*), trilliums, bloodroot (*Sanguinaria canadensis*) and lily-of-the-valley (*Convallaria majalis*)—the path here is edged with liriope (lily turf) whose arched, grass-like leaves make a perfect blind for the cats: Miss Mingus, Thelonious Monk, and Max Roach.

Here 'Dutchess of Albany's vines have almost completely devoured a dwarf apple tree. There is the patch of species cyclamens Patti bought before she learned that the dealers rustle these bulbs from endangered wild stocks—exquisite as the shooting stars of pink are, they make her sad now. By the bleeding hearts is an old wooden armchair Patti set out as a breakfast spot, though in spring she's more liable to use the bench under the wisteria, where she can contemplate the epimediums, may-apples (*Podophyllum peltatum*), and hellebores (*Helleborus sp.*). Wood asters (*Aster divaricatus* and *acuminatus*), boneset (*Eupatorium perfoliatum*), and meadow rue (*Thalictrum sp.*) carry the garden's bloom on into fall.

Patti's taste may be all-embracing, but her plants must perform. When I visited, that "dreadful lilac" didn't bloom reliably—so it was coming out. I wouldn't bet much either on the chances of the blackspot-prone hybrid tea rose that Patti called "the deadbeat." She's got space for giants as well as miniatures, but all must be able to coexist in close embrace. They have to like each other, and like Brooklyn, too. No Catskill water for this landscape.

Patti wrote in her *Wall Street Journal* column of her suspicion that "hydrophilous English-style perennial borders might not really be environmentally *echt* for the hot times to come." So who cares? Patti presides over something infinitely more interesting. She has never proposed her garden as a model, but neighbors should take note. Her "rainbow coalition" is as multi(horti)cultural as the turbulent community around it, as tough as any Brooklynite, and true to the borough's verdant heritage.

Imagine similar scapes erupting all over Brooklyn, all over New York—Patti has already assisted in the planting of a public wildflower meadow in lower Manhattan, and she long ago admitted in *The New Yorker** to encouraging the spread of "weed lots." Early in the mornings she would search her favorite wildflower hunting-grounds, harvesting bags of ripe seeds. Then when she walked the dog late at night, she'd pitch the day's harvest into neglected front yards and over the chain-link fences into the used car lots on Flatbush Avenue. She is making the city—or at least her part of it —bloom.

Is this a solution to New York's water problems? Not by itself. But reminding people that they live in a place which, though crowded, *can* be healthy and beautiful, is certainly fundamental to changing the way they treat it. We need to develop respect, and understanding too, of the place we live, whether that is Brooklyn, Palm Beach, or Santa Barbara. To do so will certainly bring a reprieve for the water supply system. With that will come all sorts of other rewards.

As gardeners we must pursue new means of water conservation. And yet, ignorance has not been the real obstacle to developing more resource-efficient landscapes. Help has been available for at least a generation. Even the Northeast, a region which is just beginning to confront this challenge, has its experts now and its step-by-step guides. You will find all sorts of materials listed in the bibliography at this book's end.

We *are* making great strides in our understanding of irrigation and plant needs, and that is wonderful. But what has been missing in the horticultural past was not know-how so much as desire. Somehow we confused precision with poverty. Standing out in the yard, hose in hand, wasting the water piped in from mountains hundreds of miles away made us feel wealthy and secure.

* "Talk of the Town," August 23, 1982.

. . .

Too often our own ingenuity has been our greatest liability as gardeners. No matter where we settled on this continent, we have brought the same vision of paradise with us, and through hard work and technical virtuosity we've always managed to re-create it around our homes. This, however, was accomplished at a terrible cost.

Leave New York City for a moment and travel to the extreme opposite coast, to the Gulf of California. Seventy years ago, before all the water projects, the Colorado River fed an estuary there that ecologist Aldo Leopold described as a "milk-and-honey wilderness," a place of egrets, jaguars, and wild melons. It's gone now. Today the Colorado dies back in the desert, long before it ever reaches the sea. How much of its water is siphoned off to keep ice plants blooming along southern California freeways?

Still, speaking as a gardener, I would say that the greatest damage our watering has done is to the gardens themselves. The effect of over-irrigation has been to make them as interchangeable as motel rooms. I believe that all the talk in recent years of the "New American Garden" only underlines how impoverished our horticultural vision has become. There shouldn't be one model. Lorrie Otto in Milwaukee should have a landscape wholly different from the ones Owen Dell is creating for Santa Barbarans—and nobody reasonable wants Brooklyn to look like Tucson.

Learning to use water wisely, to value this resource at its real worth, is something all of us will have to do if we are to enjoy our present standard of comfort in the future. And if all the answers to our nation's water problems do not lie in the garden, nevertheless, on a local level, within a city, town, or county, gardeners *can* make a critical difference. That's something I find comforting. In a era of overwhelming, global problems, I am pleased to find a difficulty I can remedy so simply as by replanning my garden. Besides, how can I resist a kind of conservation that promises me more pleasure rather than less?

Resources for the Water-Wise Gardener

Guides to xeriscaping and water-conserving gardening:

Ellefson, Connie L., Thomas L. Stephens, and Douglas Welsh, *Xeriscape Gardening*. New York: Macmillan, 1992.

Johnson, Eric A., and Scott Millard, *The Low-Water Flower Gardener*. Tucson, Arizona: Ironwood Press, 1993.

Knopf, Jim, *The Xeriscape Flower Gardener: A Waterwise Guide for the Rocky Mountain Region*. Boulder, Colorado: Johnson Books, 1991.

Landscaping for Water Conservation: XERISCAPE! Aurora, Colorado: City of Aurora Utilities Department and Denver Water Department, 1989.

O'Keefe, John M., *Water-Conserving Gardens and Landscapes*. Pownal Vermont: Storey Publishing, 1992.

Robinette, Gary O., *Water Conservation in Landscape Design and Management*. Van Nostrand Reinhold Company, 1984.

Shelton, Theodore, and Bruce Hamilton, *Landscaping for Water Conservation: A Guide for New Jersey*. New Brunswick, New Jersey: Rutgers Cooperative Extension, 1987.

Taylor's Guide to Water Saving Gardening. Boston, Massachusetts: Houghton-Mifflin Company, 1990.

Walters, James E., and Balbir Backhaus, *Shade and Color with Water-Conserving Plants*. Portland, Oregon: Timber Press, 1992.

Additional sources of information, pamphlets, etc.:
Landscapes Southern California Style
P.O. Box 5286
Riverside, California 92517

South Florida Water Management District
P.O. Box 24680
West Palm Beach, Florida 33416

Xeriscape Colorado
Denver Water Department
1600 West 12th Street
Denver, Colorado 80254

Cooperative Extension Services—Operated under the aegis of the state agricultural universities, these services (each state has one) are the best sources for all sorts of regionally appropriate landscaping information. To contact the nearest office, look under county office listings in the local telephone book.

Local water utility companies—In regions where water is in short supply, water companies commonly promote landscape water conservation and typically supply a wealth of free materials.

The current clearinghouse for information about xeriscaping and regional programs is the

American Waterworks Association
6666 West Quincy Avenue
Denver, Colorado 80235

Information about native and/or regionally adapted plants:
Diekelman, John, and Robert Schuster, *Natural Landscaping: Designing with Native Plant Communities*. New York: McGraw-Hill Book Company, 1982.

Duffield, Mary Rose, and Warren D. Jones, *Plants for Dry Climates*. Tucson, Arizona: H. P. Books, 1981.

Miller, George O., *Landscaping with Native Plants of Texas and the Southwest*. Stillwater, Minnesota: Voyageur Press, 1991.

Perry, Bob, *Trees and Shrubs for Dry California Landscapes*. San Dimas, California: Land Design Publishing, 1987.

Phillips, Judith, *Southwestern Landscaping with Native Plants*, 2nd ed. Santa Fe: Museum of New Mexico Press, 1988.

Smyser, Carol A., *Nature's Design: A Practical Guide to Natural Landscaping*. Emmaus, Pennsylvania: Rodale Press, 1982.

A Directory of Water Saving Plants and Trees for Texas. Austin, Texas: Texas Water Development Board, 1988.

Welch, William C., *Perennial Garden Color for Texas and the South.* Dallas, Texas: Taylor Publishing Company, 1989.

Xeric Landscaping with Florida Native Plants. San Antonio, Florida: Association of Florida Native Nurseries, Inc., 1991.

Xeriscape Plant Guide II. West Palm Beach, Florida: South Florida Water Management District, 1991.

For help in seeking plants native to your region, contact:
Clearinghouse
National Wildflower Research Center
2600 FM 973 North
Austin, Texas 78725
(512) 929-3600

Include return-address mailing label and $1.00 for postage with every request for information.

For help in contacting local chapters of native plant and wildflower societies:
Botanical Clubs and Native Plant Societies of the United States and Canada, New England Wildflower Society, 1993.
To order this directory, send $1.50 to
New England Wildflower Society
Garden in the Woods
Framingham, Massachusetts 01701
(508) 877-7630

Information about water-conserving turf management:
Shultz, Warren, *The Chemical-Free Lawn.* Emmaus, Pennsylvania: Rodale Press, 1989.

Information about water-conserving irrigation:
Bainbridge, David A., *Buried Clay Pot Irrigation.* Groundworks, 2825 Maude Street, Riverside, California 92506; enclose self-addressed, stamped envelope with query.

Kourik, Robert, *Drop Irrigation for Every Landscape and All Climates.* Santa Rosa, California: Metamorphic Press, 1992.

Kourik, Robert, *Gray Water Use in the Landscape.* Santa Rosa, California: Metamorphic Press, 1988.

Matlock, W. Gerald, *Water Harvesting for Urban Landscapes*. Tucson, Arizona: Tucson Water, 1989.

Information about model railway gardens:
Garden Railways
PO Box 61461
Denver, Colorado 80206
Published bimonthly.

Index

lethal yellowing, 105
lily-of-the-Nile (*Agapanthus africanus*), 40
lily-of-the-valley (*Convallaria majalis*), 251
limestone, 127
Lindheimer's Muhly grass (*Muhlenbergia lindheimeri*), 84
Lindsey, Alton A., 158*n*
liriopes, 117, 251
little bluestem (*Andropogon scoparius*), 178, 182, 187, 190
littleleaf mountain mahogany (*Cercocarpus intricatus*), 230
Living with Nature (Ludwig), 49*n*
lizards, 77
loam, 18, 125, 132
love grass, 190–91
Ludwig, Art, 49–53
Lyme disease, 202

Macleaya cordata, 249
McPherson, Jerry, 112–15, 118
marigold, 235, 250
marsh marigold (*Caltha palustris*), 249
marsh milkweed (*Asclepias incarnata*), 183, 196, 251
mastic tree (*Mastichodendron foetidissimum*), 107
Matlock, W. Gerald, 173–74
mat penstemon (*Penstemon linarioides*), 148
mayapple (*Podophyllum peltatum*), 251
meadow rue (*Thalictrum sp.*), 251
meadows, 36, 46–47
  alpine, 52, 222
  turf replaced by, 82, 202, 216
Meals for Millions/Freedom from Hunger, 141
mealy-cup sage (*Salvia farinacea*), 75, 82, 83, 147
merlins, 110
Mesiscapes, 17
mesquite, 23, 76, 146–47, 150, 152, 156, 157, 159, 178
Mexican bush sage (*Salvia leucantha*), 34, 37
Mexican evening primrose (*Oenothera berlandieri*), 37, 153
Mexican hat (*Ratibida columnaris*), 75
Mexican marigold-mint (*Tagetes lucida*), 74
Mexican oregano (*Poliomentha longiflora*), 74
mice, 202
Miller, Ray, 109–11, 112
miniature Chinese elm (*Ulmus parvifolia* 'Seiju'), 230
mini-click timers, 171
mistral, 45

mockingbirds, 73
Model Landscape Code, 103
Mohave Indians, 142
moisture-absorbent disks, 171
mondo grass (*Ophiopogon japonicus*), 104
Monet, Claude, 101
monocultures, 184
montane area, 222
Montecito, Calif., 43–44
Morton Arboretum, 188
Moses in the bulrushes (*Rhoeo spathacea*), 104
mosquitoes, 176, 243
moss, 22, 249
mountain lilac (*Ceanothus* 'Ray Hartman'), 40
mountain laurel (*Kalmia latifolia*), 84, 92
mountain sage (*Salvia regla*), 79
Moyroud, Richard, 105, 106–7, 108, 109, 110, 111–12, 114
Muir, John, 36
mulch, 65–66, 67, 75, 79, 84, 132–33, 151, 166, 213–15, 234, 237, 238, 250
Munich Botanic Garden, 220

Nabhan, Gary, 139–43
Nassau County Cooperative Extension, 29
National Arboretum, 19
National Small Flows Clearinghouse, 240
National Wildflower Research Center, 82, 88, 90
National Wildlife Federation, 115
National Xeriscape Council, 17, 56–57, 58, 62, 64, 65, 103
Native Seeds/SEARCH, 138–44
Navarro, Nick, 99
needle palm (*Rhapidophyllum hystrix*), 112
Negev Desert, 173
Nevada, 13
New Mexico, 13
newspapers, 77
New York, N.Y., 12, 247, 252
New York Botanical Garden, 28–29, 54, 60, 115
New York Botanical Garden Library, 54
New Yorker, 25
New York Times, 248
New Zealand tea tree (*Leptospermum scoparium* 'Burgundy Queen'), 42
nitrates, 12, 107*n*, 180, 201, 241
nitrogen, 50, 140, 212, 241
nodding onion (*Allium cernuum*), 198, 251
North American Prairie Conference, 187
Northington, David, 87–88

turf (cont.)
    bunchgrasses vs. sod-formers for, 207–
        208
    as default planting, 216
    dormancy of, 203, 215
    drought-tolerant, 204–5, 208–11,
        212–15
    durability of, 62–63
    fertilizers for, 201, 213, 215
    as firebreak, 201–2
    height of, 212–13
    herbicides for, 202
    irrigation for, 15–16, 30, 35, 40, 43,
        44, 60, 80, 103, 166, 201, 202–3,
        204, 205, 216, 239
    lime for, 215
    maintenance of, 46, 80–81, 201–3,
        205, 206, 212–15
    meadows as replacement for, 82, 202,
        216
    mowing of, 202, 209, 210, 212–15,
        216
    mulch for, 213–15
    pesticides for, 196n, 197n, 201
    pollutants filtered by, 202
    pre-war condition of, 203
    rainfall and, 204
    reduction of, 62, 73, 75, 76–77, 82,
        201, 215–16, 224, 234, 236
    root development of, 207–8, 209,
        210–11, 212, 215
    seed vs. sod for, 211–12
    selection of, 206–7, 210
    soil for, 210
    topdressing of, 214, 215
    uniformity of, 212
    see also grass
turk's cap (Malvaviscus arboreus), 75
turtlehead (Chelone glabra), 249
Two Forks Dam, 14–15, 55
2, 4-D herbicide, 197
typhoid fever, 239

University of Wisconsin, 132, 179
Utah, 13

Van Wyke, Phil, 151–53
variegated bugle (Ajuga reptans 'Burgundy
    Glow'), 231
velvet mesquite (Prosopis velutina), 147
Veronica Iiwanensis, 225
Virgil, 220n

Waggoner, Duke, 76, 78
Waggoner, Nancy, 76–80
Wall Street Journal, 246, 251

Walter, Heinrich, 158
washes, 154
washing machines, 238, 240
Washington, George, 247
water:
    agricultural use of, 98–99
    availability of, 11–13, 247, 252
    black, 240
    conservation of, 16–20, 33–34, 37,
        39–40, 55, 57, 67–68, 77, 84–85,
        101, 245
    cost of, 21–22, 34, 39–40, 42, 49,
        101, 117, 155, 224
    evaporation of, 32, 60, 115
    gray, 47, 49–50, 150, 238–45
    harvesting of, 150, 172, 173–75, 239,
        245
    meters for, 224, 236
    peak demand for, 16
    personal use of, 12, 238–39
    pollution of, 196, 201, 202
    pressure of, 161, 169
    recycling of, 32–33, 49–50, 51, 52,
        134, 193–97, 238–45
    shortage of, 11–17, 253
    treatment plants for, 52
Water Harvesting for Urban Landscapes
    (Matlock), 174n
water table, 24, 180
    perched, 127, 239–40
wax myrtle (Myrica cerifera), 84, 110–11,
    116
weather patterns, 13–14, 31, 68
weeding, 67, 202, 250
weeds, 61, 223, 252
    ordinances on, 198–99
    in prairies, 182, 186
    seeds from, 61
    suppression of, 65, 67, 202, 237, 250
Welch, William, 78n
wells:
    contamination of, 12, 107n, 185, 243
    irrigation from, 203
West, Margaret, 154–58
western redbud (Cercis occidentalis), 48
western sunflower (Helianthus occidentalis),
    185
wetlands, 113, 189, 196
wetteners, 134
"whirlybirds," 167
white-capped yarrow (Achillea millefolium),
    194
white Carpathian harebell (Campanula
    'White Clips'), 231
white indigo berry (Randia aculeata), 106,
    107

wild coffee (*Psychotria nervosa*), 108
wild dilly (*Manilkara bahamensis*), 108
Wild Ones, 199
wild petunia (*Ruellia brittoniana*), 73
wild plum (*Prunus americana*), 191
wild tomato (*Lycopersicon esculentum* var.
  cerisforme), 140
wild turkeys, 118
willow-leaved bustic (*Dipholis salicifolia*),
  107
wilting point, 132
windrows, 195
wing-leaf soapberry (*Sapindus saponaria*),
  108
winter honeysuckle (*Lonicara fragantissima*),
  249
Wisconsin, 179, 180
wood aster (*Aster acuminatus*), 251
wood aster (*A. divaricatus*), 251
wood storks, 112
woolly mullein (*Verbascum bombyciferum*),
  228
woolly veronica (*Veronica pectinata*), 231
World Maps of Climatology, 91
Wyoming, 13

xeriscaping, 54–85
  bibliography on, 252, 255–57
  conferences on, 56
  definition of, 55–57
  information on, 54–55

irrigation in, 60–61, 153
maintenance in, 66–69, 73, 153–54
microclimates in, 68, 212, 235–36
movement for, 56–57
mulches in, 65–66
planning and design for, 57–58
plant selection for, 63–65, 68–69, 94–
  96
popular conception of, 54–55
prairiescaping vs., 180
seven principles of, 57–67, 98
soil analysis in, 58–59
as term, 17, 54, 56
turf areas in, 62–63
water conservation in, 55, 57, 67–68,
  77, 84–85, 101, 245
zoning in, 57–58, 69
xerophytes, 26, 47, 94–96, 103, 150,
  151, 220–22
xylem, 28

yarrow (*Achillea millefolium*), 83
yellow coneflower (*Ratibida pinnata*), 191
yellow-flowered ice plant (*Delosperma
  nubigena*), 220, 225
yellow-meated watermelon, 143–44
yellow trumpet flower (*Tecoma stans*),
  79
yew, 64, 191

zoysia grass, 209–10, 211, 213

About the Author

Thomas Christopher's gardening has taken him all over the United States. A graduate of the New York Botanical Garden's School of Horticulture, he spent ten years restoring a historic Hudson River estate for Columbia University and another four cultivating antique rosebushes in central Texas, a tale told in his first book, *In Search of Lost Roses*. A regular contributor to *Horticulture* magazine, he is currently surrounding his Connecticut home with an irrigation-free meadow inspired by the hay fields of New England.